67863

JC
73
S73

Staveley, E
Greek and Roman voting and
elections

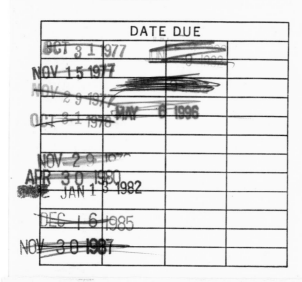
LEARNING RESOURCES CENTER
MONTGOMERY COUNTY COMMUNITY COLLEGE
BLUE BELL, PENNSYLVANIA

ASPECTS OF GREEK AND
ROMAN LIFE
General Editor: H. H. Scullard

★ ★ ★

GREEK AND ROMAN VOTING
AND ELECTIONS
E. S. Staveley

GREEK AND ROMAN VOTING AND ELECTIONS

E. S. Staveley

CORNELL UNIVERSITY PRESS

ITHACA, NEW YORK

First published 1972

This edition is not for sale in the
United Kingdom and British
Commonwealth.

International Standard Book Number 0-8014-0693-5

Library of Congress Catalog Card Number 75-37004

PRINTED IN GREAT BRITAIN

CONTENTS

PART II ROME

LIST OF ILLUSTRATIONS

PREFACE

IN DETERMINING THE FORM ~~and the scope of~~ *that ES Stavely has written in* this book I have been much influenced by the belief that it is likely to be as widely read by the student of psephology or political science as by the student of classical history. It has not, therefore, been my aim to collect together every scrap of material relating to ancient voting procedures and so to produce what would be tantamount to an encyclopaedic work of reference. Such a volume, while perhaps of some value to the scholar, would be totally unsuited to the requirements of the less specialist reader, who, I feel sure, would wish to be presented with as complete an account as possible of voting practices and elections in a strictly limited field. Instead, I have thought it right to concentrate almost exclusively upon three states—Sparta, Athens, and Republican Rome. These are the only communities concerning whose voting procedures there exists any coherent body of evidence; and they are, of course, the three ancient states with the course of whose general political development the majority of readers are likely to have at least a passing familiarity.

It is inevitable that in a book on such a subject as this a considerable amount of space should be devoted to a study of technical matter, the more particularly as the more technical problems are those on which a critical analysis of the limited available evidence throws most light. I have made some effort, however, to include much that is not unduly specialized. Perhaps at the risk of expressing a personal view with unwarranted dogmatism at times, I have sought throughout to set the voting scene which I have described in its proper historical context and to relate procedural change to contemporary political developments. I have also attempted, so

far as I have been able, to suggest some answers, however specula-
tive, to the more general questions relating to voting and elections
on which the ancient sources themselves have little or nothing to
say. It is all too easy for the scholar who is absorbed in matters of
constitutional theory to forget that there are simple and obvious
problems—such as, for example, how the Romans managed to
complete their voting process within the space of a single day—
to which readers of this book might naturally expect to find a
solution; and I am most grateful to the American political
scholar, Mr Theodore White, for bringing a number of these
questions to my attention during the course of a most fruitful
discussion which I had with him in 1966, when he was in London
to observe the British general election.

It would take up too much space here individually to acknow-
ledge my debt to the many scholars whose particular researches
into various aspects of this subject have made my task so much
easier. Almost all the works which I have consulted are mentioned
in the Notes. I should like, however, to reserve a special
mention for the late Professor Lily Ross Taylor of Bryn Mawr
College, with whom I had a most rewarding correspondence
when this book was still in embryo, and who devoted much of
her life to the study of Roman voting in many of its aspects. Her
three larger publications—*Party Politics in the Age of Caesar*, *The
Voting Districts of the Roman Republic*, and, most recently, *Roman
Voting Assemblies*—constitute an invaluable contribution to the
study of Roman constitutional and political practice, which in the
field of Greek studies still goes entirely unmatched.

Bedford College,
London, 1971

PART I

GREECE

CHAPTER I

THE ORIGINS OF VOTING IN THE GREEK WORLD

THE ORIGIN AND THE development of the vote in the political life of any community is a phenomenon which is simply explained. In the earliest stages of a state's existence power is normally vested in one person, and the rule of law is little more than the rule of superior force. There soon comes a time, however, when the interests of the ruler as well as of the ruled are manifestly seen to depend upon the peaceful resolution of differences among those who have the will and the ability to cause disruption rather than upon any continuing trial of strength. The forceful imposition of authority by one man, or by a small group, becomes a less attractive proposition either when the weight of opposition assumes formidable proportions or when what is in fact required for the success of any given venture is not so much the subservience of hostile and recalcitrant elements as their active co-operation. Mere recognition of this truth does not, of course, lead necessarily and immediately to the introduction of a formal voting process. The situation may call for little more than extensive consultation, the proffering and the acceptance of advice. But inevitably, when a ruler is forced to compromise with the principle of absolute autocracy, he prepares the ground for a progressive diminution of his power. Some of the advice which is offered must perforce be rejected. The result is a building up of discontent and a determination on the part of the opposition to seek strength through unity. The advice offered tends to become concerted advice, the essence of which is determined by the will of a majority. Common policy and attitudes are decided by a simple counting of heads, and the concept of the political vote is born.[1]

It would be misleading, of course, to suggest that voting was a purely political invention. It was surely a natural process, which was employed almost instinctively in the family and in other small social groups in order to resolve awkward differences of view concerning prospective action long before it was used in the sphere of state government. By the same token it would be equally misleading to suggest that the introduction of the practice of formal voting in the king's Council or some other such small aristocratic group was in any way directly related to the emergence of popular suffrage as exercised by the citizens at large. The circumstances which led to the extension of voting to the wider masses may indeed have been analogous to those which occasioned its adoption by the aristocratic *élite*, but they can have arisen only at a very much later date. Sizable groups among the ordinary citizens will have found themselves in a position to put pressure upon the aristocracy, as the aristocracy before them had put pressure upon the kings, only when they felt themselves free to break from the traditional bonds of clientship to the clan and when the exclusive control exercised by the family over the social and economic life of the community had long begun to be assumed by a central authority.

Our knowledge of the early history of Greek states, and in particular of the origins of their various political institutions, is extremely limited; but it may be supposed that political development followed a reasonably standard pattern. The emergence of the state—whether it be the loosely knit tribal state or the more compact city-state—was probably dictated in the first instance by the recognition of the various clan-headsmen who held sway in a particular area that there was a need for some co-ordination in matters of defence. Its most obvious manifestation was the appointment of a king whose duties were primarily those of a commander in war. In contrast to early Rome, where perhaps the less homogeneous nature of the society led to the establishment of an elective monarchy, the Greek states favoured the hereditary principle. The original choice of family was presumably dictated by such considerations as the prowess of the individual candidates and the strength of the following upon which each could severally call; but it should be supposed that the king's authority at all times depended in some measure upon the acquiescence of the other family heads who had subscribed to the mutual compact and who no doubt soon began to cast themselves in the role of advisers.

Our principal source of information concerning conditions in the regal age of Greece is Homer. Although there are still unresolved problems concerning the authorship of the two great epics, the *Iliad* and the *Odyssey*, there is today some measure of agreement that they were written between 700 and 650 BC. As Homer purported to be writing about events which took place five or six hundred years before his own time, his poems, of course, cannot be supposed to reflect contemporary conditions; but there is little doubt that he was content to rely for details of a society and political system somewhat less advanced than that of his own day upon an oral tradition which is unlikely to have reached back for more than three or four generations at the most. The conditions which Homer describes, therefore, should be regarded as those obtaining in *c.* 850 BC. What he relates of the roles of kings, aristocracy, and populace is consequently invaluable in throwing much needed light upon political developments in early Greek society.[2]

It is clear from the *Odyssey* that the king was still primarily the leader in war. When Odysseus' son, Telemachus, called an assembly in his father's absence, it was an almost unprecedented act, and it was anticipated that he had done so either to report the imminent return of the army or at least to address the people upon some other matter of public importance.[3] The dispensation of law, the provision of the society's economic needs, and even the observance of religion were still largely the concern of the clans, and not of any central authority. The position regarding the king's security of tenure is a little more confused. Certainly the hereditary principle was still accepted. The monarchy is described by one of his opponents as the 'birthright of Telemachus',[4] and the aristocrats deferred to him as he took his place upon his father's throne.[5] Nevertheless they were strong enough to plan for other things. The nature of the challenge is well illustrated by the fact that the would-be usurpers are portrayed as the suitors of

Penelope, the wife of the supposedly dead Odysseus. In order to preserve an air of legitimacy the aspirant to the throne regarded it as important that he should be wed to the former king's widow, just as in Mycenae the murderer of Agamemnon thought fit to marry Clytemnestra in order to establish his claim to the throne. In the event, as the story is told, Odysseus returned unexpectedly to put down the incipient revolt with the greatest severity. It is, however, the truculent attitude of the suitors and the apparent helplessness of Telemachus which perhaps more nearly reflect the conditions in early seventh-century Greece. In most states extensive consultation of the aristocracy was no doubt already the order of the day. Possibly the custom of taking corporate decisions by the process of counting heads was still a thing of the future; but its introduction may not have been long delayed.

If the Homeric epics offer some evidence of the growth of aristocratic influence, they offer virtually none of the emergence of popular sovereignty. Both in the *Iliad* and the *Odyssey* the popular assembly is a gathering totally devoid of power, and, to judge by Homer's story that it had met at Ithaca only once in twenty years, it does not appear to have performed any significant role, particularly in time of peace. It neither voted nor did it take decisions. When it did meet, it did so primarily to hear of decisions which had been taken by the king and also to provide a public forum for members of the nobility, who by tradition had alone the right to speak, and who used the occasion forcefully to tender their advice.[6] There are, of course, references in Homer to displays of approval or disapproval by acclamation in the assemblies, and it should be conceded that the king was sometimes interested in testing popular reaction. But that the nature of this reaction had literally no effect on policy is amply illustrated by Agamemnon's curt rejection of the priest's well-received plea for his daughter's ransom in the first book of the *Iliad*,[7] and by his quite callous response to the assembly's attitude when he deliberately made trial of the people by raising their hopes of a prospective withdrawal from Troy.[8] Indeed, the complete impotence and subservience of the non-noble population is stressed in Homer's vivid account of the manner in which Odysseus checked the army's precipitate rush to the ships on this last occasion. 'Whom-soever he met that was a chieftain or a man of note, to his side he would come and with gentle words try to restrain him . . . but whatsoever man of the people he saw and found brawling, him would he smite with his staff and chide with words, saying, "Fellow, sit thou still, and hearken to words of others who are better than thou. Thou shalt neither be counted in war nor in counsel, for no good thing is a multitude of lords. Let there be one lord and one king, to whom Chronos hath vouchsafed the sceptre and the judgments." '9

Although it seems clear enough that the people were of little consequence in the eighth century, the vehemence of the language which is sometimes used by Homer might well be taken to indicate that he could discern a trend towards greater tolerance which was already taking shape in his own time. There comes to mind the account in the *Iliad* of the unprecedented occasion when a non-noble, named Thersites, dared to flout tradition by himself taking the floor at an assembly of warriors. In so doing he incurred the wrath of Odysseus in particular; and the rebuke which the latter administered was both stern and menacing. ' "If I find thee playing the fool again, I will strip off thy raiment and thy tunic and send thee wailing to the swift ships, beaten forth from the place of assembly with shameful blows." So spake Odysseus, and with his staff smote his back and shoulders.'10 It is tempting to suppose that such interventions at popular gatherings constituted a novel, if still rare, phenomenon of Homer's own day which the poet himself found singularly distasteful.

Another episode which Homer may have introduced into his story in order to draw a sharp contrast between past and present is the account in the *Odyssey* of Telemachus' totally unsuccessful attempt to interest the assembly in his own personal quarrel with the other nobles of Ithaca. In Homer's own time, perhaps, such an appeal to the people over the heads of the nobility might well have turned out to be more rewarding. Naturally enough, in the course of time the authority of the state, as personified at one time by monarchy and later by magistracy, began to impinge more and more upon that which had traditionally been exercised by the clan. The process, of course, was a slow one; but it is possible that by the mid-seventh century the extension of centralized authority to cover not only matters military but also certain aspects of economics and law had progressed so far that it was already possible to discern the forging of a new bond between state and citizen which transcended feudal ties. Clearly, this point must not be overstated. Homer may have been voicing a protest against new and unwelcome trends, but the strong language which he uses leaves us in little doubt that any tendency to look upon the populace as an element deserving of political consideration was as yet very much in its infancy. The time when popular opinion was to be expressed and measured in terms of votes still lay some way in the future.

DEVELOPMENTS AT SPARTA

Evidence relating to the constitutional development of early Sparta is notoriously scant, and the efforts of both ancients and moderns alike to discover the truth in detail have been bedevilled by the success which Sparta's later authoritarian regime achieved in propagating the myth that almost all her institutions, social, political, and military, had been the creation of one divinely inspired individual known as Lycurgus. None the less, there is perhaps general agreement among scholars on at least one point— that before the Persian wars Sparta passed through two distinct periods of political upheaval which witnessed some measure of constitutional change. The first of these fell roughly in either the middle or the second half of the eighth century, the second towards the close of the seventh.[11]

The conflicts of the eighth century were undoubtedly associated with the struggle for power between kings and nobles. Two of the principal identifiable figures, whose names have endured, are the co-kings, Theopompus and Polydorus, of whom the latter is said to have been the victim of assassination,[12] while the former has won the reputation of having saved the Spartan monarchy, albeit in a weakened form, by making timely concessions when the very existence of the institution was threatened.[13] The story rings true of a time some fifty to a hundred years after the age which it has been supposed was characterized in the Homeric poems. The precise form of the concessions which Theopompus made is not known; but if his object was to conciliate the aristocracy, it is not unreasonable to assume that he enhanced the powers of the Council of Elders, or *gerousia*, as it was called, and perhaps gave this body recognition as an official organ of the constitution. Some support for this view may be derived from that enigmatic 'document' relating to the political forms of the early Spartan state which is known as the Great Rhetra. Variously regarded as a divine oracle and as a legal enactment, this Rhetra provided for the establishment of a new religious sanctuary dedicated to Zeus and Athena, for the distribution of the population among tribes and other local units which were called *obes*, for the establishment of a council of thirty members inclusive of the two kings, and for the calling of regular meetings of a popular Assembly.[14] Its date has been the subject of endless controversy, and there is still very little common ground;[15] but the case for linking it with the Theopompan programme of reform is nevertheless a strong one. Both the registration of the population on a local, as opposed to a kinship, basis, and the establishment of what was apparently a form of official state cult point to some extension of the influence and control of the state at the expense of the family, such as might well be dated to around the late eighth century. Once this trend had been established, it cannot have been long before the nobility began to voice a demand for a larger say in the management of state affairs as compensation for the gradual erosion of their autonomy in the clan and family circle. The formation of an official aristocratic Council, therefore, falls naturally into place in this period. The small group of leading nobles, who had earlier upheld the monarchy and tendered their advice, was enlarged, constituted as an official body of fixed size, and empowered to take collective decisions in company with the kings themselves, while the kings were as a consequence reduced to the status of *primi inter pares*.

It is possible, therefore, that a Council employing formal voting methods came into being in Sparta in *c.* 750 BC. But it was as yet only the aristocrats who were staking their claim to a political voice. The popular Assembly—the *apella*—must be assumed to have been still a body of little real consequence. The provision in the Rhetra for regular meetings of this body does not belie this view. Now that the state was assuming more control over the lives of the citizens, it was natural that gatherings of the people, which were justified even in the days of Odysseus on the ground that there was some matter of public importance to report, should have become more frequent. Furthermore, whereas assemblies had at one time been held only on the summons of a king or nobleman, it would have been a natural corollary to the establishment of some form of corporate government that the decision to call an assembly should no longer be left to the whim of the individual. A procedural change providing for meetings to be held at regular intervals in no sense implies that the *apella* underwent a change of function or indeed that it began to exercise any more power of decision than had the primitive gathering of the Homeric age.

The tendency to regard the *apella* as an active, and therefore a voting, constituent in the Spartan constitution from as early as the eighth century rests on three assumptions—that the *apella* had always been responsible for the election of members of the *gerousia*, that the emergence of the magistracy known as the ephorate, which according to tradition dated from the mid-eighth century, testifies to the early assertion of popular sovereignty, and that the early right of the *apella* both to reject and amend legislation is implied by the content of the Rhetra.[16] None of these three assumptions has very much substance.

It is very unlikely that the appointment of the twenty-eight members of the new *gerousia*, which even in later times was conducted by the most primitive method of selection (p. 74), was originally left in the hands of what was little more than a warriors' assembly. Membership of the *gerousia* was for life; and it is not unlikely that for many years the vacancies were filled by co-optation.

The classification of the ephorate as a popular magistracy and the consequent association of its origins with the rise of popular sovereignty is also misleading. In the sixth century and after, certainly, the ephors are portrayed as the all-powerful bastions of the new communal state, who, among other things, habitually watched the night sky for a sign which could be used to end the rule of the kings.[17] But Aristotle attributes the very institution of the office to King Theopompus himself. Whatever its true origins—and the ephors have been variously regarded both as early religious officials and as the headsmen of the local divisions newly created at the time of the Rhetra—there is little good reason to question the tradition that their emergence as officers of state was brought about through the agency of the kings and as a direct result of the need which they felt for assistance in shouldering their growing responsibilities. As to their mode of appointment, Aristotle nowhere suggests that they were ever elected by the popular Assembly. When they first began to assume an official role it is probable that they were nominated directly by the king or at best appointed by the *gerousia*.[18]

The most serious argument in favour of the *apella* as an early decision-making body is based on the reference in Plutarch's version of the Rhetra to the right of the Assembly to refuse its sanction. But what slight claim this may have to credence is surely undermined by the remark a few lines later that Kings Theopompus and Polydorus added a rider to the Rhetra curtailing this measure of popular autonomy and providing that the kings and *gerousia* should have power to overrule any 'crooked' decision which the *apella* took. A suggestion that an experiment in giving rein to the people was both tried and abandoned before the middle of the eighth century, when it is improbable that even the Council existed in any formal shape, is manifestly unacceptable. If there was such an experiment made, it is one which is more likely to have belonged to the sixth century than to the eighth. Just as Sparta's authoritarian leaders attempted to justify the entire social and political order of later years on the ground that it was a Lycurgan creation, so they might conceivably have tried to defend the withdrawal of a popular concession by making some obscure reference to the role assigned to the *gerousia vis-à-vis* the *apella* in the time of Theopompus.[19]

The emergence of a popular Assembly at Sparta which formally expressed itself by vote should therefore be regarded as a later development. According to both Herodotus and Thucydides, the

Spartans passed through a long period of poor government and lawlessness.[20] This can almost certainly be dated to the years between the establishment of aristocratic rule under Theopompus and the end of the seventh century—a time during which Sparta was engaged in two protracted wars against the Messenians and was also the victim of an attack launched by the all-powerful Pheidon of Argos. Not only was there dissidence within the narrow aristocratic oligarchy itself during this period; there was also a growing discontent among the ordinary Spartan citizens, who suffered from the disruption of the economy which was occasioned by the wars, and who began to derive a new sense of independence from the vital role which they played as hoplite soldiers. The poet Tyrtaeus, while quoting the Rhetra and stressing that under the rule of law authority was vested in the kings and the *gerousia*, gave voice to the demands of these hoplites for the redistribution of land and for a more efficient administration. These were eventually met by a social revolution which took place at the end of the seventh century. The defeat of the Messenians and the occupation of new territory allowed the land-hunger to be partially relieved, while the paramount need for military efficiency, accentuated by an increase in the number of Helot slaves, called for the acceptance of a discipline which could only be effectively ensured by some concession to popular demands. The outcome was the establishment of a well-ordered society of 'equals', in which it must be supposed that the 'equals' enjoyed some opportunity to give corporate expression to their views. Although the harsh discipline which the citizens imposed upon themselves was not conducive to any advance towards real democracy and indeed soon facilitated the setting up of an authoritarian regime, the Spartans appear to have established and retained some semblance of a right to take political decisions in their regular *apella*. Ostensibly they assumed some control over the appointment of councillors, and they claimed the right, however ineffective it may have been, to pronounce upon legislation and matters of policy. It is likely that it was at this stage, and not before, that the *apella* first began to register a formal vote.

DEVELOPMENTS AT ATHENS

Just as at Sparta formal voting must first have been adopted in the *gerousia*, so at Athens it will have made its appearance first in the aristocratic Council of the Areopagus. The approximate date of origin of this institution, of course, is a matter for some speculation. Thucydides and Plutarch both associate the establishment of a single council with the process of *synoekismos* and unification in Attica, and they ascribe it to the legendary King Theseus; while Plutarch adds a further detail, crediting the same Theseus with responsibility for bringing into being a privileged aristocratic caste known as the Eupatrid order, for which he reserved absolute control over government and religion.[21] It is fairly clear that events covering several hundred years have been seriously compressed by these sources and assigned *en bloc* to the days of Athens' legendary beginnings. The probable truth is that the extension of the monarchy's control over the smaller townships of Attica was a very gradual process, and that until comparatively late in the regal period the king's authority was restricted largely to the military sphere, as was the case in Homer's Ithaca. The significant element in the traditional story, however, is the hint that the extension of this centralized authority was closely associated with the institution of an official state Council to be manned by members of a particular group of families. Clearly, at this stage the trend towards a transition from monarchical to aristocratic government must have been under way. Although the fact that in later years the king archon presided over the Council of the Areopagus confirms that it was of regal origin, the very constitution of a Council which was representative of the major families in Attica must have marked an effective challenge to the regal monopoly of the Medontid clan, which had previously rested upon the support of a limited number of friends. It is unlikely to have been long after this that the aristocracy secured the regular appointment of an archon and a polemarch to take over many of the king's civil and military powers, or indeed that kingship itself was reduced in its weakened form to the status of a magistracy.[22]

To judge by the fact that the list of eponymous archons is

known to have gone back to 681 BC, it is a reasonable assumption that the establishment of a formal aristocratic Council which formulated policy and reached its decisions by vote should be dated at Athens, as at Sparta, to the second part of the eighth century. But equally, as at Sparta, the creation of a properly ordered Council and the emergence of the regular magistracy must not be taken to have heralded the almost immediate extension of the principle of voting to the popular Assembly. Almost certainly the Eupatrid body, like the patriciate of early Rome, was a definable and artificial group of families which comprised the core of the aristocracy at the time of its formation, and its very *raison d'être* was to secure a monopoly of effective power for its members to the exclusion of those who lay outside it. Although there is no trustworthy tradition on the matter, it is very probable that all the members of the early Council were drawn from this Eupatrid class, and that vacancies were filled by the Areopagites themselves by a process of election.[23] Similarly, in the case of the early magistracies it is hardly credible that the Eupatrids would have been prepared voluntarily to extend the right of appointment to any outside body. This view—that the Council of the Areopagus was originally solely responsible for the selection of magistrates—is clearly stated by Aristotle in his *Constitution of Athens*,[24] and, despite doubts which have been expressed, it appears to be confirmed rather than denied in the *Politics*; for, although Aristotle suggests that the early sixth-century lawgiver, Solon, found what he calls an aristocratic 'elected magistracy' in being,[25] he twice implies, if he does not specifically state, that it was the same Solon who was responsible for transferring the right of electing magistrates to the people.[26] The suggestion, made by one scholar,[27] that the primitive Assembly may have acquired the right to appoint the archons as the price for its acquiescence in the aristocracy's plan to abolish the life-monarchy is a fantasy which is markedly out of keeping with the lack of concern which, in Homer's portrayal, the people of Ithaca felt for the plight of Telemachus in his struggle with the suitors.

Before the end of the seventh century, then, the Assembly at Athens is unlikely to have counted for any more than the assemblies of the Homeric poems. There can have been no formal voting. The appointment of magistrates lay in the hands of the Council, and popular legislation was unknown. Nevertheless, as at Sparta, so perhaps to a greater extent at Athens the absolute control exercised by the noble families over the lives of the people must have been progressively weakened by fundamental changes in the nature of society. The principal factors which undermined the position of the aristocracy and which forced them to pay more heed to popular sentiment were three: the gradual centralization of authority in the hands of the state at the expense of the clan, the development of the hoplite army, in which common service led to the development of new associations and new loyalties, and, perhaps most important of all, the natural tendency of those excluded from the narrow Eupatrid class, both those who were themselves of aristocratic descent and those who had newly acquired status and influence through engagement in profitable commercial enterprises, to exploit popular discontent, in order to strengthen their own hand and to find support for their own claims to more active participation in government. The existence of these pressures and the instability of the Eupatrid class is to some extent evidenced by the role of the people at the time of the Kylonian conspiracy in the later seventh century[28] and by the readiness of the aristocracy to agree to the codification of the law by Draco.[29] More particularly, it is illustrated by the decision to appoint Solon as lawgiver in 594 BC.

Although the fourth-century writers erroneously portrayed Solon as the founder of the Athenian democracy, and undoubtedly ascribed to his authorship many institutions and changes for which he was not responsible, there is no good reason to reject the tradition that he gave some recognition to a form of popular Assembly, which presumably began to express itself by means of a vote. Aristotle says that he gave to the people no more power than was absolutely necessary, but that without the right of electing magistrates and calling them to account they would have been little better than slaves. Some form of participation in elections by the people is therefore probable; and, although the issue is debated, there is a case for the view that the Assembly also began to exercise certain judicial functions under the name of *heliaea*, possibly acting as a court of appeal against the jurisdiction of the magistrates, in the same way as did the *comitia centuriata* in the early Roman Republic.[30] That it did more and acted as a legislative body is less likely. There is no suggestion that any arrangements were made for regular meetings; and Solon's alleged creation of a second, elected Council, which had probouleutic functions in preparing the Assembly's business, is very questionable. Even the composition of the Assembly at this stage is in doubt.[31] The belief of Aristotle that the landless class in Athens, the *Thetes*, was officially admitted to the Assembly by Solon is not wholly acceptable.[32] Solon is unlikely to have taken the step of so radically altering the composition of a body which until his own time had been little more than the equivalent of the Homeric assembly of warriors. It is possible that the poorer elements may occasionally have presented themselves at such meetings as were held; but any official recognition of their right to a vote would appear to have presupposed a much more fully developed concept of citizenship than is likely to have existed at this time.

Solon, then, may be said to have been the first to fashion a popular Assembly which was called upon to take corporate decisions by vote. At this stage it will not have differed radically from the assembly of hoplite landowners which first began to function officially at Sparta at approximately the same period. However, whereas at Sparta a rigid self-imposed discipline and an abnegation of wealth were not conducive to democratic development, the cause of popular sovereignty at Athens was notably advanced by social emancipation and economic expansion. The tyrants, who came to power soon after the time of Solon, certainly restricted popular freedom in some sense but they also did much to weaken the authority of the aristocratic families, both by encouraging still greater centralization in the fields of administration, law, and religion, and by building on foundations already laid by Solon in promoting the growth of a profitable commercial economy. By the time of Cleisthenes the way for more complete emancipation had been well prepared, and, with his reorganization of the body politic on a local basis, there took shape for the first time a meaningful concept of citizenship which rested not upon the possession of wealth or upon any feudal attachment but simply upon registration in the local parish-like unit of the deme.

It is generally accepted that the constitution of Cleisthenes towards the end of the sixth century gave more precise definition to the powers of the Assembly than there had been hitherto. From a mutilated inscription of the late fifth century, which is considered to record a re-enactment of a much earlier provision, it has been inferred that jurisdiction was reserved for the Assembly in all cases involving the death penalty except homicide;[33] and examples of capital charges tried by the people in the early fifth century confirm this view.[34] As we have seen, the right of electing magistrates, and perhaps also of pronouncing on major issues involving war and peace, may well have existed earlier; but Cleisthenes is commonly thought to have provided for ten regular meetings of the Assembly in each year, and he obviously intended this body to play its part in policy-making and legislation.

It was almost certainly Cleisthenes also who was responsible for the creation of yet another voting body at Athens—a new, annually appointed Council of five hundred persons, to be selected in the proportion of fifty members from each of his ten new local tribes.[35] Aristotle, indeed, dated the origin of this second Council to the time of Solon, but, as there is no reason to think that the powers of the old aristocratic Council were then materially curtailed or that there was as yet an active popular Assembly for which a smaller body would be required to prepare business, there is a strong case for rejecting this as part of the Solonian legend. Only when a popular Assembly began to meet at regular intervals, after Cleisthenes, would the need for such a second Council have been felt. In practice the new body was designed to perform the useful task both of preparing the agenda for the Assembly and of shouldering part of the heavy administrative burden which with increasing centralization had begun to fall to the magistrates. In theory, it represented a compromise between the magisterial authority which Solon left virtually untouched and the trend towards popular sovereignty which was portended by the increased activity of the voting Assembly.

CHAPTER II

APPOINTMENT TO OFFICE

IN HIS ACCOUNT OF the morphology of the state at the end of the fourth book of the *Politics*, Aristotle conducts a detailed analysis of the principles underlying magisterial appointment in Greek states. He concentrates upon three variables—the identity and size of the appointing body, the rules governing eligibility to office, and the actual method of selection employed. Thus at any election the appointment is made either by all the citizens or by only some of them; it is made from out of the whole citizen body or from out of only a part of it; and it is made either by direct vote or by a process of sortition. In any one state, Aristotle continues, these three variables may be combined in a multiplicity of ways. 'Either all the citizens may appoint from out of the whole citizen body by vote, or all may appoint from out of the whole by lot; or all may appoint from out of part of the citizen body by vote, or all from out of a part by lot; or again they may appoint to some offices one way and to some in another. And similarly, if it is only a section of the citizens that is responsible for making appointments, they may do so either from out of the whole citizen body by vote, or from out of the whole by lot, or from out of part of the citizen body by vote, or from out of a part by lot, or again to some offices in one way and to others in another.'[36]

This catalogue is, of course, essentially a logical one, and it is merely introduced in preparation for a classification of the various forms of constitution typified by each method. None the less, it is likely that there was considerable diversity in the Greek world in the rules of magisterial appointment, and it is not impossible that Aristotle could have cited examples of most, if not all, of the combinations of the variables which he lists. This can be inferred from his chance and isolated references to such cases as that of Megara, where certain offices were open only to those who had previously been in exile and had fought against the democracy, or that of Mantinea, where the elections were conducted not by the popular Assembly but by an electoral college appointed by the Assembly for the purpose.[37] The fact remains, however, that the evidence relating to electoral practices in the minor townships of the Greek world is far too scanty to permit of any detailed analysis, and that a coherent account of Greek procedures can only profitably be based upon an examination of the material which relates to Sparta and, more particularly, to Athens.

In the passage quoted Aristotle suggests three of the questions which should be our concern in this chapter. What class of people was eligible for any given office? What was the nature of the electorate? And by what method, voting, sortition, or a combination of the two, was the appointment determined? There is also, however, an important fourth consideration, which Aristotle no doubt did not think fit to stress since it has less bearing upon his formal classification of constitutions. This concerns the extent to which any particular method of appointment had reference to the principle of representation. In Athens certainly, as elsewhere, there was commonly a relationship between the size of any magisterial board or other appointed body on the one hand, and the number of local administrative units into which the citizen body was divided on the other. It is clear that with few exceptions the equal, or the proportionate, representation of local units was at Athens the accepted ideal. This, of course, could be achieved by either of at least two very different methods. By one such method the state might delegate the entire responsibility for appointment to local bodies, after allocating to each a specific number of offices or seats. By another the national body might itself retain full control over the appointment procedure, while at the same time selecting the candidates with strict reference to the local units from which they came. As will be clear from the following survey of the procedures used in appointing to each of the principal offices, common use was made in the Greek state of both methods.

SPARTA—GEROUSIA AND EPHORATE

All too little is known of the rules which governed the appointment of officials at Sparta. Of the Council or *gerousia*, it can be said only that it was a body of nobles limited to twenty-eight in number, and that, at least after the reforms which can be dated to the end of the seventh century, its members were selected by a form of popular election conducted in the Spartan *apella*.[38] It is very possible that the responsibility for filling vacancies had earlier been left either to the kings or to the councillors themselves. All full Spartiates over the age of sixty were eligible for election; but no man was obliged to take office, and the list of candidates was therefore confined to those who actually sought election. This aspect of the procedure, of which Aristotle incidentally expressed disapproval,[39] is likely to have resulted in the continuance of what was virtually an aristocratic and hereditary instrument of government in a technically egalitarian state. Apart from the opportunities for bribe-taking which are presented by the tenure of any public office, the duties of a Spartan councillor were unremunerative; and it is thus probable that the majority of candidates were drawn from those who regarded a position of authority as their birthright and a successful candidature as something which they owed to their personal dignity.[40] In this sense, of course, the Spartan aristocracy will have had much in common with the nobility of the Roman Republic.

The chief magistrates of Sparta were the ephors, of whom Aristotle states that they enjoyed supreme authority in matters of highest importance and power so great that even the kings were obliged to seek their favour.[41] As has already been noted, the origins of the office are obscure, although tradition has it that they first made their appearance as state officers in the eighth century, when Theopompus conferred on them some authority as part of a general policy of compromise designed to preserve the monarchy. Their number—five—is one which features in other contexts at Sparta and one which very possibly corresponds to the number of local units which were established at the time of the Rhetra.[42] It is therefore as reasonable a suggestion as any that the ephors were originally representatives, and perhaps even headsmen, of these newly formed local divisions, to whom the kings thought fit to delegate some of their responsibilities in the fields of administration and jurisdiction. It appears that they were originally selected by the kings; but the right of appointment might well have been transferred to the aristocracy in the *gerousia* early on, especially as they could have had a particular interest in the choice of those who were now to operate in the name of the state in what had previously been their own domain.

The ephors played so prominent a role in the reformed Spartan state of the sixth century and later that they have been commonly regarded as popular leaders who must inevitably have owed their appointment in those days to the *apella*. Aristotle, however, indicates strongly that this was not the case. He remarks that the ephors were chosen from out of the entire citizen body, in the sense that every Spartan was eligible to serve, but he says nothing definite concerning the identity of the electorate; and indeed at one point in the fourth book of the *Politics*, when he is discussing what he regards as the democratic features of the Spartan constitution, he makes what appears to be a distinction between the members of the *gerousia* on the one hand, who were elected *by* the whole people, and the ephors on the other, who were elected *from* the whole people.[43] If it was not the full *apella* which appointed them, there are at least two other possibilities. One is that each was selected in his own tribe by some form of local gathering. The other, which is more likely, is that they were all chosen annually by the *gerousia*. In this latter case, it should perhaps be supposed that the candidates were listed in five groups corresponding to their tribe of origin, and that the election was held in five stages, one candidate being selected from each list in turn.

The suggestion that the members of the *gerousia* were primarily responsible for the appointment of ephors throughout Spartan history is not so much out of keeping with Aristotle's portrayal of the later Spartan constitution as might be supposed. The 'revolution' at the end of the seventh century was a popular 'revolution' only insofar as it encompassed a certain redistribution of wealth and engineered a participation in decision-making for the Assembly which was largely nominal. The regime which it established was an authoritarian one, in which, as Aristotle baldly states, privilege belonged only to the magistrates, and in which the rest of the citizens were subjected to a discipline so rigid that they found it intolerable.[44] There is, therefore, little reason to doubt that effective control in the state continued to be exercised by the old aristocratic families, who under pressure had given way to necessity and who in their common interest had countenanced a compromise which entailed the sacrifice of wealth in return for an assurance of unchallengeable authority. Just as the *gerousia* itself continued to be recruited from a traditional governing class, so must the chief magistrates have been drawn largely from the same families, even though observance of the principle of annuality and of restrictions on re-election may often have necessitated their being sought from outside the immediate inner circle which had traditionally been represented in the *gerousia*. It should be borne in mind that, when Aristotle complains of the deterioration at Sparta resulting from the supersession of aristocracy by democracy and speaks of the appointment of ephors whose very poverty lays them open to corruption, he is in fact referring to a decadent age, at least three centuries after the institution of the new order, when marked inequality of wealth had already begun to reassert itself. The very fact that he alludes in the same section to the venality of the members of the *gerousia* themselves should establish that his remarks have no bearing on the method by which the ephors were appointed.

Much has been made in recent times of the traditional hostility between ephors and kings, said to be typified by the formers' nine-yearly observation of the night sky in anticipation of ending the monarchy. Such emphasis, however, can be misleading. The nocturnal watch was possibly little more than the performance of an outdated ritual and it is unlikely to have had any serious political connotation. For the rest, the exchange of oaths between kings and ephors, the deference shown by the kings to the ephors in their presence, and the gradual usurpation by the ephors of what had once been regal prerogatives are more likely to have been symptomatic simply of that final assertion of authority by aristocracy over the royal families which elsewhere had long since led to the liquidation of the monarchy than of any enforced acceptance of the principle of popular sovereignty. Professor Andrewes has recently made the important point that it was in the reign of the strongest kings that least was heard at Sparta of the activity of the ephors—a circumstance which he ascribes to the fact that the ephors at such a time are likely to have been the king's men.[45] One might add that the kings' influence could only have extended to determining the composition of the board of ephors if the election of those officers had been conducted in a comparatively small body over which they could have expected to exercise some control. The *gerousia*, of which the kings were themselves members, was just such a body.

THE ATHENIAN MAGISTRACIES BEFORE CLEISTHENES

In pre-Solonian Athens the chief magistrates, the archons, were chosen by the Council of the Areopagus; and, although Aristotle at one point speaks in general terms of the selection of magistrates on the basis of both birth and wealth,[46] it is widely accepted that the essential qualification for the office at this early stage was membership of the Eupatrid class. It was one of Solon's most significant achievements that he substituted wealth for membership of this caste as the basic qualification for office and so made way for the recruitment both of the *nouveaux riches* and of such fringe members of the landed aristocracy as had until then been excluded. He effected this change by dividing the population into four property classes, defined in terms of annual income, and by using the individual's census rating as the criterion of his eligibility to hold the various offices of state. We are explicitly told that the office of Treasurer of Athena was reserved by Solon for members of the first property class; and, if Aristotle lists the early magistracies in order of precedence, it is likely that the archonship, which heads the list, was restricted at first to members of that class also.[47] There is a record of the office being opened to members of the third class in 457 BC;[48] and, although there is no such record of its being opened at any particular date to the second, it is an unwarranted argument from silence to suggest that it must therefore have been opened to both first and second classes by Solon.[49]

If Aristotle was right in his view that the appointment of magistrates lay in pre-Solonian Athens with the Areopagus, it is clear that the mere formulation of new rules governing eligibility would not necessarily have been effective in introducing new blood had they not been accompanied by changes either in the nature of the electoral body or in the electoral process itself; indeed, in his *Constitution of Athens* Aristotle records what in fact appears to have been just such a radical reform. 'Solon provided', he says, 'that appointment to the various offices should be made by lot from candidates chosen in advance by each of the tribes. For the archonship each tribe nominated ten candidates, from whom the final board of nine was chosen by lot.'[50] Many scholars have seen fit to reject this statement as a rationalization based by analogy upon later practice. Their case rests largely on two arguments—one, that the early introduction of the process of sortition from among candidates on a previously selected list (*clerosis ek procriton*) is out of keeping with the logical development of Athenian institutions and with the established fact that the archons were directly elected during the period of the tyranny and for some years after; the other, that certain references in the *Politics* to the 'election' of magistrates under Solon are inconsistent with the use of the lot in any form. Neither argument, however, is particularly valid. It is wrong to insist on logical development at times of violent social and political upheaval. It is also misleading to attach great importance to Aristotle's use of the word 'election' in a context where any attempt to draw a precise distinction between selection by vote and appointment by lot would have been totally irrelevant to his theme. Indeed, any reference in either of the passages concerned to the part played by sortition in the electoral process would seriously have confused the issue.[51]

A consideration of what are acknowledged to have been Solon's principal aims in his reform of the magistracy suggests that the introduction of *clerosis ek procriton* may well have been an obvious answer to his problem. The mere transference of the elections from the Council of the Areopagus to a larger and more popular body need not in itself have produced the desired result of radically changing the composition of the magisterial boards, for the social structure was still basically feudal and the traditional ties and loyalties of the ordinary Athenian were still very strong. It is noteworthy that at Rome the virtual monopoly of office held by the patriciate was not broken until the popular assembly was compelled by law—possibly against its natural inclination—to assign one of the two annual consulships to a non-patrician.[52] An equally effective way of overcoming the difficulty, however, and one which was better suited to Solonian Athens, was so to increase the number of those whom the electorate was called upon to choose as to ensure that some representatives of the non-Eupatrid element at least were included among their nominees. This is exactly what an appointment procedure such as is ascribed by Aristotle to Solon would have achieved. The popular body would have been compelled to select a little over four times as many candidates as would eventually be required to fill offices; and the use of the lot in the second stage of the proceedings would have ensured that the proportions of old and new blood among these selected candidates were duly reproduced in the final list.

It is very possible that the preliminary process of selection under the Solonian arrangements was conducted in the four assemblies of the old kinship tribes, which may well have met from time to time under the presidency of the tribal officials, the *phylobasileis*. In a society which was still feudal in structure it would have made more sense to confer the right of selecting the *procritoi* upon gatherings of manageable size, where those attending might be expected to have some knowledge of the candidates.

Solon's changes inevitably engendered discontent; and the sources hint at serious disturbance in the years which followed. One incident which Aristotle records is of particular interest in an electoral connection. A certain Damasias made an attempt to seize power by holding on to his archonship for longer than the allotted period of one year; he was eventually forced to stand down only after a compromise had been reached by the warring factions to the effect that five archons should be drawn from the Eupatrids and five from non-Eupatrid groups.[53] Aristotle appears to believe that this was a solution which had reference only to a single year; but, as he represents the archons as ten in number when in fact they were only nine, it is clear that he did not appreciate its full significance. An attractive suggestion, put forward by Cavaignac,[54] is that the compromise was of a less ephemeral nature, and that the ten persons referred to were not the archons themselves but the ten selected candidates who were appointed every year from each of the four tribes. The effect of such an arrangement, of course, would have been to guarantee the almost equal distribution of archonships over a number of years between members of the Eupatrid order and members of those groups whose interests Solon had been concerned to promote. What cannot be said with any assurance is whether this later and more rigid prescription, if indeed it has been correctly interpreted, was more or less favourable to the newer families than that of Solon.

Little is known of the other offices of these early years. The Treasurers of Athena were exceptionally appointed by a process of pure sortition after Solon; possibly they had been so appointed for many years before him, in accordance with the principle that the selection of those who had so close a connection with the affairs of a goddess should not be left in the hands of men. The other magistrates Aristotle clearly believed to have been appointed, like the archons, by a process of *clerosis ek procriton;* and there is no compelling reason to reject his view.

THE ATHENIAN ARCHONSHIP AFTER CLEISTHENES

It is uncertain how long the Solonian procedures remained in force. Thucydides affirms that the tyrant Peisistratus took steps to ensure the appointment of his own nominees to the archonship;[55] and this is confirmed by an extant fragment of an archon list for the years 528–521 BC, which indicates that the eponymous archonship at least was held successively during this period by representatives of the foremost families at Athens.[56] It is obvious that such effective control could not have been exercised if any form of sortition had been involved; and it should therefore be supposed that, if the tyrants had any respect for constitutional forms at all, there was some return to a direct electoral process. It is even possible that elections were conducted, as in pre-Solonian days, in the Council of the Areopagus, over whose members the tyrants may have found it easier to exert pressure than over any larger and less tangible body such as a state or tribal assembly.

Almost certainly the arrangements for the appointment of magistrates were affected by the sweeping reorganization of the citizen body in the time of Cleisthenes. Thus, if elections to the archonship became something more of a reality once again after the departure of the tyrants, as is to be supposed, we may be sure that the four kinship tribes, which provided the *procritoi* under the Solonian rules, no longer had any effective part to play. Elections would either have been handed over to the full Athenian Assembly or, as is also possible, to the assemblies of the ten new local tribes which Cleisthenes created. The one point which is virtually beyond dispute is that there was no immediate reversion to the use of sortition. This is indicated by the appointment of a succession of illustrious archons during the period of twenty years which followed the fall of the tyrants, and it is confirmed by Aristotle, who records that it was in 487 BC that the archons were appointed by lot 'for the first time since the tyranny'. They then began to be chosen, he says, one from each tribe, from among five hundred who had been previously selected by the demes.[57]

Two important new principles are reflected in this provision of 487 BC. One is the rule that in every year each one of the archons should be drawn from a different tribe. In a sense, of course, a precedent for this procedure had been set by Solon, who had provided that his forty *procritoi* should be drawn in equal proportions from the four kinship tribes of his day. But the motives of the later legislator in embracing the representative principle were very different from those of Solon. Whereas Solon's emphasis on the role of the four kinship tribes merely reflected his respect for the clan structure of Athenian society, the insistence of Cleisthenes and his successors that the magisterial boards should consist of a representative from each of the ten newly formed and artificial local tribes was aimed to ensure that none could again fall under the dominance of an aristocratic cabal. Exactly how this principle was applied to the board of archons, which consisted of only nine

members, is explained by Aristotle in a later chapter. Of the ten
successful candidates representing each of the ten tribes in any one
year, nine were allotted to archonships, while the tenth had to be
satisfied with the lesser post of secretary to that group of archons
known as the *Thesmothetae*.[58]

The other major innovation for which the measure of 487 was
responsible was the delegation of the task of pre-selecting candidates to the comparatively small local communities known as
demes and the consequent assignation of a far more important role
to the lot in determining the final choice. If the number of pre-
selected candidates was indeed five hundred—and it is difficult to
see how it could have been very much less, when the demes themselves numbered well over a hundred—the element of direct
election in the appointment of archons must have been all but
eliminated.[59] Even on the assumption that it was at this time that
eligibility for the archonship was extended to members of the
second property class, the total number of persons qualified to
stand in any one year is unlikely to have much exceeded a thousand; and, if due allowance is made for unwillingness to serve,
competition for nomination at deme level must have been virtually non-existent. To all intents and purposes, therefore, the deme
organizations can merely have served to check upon the credibility
and qualifications of those who presented themselves, and the
actual appointment itself must have lain almost entirely in the
hands of the lot.

The election of archons by such a process of *clerosis ek procriton*
appears to have continued throughout most of the fifth century,
although it is possible that the responsibility for pre-selection was
at some stage transferred from the small demes to the larger
tribes. At some date unknown, however, pre-selection by direct
vote at the local level was abolished, and replaced by a preliminary
process of sortition. According to Aristotle, the archons in his own
time were appointed by lot from among one hundred candidates
put forward by the ten tribes, and these candidates had themselves
at an earlier stage been selected by lot within their own tribes.[60]
The process, therefore, was twofold. First, each tribe selected ten
of its members by lot at tribe level, and then one archon was

chosen by lot from each group of ten at state level. No entirely satisfactory explanation as to why the Athenians employed this elaborate procedure has yet been offered. It is, of course, quite absurd to suggest that a people who had so little regard for tradition should have gone to the trouble of holding two lotteries purely because the principle of local pre-selection had become established in the days of the direct vote.[61] Double sortition must surely have been thought to carry with it certain positive advantages, though it is by no means certain what these can have been. It seems clear enough that the chances of any one candidate securing appointment to office cannot have been effectively altered by reason of his name going through two processes of sortition rather than one, and it is equally clear that double sortition cannot in the least have eliminated the disparity in the relative chances of candidates from different tribes who had to contend with a different calibre of opposition. Nevertheless, the procedure does perhaps begin to make some sense if it is viewed as a method of ensuring that each tribe in fact put forward ten nominations for the final sortition and of preventing thereby any attempt to manipulate and regulate nominations at the tribal level. If there had been no such requirement, it might well have proved comparatively simple for one or more influential tribesmen to buy off potential rivals within their own tribe; they might thus markedly shorten the odds against their own appointment to office by seeing to it that their tribe submitted less than its quota of nominated candidates for the state allotment. If, on the other hand, there was such a requirement, as appears likely, such manœuvres would have been effectively barred, for no person would normally have been prepared to pay highly in effort or in favours for what at best could be only a one in ten chance of success. It may not, of course, be at first obvious why a requirement that each tribe should put forward ten nominations should have necessitated a process of double sortition. There is, however, a ready answer. The responsibility for ensuring that each tribe presented ten candidates must have rested with the tribal officers; and, in the event of the number of those who presented themselves locally for nomination falling short, it must have fallen to them to make up the number by conscription. It is clear that such conscription could have been equitably effected only by the drawing of lots between all those registered in the tribe who possessed the necessary qualifications to stand.

If this is in fact the correct explanation of the use of double sortition in the appointment of archons in the later period, it has a direct bearing upon the vexed question as to whether candidature for the archonship was ever compulsory. Obviously, had it been compulsory for all those who were qualified to present themselves as candidates every year, a single sortition would have sufficed. The implications of the employment of the double sortition are two—first, that in normal circumstances the number of persons volunteering for nomination was sufficiently large as not to warrant regular conscription, and, second, that the state nevertheless reserved the right to conscript candidates whenever the number of volunteers fell short. In the event, of course, it is most unlikely that the right to conscript was at all frequently invoked. The office of archon, though it had lost much of its power by the fourth century, still retained some of its prestige, and it is likely to have been more coveted than most. Once the institution of double sortition had nullified the effectiveness of any efforts to restrict nominations by means of corrupt influence, candidates would have presented themselves in more than sufficient numbers.

THE STRATEGIA

In the early fifth century, no doubt as a direct result of the introduction of full-scale sortition as a method of appointing the archons, the chief executive authority of the Athenian state passed from the archons to the board of *strategoi* or generals. By reason of the fact that the nature of their responsibilities demanded high technical qualifications, these officers enjoyed the distinction, comparatively rare in democratic Athens, of being appointed by direct election rather than by lot.

Little is known of the early history of this office. It is very probable that the generals, or their natural antecedents, existed in pre-Cleisthenic Athens as military commanders in the four kinship tribes. In this case, when the ten Cleisthenic tribes replaced these as the principal administrative units in the state, the number of generals appointed each year would likewise have been increased from four to ten. Each general is likely to have commanded a contingent from his own tribe at this stage, and each is therefore likely to have been appointed by his own fellow-tribesmen meeting in their local tribal assemblies.[62]

The first major change in the method of appointment can be dated to 501 BC, six years after the main Cleisthenic reforms, when, according to Aristotle, 'the Athenians began to elect their generals by tribes, one from each tribe'. The orthodox interpretation of these words, which there is little reason to question, is that they refer to a change from the practice of electing the ten generals in the ten separate assemblies to that of electing them, one from each tribe, in the full Assembly of the whole citizen body.[63]

In recent discussions concerning the relative importance of archons and generals at the beginning of the fifth century, and during the period of the Persian wars in particular, the full significance of this change in the method of appointing generals has commonly been missed. The use of the full Athenian Assembly as an electoral body was something as yet unusual, if not new. It is possible, though far from certain, that for a brief period after, and perhaps also during, the tyranny the archons were elected by the entire body of citizens; but, of course, in the case of the lesser magistracies, and indeed in the case of the archonship itself both in Solonian times and after the reintroduction of sortition in 487, the most vital part of the electoral process was conducted at the local level, in demes or in tribes. If, therefore, in 501 the responsibility for appointing the generals was transferred to the state Assembly against the current trend, it can only be that the duties of these officers were already regarded as sufficiently important to require that they should exceptionally be elected by a body which could claim both to be more immune to personal and corrupt influence and to be endowed with greater collective wisdom. In other words, the change must have been dictated not by doctrinaire thinking, as has been suggested,[64] but by a consideration of the national interest. It is only natural that a need for particular care in selecting military leaders should have been felt at this time.

Sparta was hatching plots against the new regime, and as a consequence the internal security of Athens was threatened as it had not been since before the days of Solon. In addition, the collapse of tyranny had left a serious vacuum in the military command which could not readily be filled. It is true that there was still the archon polemarch; and Aristotle is careful to assure us that, despite the changes in the arrangements for appointing the generals, it was he who continued to be the nominal head of the army. But he was almost certainly assigned to this particular office by lot and without regard to his suitability to discharge it. The extent of the Athenians' reliance upon their generals is fully illustrated by Herodotus' controversial account of military decision-making at the time of Marathon some eleven years later. Whatever may have been the legal niceties of the position, it is clear that the archon polemarch was only the commander in name, and that the vital decisions were taken by the individual generals who tendered him advice.[65]

A further modification in the method of appointing the generals was made at some date in the mid-fifth century, when not only the military, but also the political supremacy of the office was already fully established. The precise nature of the change is a matter of some controversy, but its most pronounced effect was undoubtedly to make it possible for any one tribe to be represented occasionally by more than one individual on a single board of ten generals.[66] The facts are that between 441 BC and the end of the century there are at least six well-attested examples of the double representation of a single tribe in one year, and that there are half a dozen or more others for which the evidence is somewhat more tenuous. Indeed, there is even a suggestion, not firmly established, that in certain years double representation applied not only to one tribe but to two.[67]

Although there are those who have attempted to explain away double representation of a tribe in terms not of law but of accidental circumstance—the illness of a candidate, perhaps, or some form of political manœuvre designed to ensure that one tribe did not put forward a candidate[68]—it is generally accepted today that the very frequency of the attested double representation points to the implementation of some procedural reform which affected the methods of appointment. One likely motive for such a reform in the middle of the fifth century has been suggested by Wade-Gery—namely that it was primarily designed to meet the difficulties arising from the continued tenure of the generalship by one able and indispensable individual, and perhaps in the 440s and 430s by Pericles in particular. The object would have been to make it possible for the Athenians repeatedly to re-elect a man of outstanding ability without thereby depriving themselves of the occasional services of any of his able fellow-tribesmen and, perhaps more important still, without for long periods prejudicing his fellow-tribesmen's chances of holding the office. That this was indeed the aim would seem to be confirmed by the fact that in all established cases of double representation one of the two generals representing the same tribe was a man who can be expected to have commanded extensive popular support.

Wade-Gery's own reconstruction of the nature of the procedural reform, however, is less convincing. His view is that the Athenian Assembly was given the right to decide each year exactly how the elections should be conducted, and that they had before them two options. One was simply to follow the procedure of 501 BC. The other was to hold the election in two distinct phases, in the first phase choosing one general from the entire list of candidates without reference to tribe, and in the second phase selecting ten candidates from ten different tribes in the normal way, but with the proviso that of these ten the one who recorded the smallest vote should automatically be dropped to make way for the individual who had been successful in phase one. Such a procedure—which incidentally could have resulted in the double representation of one tribe, but never in the double representation of two—would have had serious flaws. Firstly, the two-phase election process would have required that the Athenians should vote twice on every candidate, once when they voted to select a single general without reference to tribe, and a second time when they voted to choose the representatives of each of the tribes in turn. Not only would this have rendered the proceedings extremely long and protracted, but the result of the first vote would inevitably have provided valuable clues as to the comparative popularity among the citizens at large of two or more candidates from the same tribe, which would thus have encouraged the adoption of undesirable electoral tactics prior to the second stage of the voting. As a result candidates placed third within a tribe could perhaps have been induced to withdraw altogether, while those running second in popular favour could well have entered into agreements with those from other tribes who were similarly placed with a view to marshalling artificial support to their mutual advantage. Secondly, the provision requiring that the 'successful' candidate with the smallest total vote should be dropped would have worked most inequitably in practice; for, as the votes of the Athenians were distributed between all the candidates of a given tribe, the 'successful' candidate who polled the fewest votes would inevitably have been either one who had a multiplicity of rivals from among his own fellow-tribesmen or one who in a straight fight had a very small majority over his opponent. In neither case would either he or his tribe necessarily have merited elimination, since an able and popular candidate might well have polled a low vote on account of the almost equal ability of his tribal opponent, whereas a candidate of mediocre quality from another tribe might have owed a high vote almost entirely to his rival's inadequacy. Finally, as has often been remarked by others,[69] it would in effect have been impossible for the Athenians to come to a rational decision each year on the procedure to be adopted in the election without thereby prejudging the outcome. If, as has been suggested, the object of the new arrangement was to devise a means whereby a specific individual might retain office over a number of years without causing embarrassment, the Athenians would have had to assume, whenever they opted for the two-stage procedure, both that a particular person would be chosen as the representative of his tribe in the normal course of events and that he would also emerge as the general chosen without reference to tribe in the first phase of the election.

A more convincing solution to the problem is suggested by what is clearly a reference to some change in the appointment procedure in Aristotle's account of institutions as they were in his

own day. 'The Athenians', he says, 'appoint all their military
officers by direct vote. The generals they at one time elected one
from each tribe, but now they elect them from out of their whole
body.'[70] Of course, these words in themselves do not tell us a great
deal about the substance or circumstances of the change in procedure; and, as Aristotle was describing a process which was still
in force as he wrote, he would have recognized no need to
elaborate further. But it is all but certain that he cannot be
referring, as has commonly been supposed, to an effective
abandonment of the principle of tribal representation in the
selection of generals. Extant lists of generals from the late fourth
century suggest that a balanced representation of tribes on the
board was still then a matter of concern to the Athenians.[71] It is
therefore not improbable that Aristotle is alluding here to the
problematical procedural change of the fifth century, resulting in
the occasional election of two generals from one tribe, which we
would otherwise have to suppose that he passes over in silence.[72]
Always on the assumption that the principle of tribal representation remained sacrosanct, the words of Aristotle in this case can
stand only one construction. Instead of voting upon candidates of
each of the ten tribes in turn, as they had done since 501, the
Athenians changed to voting upon the entire list in a single
operation and without any immediate reference during the vote
to the tribes to which the candidates belonged. Then, sub-
quently, in determining the results of the voting, they awarded
places on the board of generals to the ten candidates, *each from a
different tribe*, who were severally found to have polled a higher
vote than the other candidates from their own tribes. In view of
what is known about the composition of the boards of generals in
the later fifth century, it is probable that this change in procedure,
which in itself could have served little useful purpose, was
accompanied by some further provision which made possible the
occasional double representation of one or more tribes and the
consequent exclusion of others. The precise formula must remain
a matter for speculation, but the likely gist was simply that any
candidate who under the revised procedure received a stipulated
minimum total vote should automatically be declared elected

without detriment to the chances of any other candidates from his own tribe. The remainder of the board of ten would then be constituted by the most successful representatives of as many different tribes as there were places to be filled, the tribe (or tribes) to be excluded being that whose most successful candidate scored the lowest total vote.

If this was indeed the essence of the change in electoral procedure which the Athenians adopted in the mid-fifth century, they devised a most satisfactory method of dealing with their immediate problem. The decision as to whether to appoint one or more generals without reference to their tribes in any one year was not taken independently and prior to the election, as Wade-Gery suggests. It was taken during the course of the election itself, and, being geared to the overall popularity of one or more candidates, it was reflected in the voting figures. Furthermore, it may reasonably be supposed that any tribe which under this procedure ended up without a representative on the board owed its exclusion to a genuine lack of enthusiasm among the Athenians for any one of its nominated candidates; for, once the principle had been established that the election of two candidates from a single tribe was theoretically possible, the voters, so far from feeling logically bound to vote for only one candidate from each tribe, would have felt perfectly justified in voting for two or more candidates from one tribe, and for none from another. Indeed, it is possible that they were no longer constrained to restrict their votes to ten, and that, in the absence of any enforceable restrictions on the number of votes cast, they merely refrained from voting for those candidates whom they held in low esteem.

Although, as suggested, the principal purpose of such a change must have been to make possible the repeated re-election of one man without seriously interfering with the principle of tribal representation, this need not have been the sole motive. The reform may also have gone far towards curbing the candidates' opportunities of indulging with any success in undesirable electoral manœuvres. The system of 501, whereby generals were selected one at a time from the individual tribal lists, must have lent itself to joint electioneering. Candidates from different tribes must have tended to join forces with a view to the pooling of votes in the Assembly at large. Clearly, the effectiveness of such manœuvres would have been severely restricted by a change in procedure which enabled the voters to select from the complete list in one operation. In the majority of cases tribal loyalties would have been strong enough to induce voters to vote for two or more candidates from their own tribe, and this alone must have robbed the would-be manipulator of what had previously been an effective basis for mutual bargaining.

THE ATHENIAN MINOR MAGISTRACIES

In addition to the archons and the generals, the Athenians annually appointed a large number of lesser magistrates, most of whom, after Cleisthenes, were constituted either in boards of ten composed of a single representative from each tribe, or in boards of five on which each of the ten tribes was represented over a two-year cycle. No complete list of such officers exists for the fifth century, but it is probable that the majority of those catalogued by Aristotle in his *Constitution of Athens* were of reasonably long standing.[73] These are classed in two groups. Into one category, which was by far the smaller, fall those who were appointed by direct election. These included the military officers—the taxiarchs and phylarchs, who commanded tribal battalions of hoplites and cavalry, and the two hipparchs who had a wider responsibility for cavalry command—and also a small group of civil magistrates who had very specialized duties and who were in many cases appointed for a four-year term. The Athenians were obviously prepared to recognize that there were some tasks which demanded special qualities, and that the appointment of the magistrates concerned by direct vote was essential, if they were to be competently performed. For the same reason direct election was also employed from time to time for the purpose of appointing members of special commissions set up to deal with matters of urgent national concern. Notable examples are foreign legations, and special boards such as the *syngrapheis*, appointed to suggest revisions in the constitution, and the *teichopoioi*, appointed to build up the city's defences at a time of crisis.

Into the other category fall those who were selected by lot. In the isolated case of the Treasurers of Athena, sortition, albeit from among a very restricted group of citizens who were registered in the first property class, was of pre-Solonian origin. In most other cases it is likely to have dated from the time of Cleisthenes, or of course from the creation of the office, whichever was the later. It would serve little purpose here to list all the various known officers in this class or to detail their duties, and it should suffice to note that their functions generally amounted to little more than the superintendence of various departments of state administration in accordance with a strict code of rules and in such a way as did not demand the display of any outstanding talent or initiative. The exact number of these boards at any particular period is not known for certain, but it may be said that in Aristotle's day there were at least eleven boards of ten members, as well as two boards of five and one of forty, appointed each year.[74]

There is little which is problematical about the procedures which were adopted for appointing magistrates elected by direct vote. Originally, in the case of the older offices, it is probable that the local tribal assemblies were the electoral bodies employed; but the transference of the election of generals to the state Assembly in 501 is certain to have established a pattern which was soon followed in most, if not all, other cases. The trend in democratic Athens was to distrust smaller bodies on the ground that they were more subject to corrupt pressures.[75]

The procedure adopted for appointing the allotted officers is considerably more obscure. In a short and somewhat enigmatic passage in his *Constitution of Athens* Aristotle draws a distinction between two categories of allotted magistracies—those, including the archonship, for which the candidates had always been drawn from the tribe as a whole, and those which had at one time been distributed over the demes. The latter group, he continues, were in his day treated in much the same way as the former; the demes had made a habit of selling their quotas and it had therefore been found advisable to draw candidates in these cases also from the whole tribe.[76] It is a reasonable assumption that Aristotle's first group included only the more important offices which, like the archonship, were restricted to persons with a certain minimum property qualification, and that most of the minor magistracies fall into the second category. But what then is meant by the statement that these offices were at one time 'distributed over the demes'? One suggestion is that the demes all contributed to a common tribal pool of candidates in accordance with the size of their population, and that it was from this pool, totalling possibly fifty, that the tribal representatives on each of the fourteen or more annual boards of magistrates were selected by lot.[77] The constitution of each deme's quota was in this case presumably determined, if there was any competition, by a direct vote in the deme assembly. It is easy to see, however, that this procedure would have had severe disadvantages. In the first place, it would have involved a double process of selection—at deme level by vote, and at tribe level by lot—and it would possibly have necessitated the attendance of some five hundred persons, fifty from each tribe, at the final allotment. This might not have meant any great hardship, but it would have been unnecessarily troublesome when a simpler method could have been devised to achieve the same end. Secondly, the equitable operation of the lot and the arrangements designed to give each deme a chance of representation proportionate to its size would have been badly upset when the lot for a particular office fell upon someone in the pool of candidates who had already held the office and who, because of the ban on holding the same office twice,[78] was therefore ineligible to take up his appointment. Ways could, of course, have been found of avoiding such a complication, the simplest perhaps being to exclude from the lot for any particular office all those who had previously held it; but such methods would have made nonsense of the proportionate chances of the various demes, the achievement of which would presumably have been the whole purpose of such a complex procedure. And there is a third difficulty arising out of this interpretation. According to our information, the scheme was scrapped because the demes sold their quotas; and on this view the trade would have been not in the quotas of offices, but simply in the quotas of candidates which each deme was entitled to present at the tribal allotment. But, as it would have been impossible for any individual candidate to profit by such a transaction (his chances would always have been approximately 14 in 50), it is difficult to see who would have been the buyers. It is just possible that some demes had such corporate pride in being well represented on the magisterial boards that they were willing to use their funds to this end; but, against that, if deme pride did run so strong among the Athenians, it is unlikely that there would have been many sellers.

An alternative and eminently more sensible procedure is indicated by the evidence of allotment tokens, whose significance is discussed in detail in the next chapter. What these tokens suggest is that the allotment conducted in the Theseion to which Aristotle refers constituted not the final stage, but a preliminary one, in the appointment procedure. It did not determine the identity of the various magistrates for the following year; it merely marked out the particular demes within each tribe to which the responsibility for appointing each magistrate should be assigned. The allotment was scrupulously conducted so as to pay due regard to the proportionate size of each deme and to ensure that a deme which, for example, had twice the population of another should enjoy double the chances of being allocated an office in the lot. Once this allocation of offices was over, it presumably fell to the deme organizations to invite applications for the office or offices which they were empowered to fill, and, if necessary, to conduct a sortition at deme level to determine the successful candidates. It should be noted that this procedure would not only have been fairer and more simple to operate than the other; it would also have led naturally to the bargaining to which Aristotle refers. Both because the individual offices which were at the disposal of a deme were identified and because the final selection of the magistrate was made at local level, it is very credible that a wealthy demesman who aspired to the office in question should have attempted to buy his deme's good services in procuring it for himself.[79]

With the change to a tribal allotment of the minor magistrates at some date in the fourth century, the demes presumably lost all control over candidacy, and any attempt to guarantee a fair representation of the demes was abandoned. Candidates now presented themselves at the tribal level, and the representatives of the tribe on each of the boards were no doubt drawn by lot in turn. Under this procedure the ban on re-election to the same office would have caused no difficulties, since the draw for each office would have been based upon a separate list of candidates composed only of those who were eligible and willing to serve.

Two further questions which have been raised in connection with the minor magistrates are whether a candidate could offer himself for a particular office rather than for office in general, and whether any citizen could be compelled to stand against his will. The first of these is one which, for the earlier period at least, cannot be considered apart from the problem of the appointment procedure; for the view that a candidate had to be prepared to accept any office for which he was legally eligible is no more than a corollary to the theory that there was a candidates' pool. If, as is more likely, demes were assigned the responsibility for filling particular offices, then clearly applications were invited at deme level for those offices and for those offices alone. When the allotment was later transferred to the tribes, of course, it is conceivable that willingness to serve on any board for which one was eligible was a pre-condition of candidacy; but this is not very likely. Most of those who aspired to these magistracies, which conferred status rather than authority, may in any event have been prepared to accept what was offered and to submit their names for multiple sortition without pressure being brought to bear.

The second problem is related. It is possible that the tribe or the deme had powers to compel citizens to stand by drawing lots among all those who were eligible, but, if so, it is doubtful if such powers were used. Voluntary candidature is well attested;[80] and the pressure which may have been put upon demes to sell offices which were at their disposal does not suggest that they were frequently saddled with a responsibility in magisterial elections which they could not readily discharge.

THE COUNCIL OF FIVE HUNDRED

There is a tradition that it was Solon who first brought into being a second Council to work alongside the aristocratic Council of the Areopagus. The alleged complement of this body was four hundred, made up of one hundred members from each of the four kinship tribes. However, the existence of such a body is highly suspect and it would serve little purpose to speculate on the methods which might have been employed to appoint its members. A politically active second Council is first attested in the fifth century, and because of this body's association with the ten local tribes and of the tradition that the councillors' oath was instituted in 501 BC[81] it is generally accepted as being a creation of Cleisthenes.

In their main essentials the regulations which governed the appointment of councillors in the fourth century are likely to have been original. At that time every citizen who had attained the age of thirty was eligible to stand, and no one person could serve for more than two annual terms. The method of selection was by lot. Fifty councillors from each of the ten Cleisthenic tribes were chosen every year from among candidates who presented themselves at the deme level.[82] Furthermore, a second group of persons—according to one source yet another fifty— was allotted in the same process to act as reserves who might step into the shoes of those who either died in office or failed to pass the official scrutiny.[83]

As in the case of the minor magistrates, our sources do not make it at all clear how this process of selection operated or what exactly was the role of the demes. One popular view is that there was a single sortition, held centrally each year in the Theseion, which determined who were to be the councillors from each tribe, and that to this allotment each deme within a tribe sent in a fixed maximum quota of candidates, which was determined by reference to the size of its population. The total number of candidates who assembled to draw lots on this view was therefore in theory the sum of the various deme quotas, amounting possibly to at least one hundred men from each tribe or twice the number of councillors required. Apart from the fact that it implies a process of pre-selection at deme level for which there is no direct evidence, this interpretation is open to one major objection. It implies a flow of candidates for service on the Council in excess of that which Athenian society might reasonably be supposed to have been able to produce. It has been estimated that the number of citizens attaining the age of thirty each year at the beginning of the fifth century fell short of a thousand, and that it was perhaps as low as five hundred in the fourth.[84] This means in effect that the number of those eligible for Council service can never have been more than twenty times the number of those required, and never more than ten times the number of candidates which on this view the demes were called upon to put forward. Inevitably, therefore, it would have proved difficult, if not impossible, for many demes to present their full quota of candidates. Although conscientious citizens who had private means might well have been prevailed upon to discharge their civil responsibilities, candidature must have remained essentially voluntary, and there is likely to have been a large majority who, even after the introduction of a limited payment for Council service,[85] could not afford the considerable financial burden and disruption of life involved.[86] Of course, any deficiency in the number of candidates put forward by the demes would not have rendered an allotment process at the tribal level inoperable; for a sortition would always have been meaningful so long as there was an excess of candidates over Council seats, however small. If, however, there was a considerable variation in the meeting of quotas by individual demes, this would have made a nonsense of any pretence to distribute the seats equitably among them. Yet this was a matter on which the Athenians apparently held strong views; for, when the principle of deme representation was abandoned for the minor magistrates, it was exceptionally retained for the selection of the councillors.

An alternative and more acceptable suggestion is that what took place in the Theseion was not a single tribal allotment, but a series of deme allotments designed to determine the composition of the various deme contingents. It might well be thought that such allotments could have been conducted locally by the demes themselves, if indeed each deme was allocated a fixed quota of seats. But there was one good reason why this should not be done. If the allotments had taken place locally and one or more demes failed to produce as many candidates as there were seats to which it was entitled there would be no ready means of filling the vacancies. If, on the other hand, they took place centrally, it would be a simple matter to allot the unclaimed seats to other demes who were seen at the time to have an excess of candidates. The view that this is in fact what happened derives some support from the evidence of inscriptions. Extant lists of tribal contingents on the Council from different years show that one or two smaller demes were repeatedly without representation. They show too that the representation of larger demes, though roughly similar in size from one year to another, was yet not in all cases exactly the same. This variation is likely to have been the outcome of supplementary allocations to the deme in question of seats which had not been claimed.

It should be stressed that this method of appointing the councillors would have been wholly consistent with the insistence of the Athenians on maintaining deme participation. The fact that some demes may occasionally have put forward no candidate, or fewer than their allotted quota of seats, may have resulted at times in the Council not being a truly representative body. But the essential point is that all demes were given an opportunity to be represented in small or large measure according to their size, so long as they had sufficient candidates to offer.

THE PRINCIPLE OF SORTITION

The extensive use which the Athenians made of sortition has led to a wide acceptance of the view that the principle of the lot was itself the very corner-stone of radical democracy and embraced by the Athenians on purely doctrinaire grounds. The object, we are asked to believe, was to ensure mediocrity in office. In the words of one writer, the first stage was the introduction of *clerosis ek procriton*—a hybrid invented by those anxious to substitute sortition for election but not prepared to press the change to its logical conclusion. By increasing the number of magistrates later radicals were able to limit the competence of each of the boards and so to do away with the element of pre-selection altogether.[87]

As so expressed, this is a misleading doctrine. It cannot be denied that by the fourth century the use of the lot in the appointment of councillors and the majority of magistrates was accepted as sacrosanct, and that those who, like Socrates, had the boldness to call for its abandonment and for the establishment of an administration of experts were regarded with the gravest suspicion by their contemporaries. What the Athenian people, or at least their leaders, were intent on preserving was the overriding supremacy of the popular Assembly: what they most wanted to avoid was the emergence of an identifiable governing class, whether represented in the Council or the magistracies, which would be strong enough to wrest control from the Assembly and maintain a general supervision of policy. This was of the essence of oligarchy; and oligarchy was anathema to the orator and demagogue who throve on his influence over the citizens at large. It is a mistake, however, to suppose that it was basically sortition which kept the democracy in being and ensured that power remained at least nominally with the popular Assembly. More fundamental by far was the principle of rotation—the rule, applied in all but a few cases, that no citizen should hold any one office more than once in his lifetime. It was the strict enforcement of rotation which resulted in the mediocrity attacked by Socrates, and it was its strict enforcement also which may be held responsible for the wide application of sortition. When Hignett writes that it was not because the number of Athenian officers was large but because their functions were so unimportant that they had to be appointed by lot, he tends to mistake cause for effect and to obscure the issue. The use of the lot and the diminution in the authority of the magistracy were both alike the logical corollaries to rotation, a principle which rendered it inevitable that the competence of a candidate should not be a determining factor in his selection. Wherever, as at Athens, office is open to the whole or to a large section of the citizen body, the adoption of the principle of rotation must render any system of direct election an almost futile exercise.[88] Thus, at Athens any direct election of councillors or of minor magistrates would have been virtually meaningless, since the candidates, in so far as they exceeded the number of places to be filled—which was not always the case—would have been nonentities, and the voting body as a consequence would have had no useful criterion by which to choose between them.

There is therefore a strong case for regarding the use of the lot on a large scale as dictated by rotation rather than by any democratic principle. It is likely that Cleisthenes recognized the paramount need to protect his new and emancipated Assembly from any usurpation of its sovereignty by a ruling class, whether old or new, and therefore insisted on rotation in all offices but those which required the exercise of special skills. It was essential too that his new Council should not develop into a second Areopagus, and this could be guaranteed only by ensuring that it should have no permanent or even semi-permanent membership.

On occasions, of course, sortition was introduced in the appointment of magistrates for more particular reasons. In the aristocratic state the lot had a firm religious base; the notion that it signified divine sanction is the probable explanation for its traditional use in the appointment of the Treasurers of Athena. Aristotle, too, refers to the use of the lot in Heraea as a means of avoiding dissension between hostile factions;[89] and it is reasonable enough to suppose that at Athens the practice of employing sortition to allocate particular functions to members of the board of archons should be explained in terms of a readiness to call for a divine decision in a matter which the governing class could not resolve without undue friction.[90]

As has been suggested, Solon may have introduced sortition into the procedure for the appointment of archons for a special reason of his own. His purpose in sanctioning *clerosis ek procriton* may well have been to compel the tribesmen to select from a wider circle than they would have been required to do if their function had been to nominate only nine persons rather than forty. In other words, given that it was desirable to have a larger number of candidates elected than there were places to be filled, the lot was simply the most natural device for reducing that number to the smaller number of archons actually required.[91]

In 487 BC, when the lot was brought back for the election of archons 'for the first time since the tyranny', the motives behind its reintroduction would have been different again. When sortition had been introduced, probably by Cleisthenes, for the minor magistrates and the councillors, the procedure for the appointment of archons remained elective. The reason for this was the simple one that it was considered essential to select these officers, who were still regarded as the chief executive magistrates of the state, with a due regard for the general competence of the candidates. If therefore a decision was taken in 487 to throw this office also open to the lot, this can only be explained as a deliberate move designed to undermine its authority and standing.[92] There was undoubtedly a connection between this change and the rise in prominence of the board of ten generals, which had considerably enhanced its prestige during the Marathon campaign three years earlier. The generalship was an office which called for exceptional talent, and one therefore to which even the principle of rotation could not reasonably be applied. It was consequently destined in time to replace the archonship as the senior state magistracy. If steps were taken so soon to speed up this process of transition, this was almost certainly due to the activity of one or more of the generals of the time, who sought to weaken any effective opposition to their policies from among the archons' ranks. Themistocles in particular is likely to have been involved—the man who had held the archonship himself some years before and who was intent both on furthering his own career and on guiding Athenian policy along very definite lines in preparation for the renewal of the conflict with Persia. The sudden spate of ostracisms which secured the temporary removal from Athens of several other notable political figures in the 480s is commonly regarded as having been due to his efforts, and it is probable enough that he also took steps to ensure that he would not meet with undue interference from the incumbents of the archonship.[93]

THE SCRUTINY

No account of the selection of Athenian magistrates would be altogether complete without a brief reference to the process of scrutiny known as the *dokimasia*. This took the form of an examination which all appointed officials, magistrates and councillors, whether selected by lot or by vote, were required to undergo before they could take up their office. In the case of the nine archons, exceptionally, a twofold scrutiny was involved, a preliminary one held in the Council of Five Hundred, and a second one held in the popular courts.[94] In the case of all other officers there was just the one, which was conducted for the magistrates in the popular courts and for the councillors before the outgoing Council.[95]

The form of the examination used for the archons, which is likely to have been basically similar to that used for the other magistrates, is detailed by Aristotle. The potential officer was required to establish that his family had been citizens for three generations, and to show that he had a family tomb and observed the traditional religious rites of Apollo and Zeus. He also had to submit to questioning on such matters as whether he had paid his taxes, whether he had done his prescribed period of military service, and whether he treated his parents with respect. After witnesses had been produced to give evidence on these points, an open invitation was extended to any of those present to challenge the candidate's credentials or to lodge a complaint; in the event of a complainant coming forward, a form of legal trial was staged, involving the use of both prosecution and defence counsel, before a final verdict on the candidate's suitability was taken by vote.

It is clear enough that this procedure was regarded as something more than a formality. This follows from its very thoroughness and complexity. It is indicated too by the number of attested occasions in the fourth century when a candidate's credentials are known to have been seriously contested. It is noteworthy that the inquisition detailed by Aristotle does not contain the more obvious enquiries concerning the candidate's property rating or concerning the offices which he had previously held. That he possessed the correct qualifications in these respects had presumably been confirmed at deme or tribe level before his selection. The questions asked were of the more probing type to which in some cases it may not have been possible to provide a wholly verifiable answer. The orator Lysias summed up the situation when he remarked that in his view it was right that a candidate should be called upon at the *dokimasia* to give an account of his whole life;[96] and orators certainly thought it relevant to ask a court to take note of one candidate's undemocratic political activities and of another's immoral mode of living.[97] Whether the sustaining of charges such as these was in itself sufficient to ensure a candidate's disqualification from holding the office to which he had been appointed, or whether, as Hignett prefers to believe,[98] these unsavoury details were merely introduced by prosecutors to bias the minds of the jury, it remains beyond dispute that the form of the questioning was designed to do more than provide confirmation of verifiable facts; and the whole process of the *dokimasia* therefore gave considerable scope to those who wished to challenge the decision of the lot or the voters.

If then the *dokimasia* represented something more than a formal sanction in the hands of Council or courts, for what purpose was it designed? The answer, of course, must depend upon its date of origin. The fact that the preliminary *dokimasia* of the archons was held before the Council of Five Hundred rather than the law-courts has encouraged the view that the process dated from a very early period, and that the Council was in this instance exercising a right of sanction which had at one time been vested in the Areopagus. This, however, is far from certain. What does appear likely is that the Council at one time enjoyed the right to conduct the *dokimasia* for all magistrates, and that this responsibility was transferred to the law-courts later, when the number of magistrates multiplied and the activities and competence of the popular courts were extended. In this case the *dokimasia* could well have been the creation of Cleisthenes, concomitant with the establishment of the new Council of Five Hundred and with the new provisions for the appointment of minor magistrates and councillors by a process of sortition.[99]

The suggestion that the original object of the *dokimasia* was to mitigate the worst effects of the Athenian system for appointing officers, and of the use of the lot in particular, is one which has come in for sharp criticism.[100] But we should not be misled by the fact that the institution is represented in fourth-century literature as a facet of extreme democracy and as a political weapon to be used in the power game by unscrupulous demagogues. All institutions are, of course, subject to abuse, and later abuse often obscures their original purpose. It is indeed very possible that Cleisthenes should have felt qualms about allowing his new procedures for the appointment of officers to operate without check. Even where direct election was involved, he may have seen some danger in the breaking down of the feudal structure of the local assemblies, for which he had been responsible, and in the consequent removal of the salutary influence exerted over the voters by men of political expertise and experience. But, where the use of the lot was involved, the dangers were even more acute. Sortition, it has been suggested, was introduced for a variety of reasons, principally, at the time of Cleisthenes, as a natural corollary to rotation in office. But, while the acceptance of rotation may imply some faith in the ability of the majority competently to discharge the responsibilities of office, it implies no such faith in the ability of all to do so. By all but the most misguided idealist some protection must have been seen to be needed against the appointment by lot of the truly incompetent. The procedure of the *dokimasia*, which gave to a large group of citizens, whether in the Council or a court of law, the widest discretionary powers in interpreting its terms of reference, was no doubt as effective a method of providing that protection as any which could be devised.

CHAPTER III

THE OPERATION OF THE LOT

IN VIEW OF THE very important part played by the lot in the appointment of officers at Athens, it is rather surprising that literary sources tell us so little about the methods used in making an allotment. Almost our only detailed information is derived from isolated archaeological finds and from an extended passage in the *Constitution of Athens* in which Aristotle describes the allotment of jurors.

In the early days of official sortition it is clear that the Athenians used white and black beans for the purpose, and indeed as late as the end of the fifth century Thucydides can refer to a councillor owing his seat 'to the bean'.[101] The procedure employed was presumably to use some form of container with an open top through which a hand could be inserted, and to pour into it white and black beans equal to the total number of candidates. The number of white beans would correspond exactly to the number of places which were to be filled, and the number of black beans to the number by which the total of candidates exceeded that figure. Some such method is likely to have been employed at all levels—at state level for the appointment of archons and the senior officers, and at tribe and deme level for the appointment of minor magistrates. Thus, for the appointment of archons in Solon's time forty beans will have been used corresponding to the forty pre-selected candidates, thirty-one of them black and nine of them white; later, when the archons were appointed on a strictly tribal basis, there will have been ten separate allotments, one for each tribe, with one white and nine black beans being used in each case. In the local allotments, of course, the number of black beans used will have varied with the number of candidates who presented themselves for any given office.

It is not certain how the beans were drawn, and there may well have been a change of practice. One possibility is that the candidates themselves participated in the allotment by drawing the lots. Another is that the tribal or state officers assumed responsibility for the drawing of lots themselves, drawing them in fact against a predetermined order in the list of candidates. Clearly, the second procedure would have been more open to abuse, unless there was provision for stringent supervision; but, of course, insofar as even the candidates themselves would have had to draw in some arbitrarily predetermined order, the scope for abuse must have been appreciable in either case.

By contrast, the arrangements made for sortition in the later period of the democracy were highly complex. The most significant innovation was undoubtedly the use of the allotment machine, or, as it was called by the Athenians, the *cleroterion*. The first known mention of such machines is made by Aristophanes in a play which he produced in 390 BC,[102] and, as he speaks of them being moved into the market-place, it must be supposed that they were at that time constructed of wood. Aristotle also refers to their use in his own day in his detailed account of the selection of jurors.[103] But it is from the archaeological evidence that most can be learnt about the form which they took and the way in which they were used. We are extremely fortunate in that a number of stone machines of second-century date have recently been unearthed in excavations at Athens.[104] They are of greatly varying size, and they were clearly used for different purposes, but the general pattern of them all is similar. They are of an oblong shape, in the form of a large gravestone with a projecting surround. On the face are elongated slots which are ordered symmetrically in horizontal and vertical rows. The floor of these slots inclines slightly into the stone, and it is clear that they were designed firmly to hold objects inserted into them. Their number varies considerably from one machine to another. Thus, on one there is a single vertical column of twelve slots; on another there are eleven vertical columns each containing as many as fifty slots or more; and on others again there are five vertical rows with at least twenty slots in each. In the top surface of the stonework, on the left side as one views the machine, there is carved an inverted cone which leads to a small circular outlet in the projecting head surround, and it is a fair assumption that there was connected to this outlet a form of tube which ran vertically down the front of the machine to the side of the rows of slots and which, to judge from markings on the face of the stone, was secured at top and bottom by clamps. It seems clear that such a tube must have been designed to accommodate small, spherical counters, which could be inserted at random through the funnel at the top of the stone, and which could presumably be released one by one at the base, either by the operation of a simple catch mechanism or, as has been recently suggested,[105] by the withdrawal of one of two pins which passed through the tube into slots in the stone and so held the bottommost of the counters firmly in position (Fig. I).

In his account of the selection of jurors Aristotle throws a great deal of light on the way these machines were operated and on the part they played in the full allotment procedure.[106] In fourth-century Athens all citizens over the age of thirty qualified for jury service and were permanently assigned to one of ten dicastic groups, which were identified by the letters A to K. Each day that the courts sat, those who were anxious to serve and so duly to collect the jury payment provided by the state offered themselves at the courthouse for selection. The entire process of jury selection was long and complex, and it fell into two stages—first, the selection from among the applicants of as many as were required to man the courts for the day, and second, the assignment of the jurors so selected to particular courts and cases. In both stages sortition played an important role, but it was in the first that use was made of the allotment machine.

The would-be jurors entered the courthouse through a doorway marked with the name of their tribe. Inside they found ten boxes lettered from A to K, corresponding to the ten dicastic sections in which they were severally enrolled, and they were required to place in the appropriate box their personal identity ticket, which bore on it their name, their tribe, and the letter of their dicastic section. The tickets of all the applicants were therefore at this point distributed in as many as a hundred different boxes, ten of them at each tribal entrance. The next move was for the archon who was in charge of each tribe to draw one ticket at random from out of each of the ten boxes in his division, and to designate the persons named on the tickets so drawn as 'ticket-setters' for their own dicastic section. The task of this ticket-setter was then to make a random draw of the tickets in his own box (i.e. the box marked with the letter of his section), and to fix these in a single vertical row of slots in one of two allotment machines which stood in each tribal compartment, presumably starting by inserting the first ticket drawn in the top slot and working downwards until all the tickets were exhausted. It must be supposed that there were five columns of slots in each of the two allotment machines, making ten in all, and therefore that at the end of this part of the operation the tickets of all applicants from the same tribe and the same dicastic section were arranged in a random order in just one of these vertical columns.

At this point the allotment proper began. The mechanism used may have been more primitive than that used on the later, excavated machines, since Aristotle refers to the counters as dice rather than balls, but the general principle is likely to have been the same. The presiding magistrate shook up and poured into the funnel of the machine at random a number of black and white counters corresponding in total to the number of rows of slots on the face of the machine which had been completely filled with tickets, and as each counter was released in turn its colour determined the fate of all five people, each from a different lettered section, whose tickets were arranged in a single horizontal row. The first counter, of course, referred to the first row, the second to the second, and so forth, until a counter had been released for each of the completed horizontal rows in turn. The number of white counters inserted in each allotment machine was naturally determined by the total number of jurors required for the courts on the day in question. As twenty machines in all were used, two in each tribal division, each machine must have been called upon to select five per cent of the jurors; and, as each counter selected five persons at once, the number of white counters inserted in each machine had to be exactly one per cent of the number of jurors required.

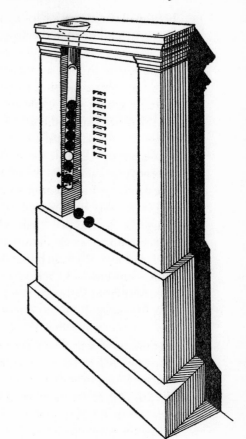

Fig. I *Reconstructed drawing of an Athenian allotment machine designed to demonstrate its mode of operation. For purposes of illustration the outer cover of the tube has been cut away to reveal the counters not yet released.*

Such a simple machine as this, having only ten slots on the face, could have been used both to allocate particular offices to members of the board of archons and to determine the order in which the tribal sections in the Council were to take their turn as prytaneis.

The reason for the use of two allotment machines in each tribal division, each catering for five of the lettered sections, can only be guessed, but Sterling Dow has given as convincing an answer to the problem as seems possible on the present evidence. He points out that the extreme alternatives to this method would have been either to use one machine with a single vertical column of slots for each section, and thus ten for each tribe, or to use for each tribe a single machine containing ten vertical columns of slots. The former alternative was ruled out because it would have involved either an intolerable delay, if the allotments for each section had been made in succession, or a multiplicity of responsible officers to supervise and operate the allotments, if made simultaneously. As the Athenians employed the nine archons and the secretary to the *Thesmothetae* to look after each of the tribal divisions, it is clear that they were concerned to vest the responsibility for supervision in those whom they could most surely trust. The latter method, on the other hand—the use of one machine with ten columns of slots—would have had two major disadvantages. It would have made it more difficult for all the interested parties to witness the proceedings since they would have had to congregate around the one machine. Perhaps more important, it would have resulted in a larger number of persons being ruled out of the main allotment altogether by reason of their belonging to sections which yielded a larger number of applicants than the minimum and so having their tickets inserted in horizontal rows which were not complete. This point can be simply illustrated by considering the effect on the allotment of a below average yield from one section of, let us say, fifteen applicants as opposed to the average yield of twenty-five for the remainder. If one machine had been used for all ten sections, no fewer than ninety persons would have been drawn in uncompleted rows as a consequence. With the use of two machines, on the other hand, the number of persons accidentally disqualified in this way would have been reduced to forty. It is obvious that, had time allowed, the ideal answer would have been to use one machine for each section; but the use of two machines for each tribe was a sensible compromise, which had the effect of lessening the unfair consequences of a small turn-out in any one section or sections, of providing for the allotment to be properly observed by all those concerned, and of allowing the whole process of allotment to be conducted by one responsible and trusted individual.

Two of the allotment machines which have been unearthed at Athens correspond very closely to those which must have been used in the Aristotelian procedure. They have five vertical columns of slots, and they are almost certain to have been designed for the daily selection of jurors. But the fact that there are others in this small collection which were both smaller and larger, and which contain a varying number of rows, both vertical and horizontal, is enough to prove that machines were widely used for a multiplicity of purposes, and that from the fourth century onwards they became the standard instruments for most processes of sortition.

One of the great advantages of the procedure detailed by Aristotle is that it made use of what was in effect a double sortition. The final and decisive part of the operation was, of course, the releasing of the black and white counters from the apparatus affixed to the side of the machine; and this was the improved and more foolproof equivalent of the earlier and more primitive process of drawing beans from an open container. But before this came another allotment represented by the random drawing of tickets from the boxes by the ticket-setter, and it was this which determined the order of names against which the final allotment was to be made. There are at least two reasons why the Athenians should have considered this double process of sortition desirable. The principal one, perhaps, is that it rendered manipulation of the lot more difficult than when lots were drawn by or on behalf of candidates in a predetermined order. The other is more psychological than real. Mathematicians may regard it as self-evident that the starting odds against any one of a number of candidates drawing a particular counter from out of a fixed number is not in any way affected by the stage at which his lot is drawn. But the average Athenian may not have been so rational, and he may well have been glad of some assurance that the order of the draw had not been fixed to his apparent disadvantage.

Those who have tended to look upon the slots in allotment machines as mere receptacles in simple electoral sortitions for the tickets of successful candidates or tribes appear to have missed this vital point that the machine was designed to provide for a twofold allotment. On the analogy of the jury selection process, the procedure adopted at the appointment of magistrates is likely to have been something like the following. The identity tickets of all the candidates will have been thrown into a container, shaken up, and drawn individually at random. They will then have been placed in the order in which they were drawn in a column of slots on an allotment machine. A number of counters equal to the total of candidates, and including as many white counters as there were places to be filled, will then have been poured into the funnel and tube and released one by one to signify the success or failure of the candidate whose ticket was in the corresponding slot. This procedure, requiring only a small machine with a single column of slots, is the one which is likely to have been employed for such purposes as the appointment of deme representatives on the Council and for the determination of the ten candidates which each tribe submitted for the final sortition for the archonship. Such too, no doubt, was the method used to determine such matters as the order in which the tribal sections of the Council— the *prytaneis*—should take their monthly turn of responsibility.

In some cases, particularly at the state level, the appointment procedure must have been more complex. It is probable, for example, that at the final sortition of archons a machine was used with ten vertical columns of ten slots each. Each column will have contained the tickets of all ten candidates from a single tribe, arranged in an order decided by a random draw, and the emergence of the one white counter from the tube will have determined the identity of the entire college of archons by designating one complete horizontal row of tickets, each one of necessity bearing the name of a candidate from a different tribe. This will not, however, have been the sum of the proceedings, for there will have remained the important task of assigning the particular offices on the board to the successful candidates. For this purpose it would have been possible for the Athenians to place the names of the ten offices in a column of slots on a machine in an order determined by a draw, and then to release counters against each ticket for each of the ten tribes in turn, either using one white counter among nine black counters on nine different occasions, or simply using counters inscribed with the names of the tribes. In view of the meticulous concern of the Athenians to take every precaution, however, it is likely that they made use of what was called *synclerosis*,[107] or simultaneous sortition, for which purpose two allotment machines were employed together. In one will have been inserted in a random order the tickets of the ten successful candidates, and in the other the tickets representing the ten offices to be allocated. Ten counters, one white and nine black, will then have been placed in each machine and released simultaneously until in each case the white counter appeared. The magistrate designated by the white counter on one machine will then have been matched to the office designated by the white counter on the other. At this point the tickets of this magistrate and office will have been duly removed from their respective slots, and the process will have been repeated with the use of nine, eight, seven counters, and so on, until every magistrate had been assigned to a particular office. As without some elaborate form of collusion the official responsible for operating one machine could not technically have had knowledge of the order of tickets on the machine operated by the other, the chances of fraud will have been reduced to a minimum.

It has been suggested that in the case of the archonship the Athenians strictly observed tribal cycles, and that consequently over a set period of ten years each of the various offices on the board went in turn for one year to a representative of each of the ten tribes.[108] The case is by no means proved; and indeed, in view of the emphasis which the Athenians placed upon the lot, it is difficult to see what advantage they could have thought was to be gained from adhering to a principle which can only have resulted in potential candidates towards the end of any tribal cycle knowing to which particular office they would be assigned if they should be successful in the lot. But, even if such a system of tribal rotation was introduced, the process of simultaneous sortition just described could easily have been suitably adapted. The number of counters used in the second machine at any allotment could simply have been restricted to the number of years left in the tribal cycle. Then, when the release of a counter on the first machine marked out a candidate of a particular tribe, the allotment on the other machine would have been conducted without reference to the tickets of those offices which a representative of that tribe had held during the current cycle.[109]

It was suggested in the last chapter that in the fifth century at least the method of appointing many of the minor magistrates at

Athens followed a rather different pattern. Although candidates may have been chosen by lot for particular offices at deme level, there was a prior process of allotment which was conducted centrally, probably in the Theseion, and which resulted in the allocation of particular offices to the demes. This is what Aristotle implies; and it is confirmed by the recent discovery of a hoard of pot fragments in a pit behind the Stoa of Attalus which have every appearance of having been at one time parts of what can only be called allotment tokens.[110] These pieces are all of fairly uniform width and length and show little sign of repeated use. They are clearly all upper or lower halves of what must at one time have been rectangular wholes, and they have all been divided from their other halves by an irregular, although properly finished, jig-saw cut. Letters have been painted on both sides before firing. On one side, running across the cut so that the letters can be read on both halves of the token, appears the abbreviation for an Athenian tribe. On the other side, the upper halves contain the abbreviated name of a deme, while the lower halves are either blank or contain the letters POL, which have reasonably been taken to be an abbreviation for the magistrate known as the *poletes* (Fig. II). It is difficult to resist the obvious conclusion that these tokens were designed to match together two entities with the same tribal connection, the deme, which was of course a sub-division of the tribe, and, very probably, a particular office which it was the responsibility of the tribe to fill.

We can only speculate as to how an allotment process which made use of tokens such as these may have operated. At the annual sortition in the Theseion, it may be suggested, each tribe disposed of as many of these tokens as could conveniently be divided among its demes in a manner which took strict account of the relative size of their population. Since the tribal allocation of fifty members of the Council was distributed over the demes on this basis, it is very possible that the number of tokens was also fifty.[111] The name of the tribe having been painted on one side of each, they were then cut into two, each one by a different and individual jig-saw cut, and the upper and lower halves assembled in two independent heaps. On the reverse of the upper halves

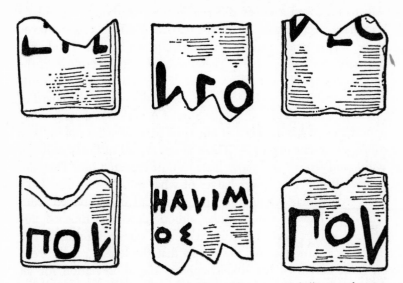

Fig. II *Halves of allotment tokens probably used for purposes of allocating the minor magistracies to the demes in fifth-century Athens.*

were painted the names of demes, those of the more densely populated demes on several, and those of the more sparsely populated on only one. From the lower halves as many were picked out as there were offices to fill, which was in the region of fourteen, and on each of these was painted the title of one particular office. The remainder of the lower halves were, of course, left blank. All the pieces were then sent away for firing. On the day of the allotment they were again produced and were presumably laid out with the tribal names uppermost so that the upper and lower halves could be pieced together—a process which will have been facilitated by the lettering of the tribal abbreviation which had been painted across the whole upper face before the jig-saw cut had been made. Once the halves had been reunited, it no doubt fell to the presiding official to turn them over for his own and the public's inspection, and, concentrating his attention on those which had lettering on the lower half of the reverse side, to make an announcement that the responsibility for filling the office named in the lower half had fallen to the demes named in the upper half in each case.

It cannot be said when, or for how long, this was the standard procedure, and indeed it is possible that it was only a temporary experiment. Certainly other methods are likely to have been used. At first the various deme officers may merely have drawn lots from an open container, one or more according to the size of the deme's population. Later, with the coming of the allotment machines, it is likely that these began to be used for the purpose, and that the somewhat troublesome method of working with half-tokens was abandoned. The process of *synclerosis*, involving the use of two machines, would have been most suitable for this operation. In one machine could have been inserted tickets bearing the name of demes, in the other a ticket for each of the various magistrates to be chosen. Into the first machine would be poured as many counters as there were deme tickets, including as many white ones as there were offices to be allotted, while into the second would be poured as many counters, including only one white, as there were offices which at any given stage remained unallotted.

CHAPTER IV

VOTING PROCEDURES

THE SPARTAN APELLA

ACCORDING TO THE GREAT RHETRA, provision was made for the Spartans to meet in full Assembly in an open space between the brook Knakion and the bridge Babyka once every month at the full moon. In the earliest days these gatherings were probably almost the only ones held, and they are likely to have been presided over by a king, although of course it may always have been feasible, in accordance with well-established Homeric practice, for an additional assembly to be summoned at a time of crisis by other persons of noble birth. Later, however, in the fifth and fourth centuries, the little evidence we have seems to suggest both that Assemblies could readily be called at will and without reference to any fixed date, and that by then it had become accepted practice for the Assembly to be summoned and presided over by one of the ephors. The most notable example was the Assembly summoned just before the outbreak of the Peloponnesian War, at which the ephor Sthenelaidas took complete charge of the proceedings.[112] Whether it was still within the rights of the kings to call and preside over an Assembly themselves is not known; but Xenophon's repeated references to the decisions of 'ephors and Assembly' imply that these two organs of the constitution acted in close association,[113] and the account of the third-century ephor who was asked by the king to introduce a measure before the Assembly on his behalf certainly implies that by then at least the king's direct dealings with that body had become something of a dead letter.[114]

The only elections for which the Assembly is known to have

been responsible were those which were held to fill vacancies in the *gerousia*, and it is to be supposed that these were held at the next convenient meeting after a councillor's death. The procedure was primitive, and it was dismissed by Aristotle as 'childish'.[115] The candidates proceeded one by one before the assembled citizens in an order which was determined by lot, and, as they did so, the people expressed the extent of their approval of each by shouting. Meanwhile, a small group of men were confined in a nearby building from which they could see nothing of the proceedings, and there they noted on tablets their impression of the relative loudness of the cheers raised for each of the candidates as they passed by. When all was done, the numbers written down by the judges were checked against the names of the candidates to which they corresponded, and the one who was judged by the panel to have received the loudest acclaim was declared elected. This account, which comes from Plutarch,[116] of course leaves many questions unanswered. He does not tell us how or when the lots were drawn to determine the candidates' order of appearance, how many were the judges, whether they were required to consult together and reach a unanimous verdict, or whether they were required to submit their verdicts independently with the resultant risk that they might reach no definite decision. The first question is perhaps the most significant, for the order in which the candidates appeared was the key to the whole proceedings. Despite the opportunities which an allotment behind closed doors might have presented for collusion, it is most unlikely that lots were drawn in the presence of the Assembly itself, if only because foreknowledge of the order in which the candidates would present themselves would inevitably have detracted from the element of spontaneity in the shouting which was so necessary to the credibility of the vote.

Evidence on the rules governing the activities of legislative assemblies comes largely from the Rhetra and from comments in Aristotle's *Politics*. The Rhetra provided that the Assembly should have the final decision on matters put before it by the kings and the *gerousia*, although a rider was added which recognized the right of the *gerousia* to reject any 'crooked' resolution passed by the larger body. Whether or not this implies that the Assembly possessed a right of amendment, this is clearly not what Aristotle believed; for when comparing the Spartan with the Cretan and Carthaginian constitutions, he specifically denies either that the Assembly had any power other than to accept or reject, or that its members had any freedom to express criticism.[117] It is hard to believe that Aristotle was mistaken on so important a matter, and the rider to the Rhetra may well have to be taken to mean that the *gerousia* reserved the right to override the Assembly in an emergency, if it refused to assent to a particular course of action. As regards debate, our meagre information suggests that there was frequently discussion immediately prior to the taking of a vote. Aristotle cannot therefore mean that there was no right of criticism at all at Sparta. Rather should his words be taken to imply that comment was restricted to the notables—no doubt the kings, ephors, members of the *gerousia*, and of course others, such as foreign envoys, who may from time to time have been invited by the ephors to address the Assembly. It would appear that the situation differed little from that which prevailed in the gatherings of the Homeric age, when the right of any person to address the Assembly was conferred by the president and nonentities such as Thersites were traditionally debarred from voicing their opinions.[118]

There has been a tendency recently to play down the importance of the probouleutic role of the *gerousia*, which is stressed in the Rhetra, and to suggest indeed that the Spartan Assembly could proceed to the vote at the instance of the ephors alone, and on a motion not previously considered by the *gerousia*.[119] This view is based on the comparative silence of the sources on the role of the *gerousia* in the later state, upon the repeated emphasis which is laid on the association of Assembly and ephors, in whose joint names resolutions were carried, and upon reports of open discussion in the Assembly which is stated to have preceded any vote in the *gerousia*. Despite all this, however, the fact has to be faced that as late as 242 BC a move on the part of King Agis to implement important reforms was thwarted because the measures had not been approved by the *gerousia*, 'with whom', as Plutarch says, 'lay the power in making the preliminary resolution'.[120] The truth seems to be that the Assembly came to be used increasingly as a forum for the airing of views by persons in authority before any motion had been put before the *gerousia*. These debates did not culminate in a vote, and the purpose of those who initiated them was probably merely to test sentiment, or, as is attested for 242 BC, to influence the attitude of the councillors in advance.

The more radical suggestion that the Assembly was peculiarly the mouthpiece of the ephorate is misguided and is based upon the misconception that the ephors and the *gerousia* were natural enemies. In fact, the opposite is likely to have been the case. Ephors and *gerousia* are frequently represented as working in close harmony, and the ephors may well have presided over the councillors and even owed their own election to them.[121] If the sources stress the role of the ephors in legislation, this is presumably because they were regarded as the executive arm of the body which was ultimately responsible for the making of decisions. There is a marked parallel in this respect between the role of the ephors at Sparta and that of the official magistrates of middle Republican Rome, who despite their individual differences of outlook implemented in the main the decisions taken by a majority in the Roman Senate.

As is clear from the account of the Assembly in 432 BC, formal proposals were put to the Assembly in later times by one of the ephors. Voting was normally by acclamation; but if this method left any room for doubt the president appears to have had the right to call on the citizens to divide by taking up places on either side of the arena according to their individual point of view. This right was invoked by Sthenelaidas in 432 BC, perhaps for his own protection, since the issue was so crucial;[122] but, in view of the confusion which must have resulted from such movement in a gathering of several thousands, this is not a procedure which is likely frequently to have recommended itself.

THE SPARTAN GEROUSIA

The principal functions of the *gerousia* were to prepare legislation for approval by the Assembly, to act as a high court in serious cases such as those of homicide,[123] and possibly also to make annual appointments to the ephorate. In all cases some form of voting was involved.

The sole clue as to the way in which the councillors cast their votes on judicial matters comes from an account of the trial of King Pausanias by a court consisting of the five ephors and the councillors.[124] The fact that our source can quote the exact details of the vote—fourteen councillors and one king for condemnation, and fourteen councillors and the five ephors for acquittal—establishes that the vote was counted and the result made public. As the numbers involved were small, it is very probable that the vote was taken by calling the roll, each juror pronouncing his verdict as called upon to do so by the president. That this was the procedure is to some extent confirmed by a somewhat cryptic passage in Thucydides, in which he claims that, contrary to a popular misconception, the kings of Sparta 'had only one vote for each of them added to the rest, and not two'.[125] The use of the word 'added' suggests consecutive voting, with the kings casting their votes last of all.

This same general reference of Thucydides to the voting rights of the kings may also be taken to indicate that voting on legislative matters was conducted in a similar fashion. It further provides an interesting commentary on the nature of the *modus vivendi* which was established between kings and *gerousia*, possibly at the time of Theopompus. Care was taken to ensure that the kings did not lead the *gerousia* in the voting, although, of course, their right to participate in it was paramount, as witness the special privilege which was afforded to them of voting in their absence through the medium of a proxy.[126]

Nothing is known of the procedure adopted at the appointment of ephors. Aristotle has much the same to say about it as he does of the method employed in selecting councillors, dismissing the whole process as 'altogether wrong and unspeakably childish'.[127] Plato refers to the election of ephors as 'to all intents and purposes a lottery'.[128] Suggestions that he is to be taken literally and that some element of divination or taking of auspices entered into the appointment procedure seem to be ruled out by Aristotle's insistence that the choice was made by election and not by sortition; it is possible that the selection was made by an assessment of shouting, as in the case of the councillors. To appoint all five ephors together by this method would, of course, have been impossible; but if each ephor was appointed in turn from among a group of candidates representing one tribe or local division there should have been little problem.

THE ATHENIAN ASSEMBLY

The sovereign body of the Athenian democracy was the popular Assembly or *ekklesia*. This was open to all males who had reached the age of eighteen and who, at least after Pericles' citizenship law of 451, could claim to have both an Athenian father and an Athenian mother. No census qualification was demanded, and the only born Athenians debarred from attending were those from whom citizen rights had been either permanently or temporarily withdrawn. Despite this, the number of those who actually did attend was comparatively small. Although the total citizen population at the time of Pericles has been estimated at between 50,000 and 60,000, Thucydides suggests that an attendance of as many as 5,000 at any vote was a rare occurrence.[129] This is undoubtedly something of an exaggeration, for we know that there were certain decisions affecting individual citizens which the Athenians could take only when a quorum of as many as 6,000 was present; but 2,000 to 3,000 was probably the normal size of the attendance at the ordinary meetings of the Assembly. As both Aristotle and the contemporary Aristophanes imply,[130] this number was predominantly made up of craftsmen and artisans domiciled in the city itself. The middle-class farmers were for the most part too busy to make the journey to Athens in order to attend debates, and the attitude of the more leisured aristocracy appears to have been that it was neither fitting nor useful to take part in votes at which they were hopelessly outnumbered by an urban proletariat. During the fifth century, perhaps, the very lowest-paid members of Athenian society were deterred from attending by the fact that they could not readily afford to forgo their daily wage; but when in the name of total democracy payment was introduced for attending, at the beginning of the fourth century, the opportunity to put in an appearance was denied to none.[131] The inevitable consequence was that the Assembly came progressively to be dominated by those elements in society which had little sense of responsibility—those among the self-employed who had the least concern for their trade, and those in another's employment who had the fewest qualms about absenting themselves from work.

In the earlier period of the democracy the Assembly normally met on only ten occasions during the year, once in every prytany. Later, this proved to be insufficient, and the number of regular meetings was increased to forty, four in every prytany, of which one—the first—was known as the 'principal meeting' of the prytany. In Aristotle's day the basic programme of business for each of these four meetings was predetermined; and, although an Assembly was competent to deal with any matter provided that it appeared upon the agenda, each had a particular responsibility for conducting certain regular and recurring business. The actual dates were not fixed, and time had to be found on days which were not reserved for public holidays and which were not designated 'unlucky'. Except in the case of extraordinary Assemblies necessitated by a crisis, which could be summoned at a moment's notice by the blast of a trumpet and the lighting of a bonfire, the accepted procedure was for a summons and an agenda to be posted publicly at least five days before the projected meeting. This was the responsibility of the Council of Five Hundred, or more particularly of that tribal section of the Council, known as the *prytaneis*, which was currently acting as the Council's executive committee.[132]

The place of assembly varied according to the type of business to be transacted and also according to the period. The infrequent plenary Assemblies, at which the minimum attendance was six thousand, were held in the market-place.[133] From the time of Demosthenes it became increasingly common to hold Assemblies in the theatre, or, if their principal business was to discuss naval matters, in the port of the Piraeus.[134] But the chief meeting place in the fifth and early fourth centuries, and the venue for at least the electoral Assemblies even after that period, was the large natural amphitheatre on the hill of the Pnyx, the centre of three hills overlooking the market-place and the Acropolis from the south-west, where there was seating accommodation for many thousands both on specially constructed wooden benches and on the rock terraces. This was the venue which came to be regarded as the chief arena of the radical Athenian democracy.[135]

There is some confusion about the methods used to control entry to the place of assembly and to ensure that only those qualified participated in the voting. The responsibility for seeing that no unauthorized person attended a meeting, and also, after the introduction of state pay for attendance, that no person drew pay who did not take part in the vote, lay with six officials known as lexiarchs, who were in turn assisted by thirty more known as 'collectors of the people'.[136] But how and when they made their checks is not made clear. Reference in certain authorities to the use of a dyed rope by the Assembly police,[137] and an indication in Aristophanes that late-comers received no payment voucher,[138] have given rise to the conjecture that the scrutiny was conducted as the citizens actually entered the place of assembly. But there is much to be said against this. For one thing, the roping off of so large an area as the market-place or the Pnyx to prevent entry except through one or two narrow openings would almost certainly have been impracticable, and would have involved the employment of a police force far larger than that which was in fact used. Indeed, the impression conveyed by the sources is more of a somewhat disordered convergence upon the place of assembly than of an organized queueing for admission. Authoritarian as the procedure may appear, the purpose of the red-dyed rope used by the police is expressly said to have been to drive loiterers from the open market on to the Pnyx. By surrounding the area and contracting the rope, thereby threatening to stain with the dye all those who allowed themselves to come in contact with it, they presumably succeeded in inducing people there assembled to make off in the direction of the Pnyx. A second point to be borne in mind is that checking against an official list of citizens at one or two points of entry would have been an impossibly protracted procedure, and one which could hardly have been effectively shortened by the employment of a plurality of checking officials. The use of the thirty 'collectors', who together were responsible for scrutinizing the attendance, can only be satisfactorily explained if each official was charged with checking the credentials of approximately a thirtieth part of the gathering; and such a division of labour could only have been effectively organized after the citizens had already been admitted to their place of assembly.

This raises a further interesting point of controversy. Were the Athenians in any way ordered into groups in their Assemblies? It is clearly attested that in the plenary Assemblies held in the market-place, where votes were taken which affected the rights of individuals, the citizens were grouped strictly according to their tribes.[139] But that they were so ordered in the other Assemblies held on the Pnyx and elsewhere is often denied, largely on account of references in the sources to the tendency of political friends to group themselves together in the Assembly. Thus, Plutarch records that Pericles' opponent, Thucydides, son of Melesias, induced the nobility not to mingle with the masses but to seat themselves apart; and Thucydides asserts that the followers of Alcibiades banded together in the Assembly at the time of the great debate on Sicily.[140] This evidence, however, is not decisive, for both writers can be held to mean simply that political cliques held themselves apart only so far as the acknowledged division of the gathering into tribal groups allowed. Recent excavations on the Pnyx have revealed rock beddings for posts, which look as if they may have served to mark off one part of the seating arena from another;[141] and, if such divisions there were, it would be not a little odd if they bore no relation whatever to the tribes. For the purposes of facilitating the counting of votes, perhaps, any chance division of the citizens would have served, but for the purpose of checking the credentials of those who voted a division by tribes would have been invaluable. It is significant that the thirty 'collectors', who conducted the check, were themselves selected by the Council, three from each tribe; and it would have been a sensible arrangement for each tribal contingent of three to have been equipped simply with a list of citizens enrolled in the demes of their own tribe. Any fuller list it would have been virtually impossible to carry around. As it was, if the citizens were ordered in the Assembly in tribal groups averaging two to three hundred men, the task of the scrutineers in checking the names of those seated in a given tribal area against their lists would have been perfectly feasible.

The arrangements made for the distribution of pay vouchers in the fourth century remain problematical. Some could well have been handed out as citizens took their seats, but, as it appears to have been possible to defraud the state by claiming pay to which one was not entitled, it is conceivable that others were claimed and distributed in advance. It is likely that the 'collectors' made themselves responsible for satisfying the demands of their own fellow-tribesmen, and, of course, only if the citizens sat by tribes will it have been at all an easy task for them to have checked upon the attendance of those to whom vouchers had been issued.

Procedures in Athenian Assemblies varied to some extent according to the purpose for which they were called, and in the survey which follows the three principal types of Assembly, the routine legislative Assemblies, the electoral Assemblies and the special plenary Assemblies, are separately treated.

Before c. 380 BC responsibility for the conduct of affairs in the routine Assemblies lay with the fifty members of the Council who constituted the *prytaneis*, or executive committee, for the month in which the meeting was held. They sat on the front benches and were responsible for the maintenance of order, while the actual presidency of the Assembly fell to that one among them who had been selected by lot as *epistates* for the day.[142] After 380 the arrangements were slightly more complicated. The *epistates* of the ruling prytany on the day of the Assembly himself selected by lot nine presidents or *proedroi*, one from each of the other non-ruling prytanies in the Council, and these then formally assumed charge of the proceedings, the single presidency being handed over to one of their number who was again selected by lot.[143] It is important to distinguish between the functions of the single individual who actually presided over the Assembly and those of the larger group, whether it be the fifty *prytaneis* before 380 or the nine *proedroi* after that date. The former's job was to preside over any discussion, to decide the time when any matter should be put to the vote, formally to put the question through the agency of his herald, and to announce the results of the voting. The responsibility of the latter, on the other hand, was, among other things, to adjudge whether a vote on any matter was admissible under the law and to satisfy themselves that the official assessment of the outcome of a vote was correct.

The form of voting employed at all such Assemblies was a show of hands.[144] This, of course, was far from ideal. It did not respect secrecy, and, in view of the natural tendency of a mass to follow a lead rather than think out the arguments for itself, it was not particularly conducive to independence of judgment. But the principal reason for its use will have been that the volume of business and the form of the proceedings allowed little time for anything more complex. In marked contrast to Roman practice, the number of votes which any one Assembly may have been called upon to register was considerable. First of all there was a certain amount of regular business which every Assembly was required to discharge before the citizens could turn their attention to more specific matters; much of this involved the taking of decisions by vote. Thus, for example, at no less than nine meetings each year it had to vote its approval or disapproval of the manner in which the various magistrates were conducting themselves in office; and again, at the principal meeting of the sixth prytany, it was required to vote as to whether it thought it necessary or advisable to invoke the law of ostracism.[145] When all this preliminary business was done, the Assembly began to turn its attention to the proposals embodied in *probouleumata* of the Council—measures initiated by the Council itself, by magistrates, or, as often as not, by private citizens who had given the matter an airing at a previous meeting and had succeeded in having it referred to the Council for official presentation. Of these *probouleumata* there could be several at each meeting, and for each one individually the same procedure was adopted. First came a preliminary vote on the simple issue of whether the motion should be accepted as it stood without discussion or whether it should be thrown open to debate with a view to possible amendment or rejection. This was known as the *procheirotonia*.[146] No doubt in many cases, indeed in all cases except those in which the Council had drafted a detailed and definitive proposal, which it frequently did not do, the decision was in favour of discussion. There then followed a debate, during which it was open not only for the author of the proposal to speak for his motion but also for others to suggest formal amendments; and, when the president decided that the time had come for a final decision, the voting must often have been complex. The people were called upon not merely to give one simple 'yes' or 'no' verdict, but to vote in turn upon a number of conflicting amendments.

It is thus clear that the multiplicity of corporate decisions which the Athenians were commonly called upon to take at their legislative Assemblies goes far to explain their failure to adopt any formal system of voting comparable with that adopted either at Rome or indeed in their own popular courts. An interesting question is raised, however, by their use of the word *psephisma*, derived from *psephos* (a pebble, a balloting token), to designate their formal resolutions in Assembly. Busolt chose to dismiss the problem by suggesting that the word was simply borrowed from the terminology of the courts,[147] but in view of the equally important role played by the popular Assembly in Athenian public life this is, to say the least, a doubtful answer. The alternative view is that in the earlier Assemblies *psephoi* had in fact been used by the voters, and that pressure of business had later rendered their use impracticable. This is not so far-fetched an explanation as it may at first appear. It is true that the trend in any democratic society is towards the observance of greater secrecy in the recording of the vote rather than less; and, if the use of *psephoi* were necessarily to be associated with the principle of a secret ballot, its abandonment by the radical democracy would therefore appear most improbable.[148] But in fact the use of voting pebbles does not imply secrecy. This point is clearly illustrated by vase-paintings which have survived, depicting the vote which is alleged to have been taken to decide whether Odysseus or Ajax should be allocated the arms of Achilles. While the two contestants stand in the wings, the goddess Athena is portrayed as presiding over a vote at which the voters process in front of a low table and deposit a pebble in one of two rows situated at either end of it (Fig. III).[149] This is indeed an open vote, probably to be construed as less secret than the raising of hands in a crowded Assembly, if the voting table

Fig. III *Vase-painting which depicts the vote on the award of the arms of Achilles. The voters place their pebbles openly in one of the two groups situated at either end of the tribunal.*

was under the close scrutiny of those who were most concerned to influence the outcome. There is in fact a parallel here with the similar procedure which was introduced into the courts by the Thirty oligarchs in 404 BC, when the jurymen were required to cast their ballots on an open table in front of the judges.[150] It is therefore not at all unlikely that in the early days of the popular

Assembly, and perhaps in the still older local assemblies, votes were taken with the aid of pebbles in a manner very similar to that depicted. Such a method would have rendered individual voters more liable to supervision by their superiors. It would also have greatly facilitated the process of the count.

The method used to count votes in the Assembly is another matter about which we know little. At some votes, as for example in many preliminary votes taken on the Council's *probouleumata*, the sense of the Assembly's decision may have been abundantly clear on the show of hands, and the taking of an exact count may have proved unnecessary. At others, however—in the voting on alternative resolutions, in close voting on matters of policy and more particularly at elections—it will have been essential to take an accurate count. Before 380 it would seem that the fifty members of the prytany took collective responsibility for this task, which they may have apportioned among themselves. After 380 it appears to have been the job of the nine *proedroi* to conduct the count; and it is likely that they joined with the *epistates* of the ruling prytany, who had been responsible for drawing them by lot, in each taking charge of the count in a particular section of the gathering. This would produce ten enumerators, each one representing a tribe, and it may be suggested that they severally concerned themselves with the counting of the votes of their own tribesmen. Of course, even the counting of some three hundred hands with absolute accuracy is no simple task, and, in view of the attested difficulty which the Greeks encountered in counting in their heads,[151] the tellers may well have used pebbles as aids, perhaps dropping one beside them for each hand which they counted and so allowing themselves to give their undivided attention to the job in hand. Such a practice could have been suggested by the earlier supposed procedure, which has just been described, in which pebbles were deposited not by the tellers but by the voters themselves.

It should, of course, be emphasized that, although the votes were almost certainly counted in sections, and very possibly in tribal sections, the totals of votes cast in each section or tribe were of no consequence in themselves. In direct contrast to the procedure adopted at Rome, it was the sum total of all votes cast in the Assembly at large, and not the totals of the votes in the individual groups, which went to determine the final verdict. The officials responsible for counting the votes in each section presumably reported the totals of votes cast both for and against a motion to the president of the Assembly. He then simply aggregated the figures and determined the overall result, which he caused to be publicly announced.

The electoral Assembly was normally held annually in the first prytany after the sixth when the auspices were favourable. Nothing very definite is known about the arrangements made for producing and publicizing a list of candidates for the various offices to which appointment was made by direct vote. In the case of extraordinary offices, certainly, nominations were frequently accepted and voted upon at one and the same meeting;[152] but it is unlikely that this was the practice with the regular, annual magistracies. In these cases a formal list of candidates must surely have been completed before the election day, probably by the *prytaneis*, and possibly incorporated in the *probouleuma* of the Council which authorized the electoral proceedings. Such a list of names must also obviously have been read out to the meeting before the vote. A small complication is raised by a statement of Plato to the effect that at the election of the generals it was open to anyone present in the body of the meeting to propose the substitution of a candidate of his own naming for one who was included in the official list, and to ask for a vote to be held prior to the election itself in order to determine whether such a substitution should be effected.[153] Why, it may be asked, should the acceptance of such a late nomination have necessitated substitution at all and the displacing of one who was already on the list? It is difficult to believe that the original list was strictly limited to a certain number of candidates from each tribe, for without the use of the lot there was no basis on which any qualified person applying for nomination could have been excluded. One possible explanation of the procedure, which is wholly consonant with the democratic principle, is that the right to call for a substitution, to which Plato refers, was in fact limited to those cases where the number of listed candidates did not exceed the number of places to be filled and where, as a consequence, the Assembly had been offered no freedom of choice. In such circumstances—as, for example, when there was only a single candidate from one tribe on the list for a place on a board of ten—the admissibility of a substitution at the last minute would have been eminently reasonable. Obviously, it would not have done to accept additions to the list, for a proliferation of late nominations could easily have been engineered to produce vote-splitting and to thwart the will of the majority; but a vote on substitution would simply have been tantamount to a straight trial of strength between the supporters and opponents of the official candidate.

The taking of the vote in electoral Assemblies was invariably by show of hands; if a plurality of tellers and the use of pebbles as an aid to counting were necessary for legislative votes they will naturally have been the more necessary at elections, when there might be many candidates and the margin between success and failure in terms of votes may frequently have been small. The procedure at most elections, when the Assembly was required to choose one or more candidates from each tribe, was for voting to take place in turn on each of the tribal lists of candidates. In the case of the election of generals after the middle of the fifth century, however, a somewhat different procedure may have been adopted. It was suggested earlier that the Assembly voted in succession upon the entire list in a single exercise, that a tally was kept of the votes accorded to each candidate, and that as a general principle places were awarded to those from each of the ten tribes who had received the highest vote.[154]

The plenary Assemblies of the Athenians fall into an altogether different category, and were held comparatively infrequently for one of three principal purposes: to decide who, if anyone, should be temporarily expelled from the city under the law of ostracism —this only in such years as an ordinary Assembly had already voted in favour of an ostracism being held—to bestow *adeia*, or immunity from the law, upon a citizen who had incurred a loss of rights or who wished to introduce an 'unlawful' proposal, and, in the fourth century at least, to agree upon the conferment of citizen rights. They had several distinguishing features. They had to be attended by at least six thousand people, and therefore by a fair proportion of the rural population of Attica; they were held in the market-place, where there was ample room for so large a number to manœuvre; they were summoned and presided over by the nine archons and the whole Council; and they culminated in a vote which was taken by ballot.[155]

Most of our detailed information concerning the procedures adopted at these Assemblies comes from accounts of votes on ostracism; but, although there must have been certain distinctive differences between votes on ostracism and votes on one of the other two matters, particularly in the form of the ballot, it is a reasonable assumption that the general arrangements made for ordering the voters were much the same in all cases. In the central part of the market-place was erected a circular enclosure constructed of a wooden material, in which there were ten openings. In order to cast their votes the citizens passed through the particular opening which corresponded to their tribe and deposited their ballots in vessels inside the enclosure. The actual voting was supervised by the nine archons and the secretary of the *Thesmothetae*, each of whom presumably made themselves responsible for one particular tribal section. It will have been their duty, perhaps assisted by selected members of the Council, to ensure that no unqualified person voted and that no person entered the voting area more than once, and furthermore to satisfy themselves that no voter cast more than a single ballot.[156]

At an ostracism the form of ballot used was not an official token, but a plain piece of tile or potsherd. Hoards of such *ostraka*, as they were called, have been discovered in excavations at Athens, and it is clear from the different shapes and sizes of the finds that the voters made use of any plain surface of pottery on which they could conveniently lay their hand. On it they simply inscribed the name of the statesman whom they wished to see ostracized (Fig. IV). Whether they did this at home or in the voting arena was apparently their own concern; indeed, if they were themselves illiterate there was nothing to prevent their asking another to write in the required name on their behalf.[157]

There are two contradictory traditions about the counting of the *ostraka* and the determination of the result. According to Plutarch, the total number of *ostraka* deposited in the receptacles was first counted without reference to the names that were written upon them, and the actual reckoning of the votes cast against each name was only made if it was found that at least six thousand citizens had voted. Philochorus and others,[158] however, imply that it was necessary for at least six thousand votes to be cast against one individual before an ostracism could be validated, and they therefore quite naturally make no mention of any preliminary count. The arguments which have been used to discredit Plutarch's version are principally two: first, that in multiple contests, such as are attested by both the literary and the epigraphical evidence, it would on this view have been very possible for a person to be ostracized on a minority vote; and second, that if a quorum were all that was required the desire of a large majority group to ostracize a particular individual could easily have been thwarted by the action of a minority opposition in absenting themselves with the express purpose of ensuring that the quorum was not attained.[159] But the force of both these arguments is more apparent than real. The first does not take into sufficient account the fact that no vote of ostracism could take place at all without a prior recommendation from the regular Assembly, and unless six thousand people were ready to act on that recommendation and present themselves at the vote. The fulfilment of both these conditions would normally imply that feeling was running high against one or at the most two individuals in particular. The second is based on a glaring logical fallacy: for, if it is argued that the absenteeism of an opposition could effectively thwart the attainment of a quorum of six thousand voters, how can it consistently be maintained in the same breath that no vote on ostracism could be valid unless six thousand voted against the same person? Indeed, it is just such a consideration of the numbers who attended at the votes on ostracism which renders the Plutarchean account so much more credible. Thucydides tells us that in his day attendance figures at the Assembly never approached five thousand. He refers, of course, to the regular Assemblies; but it is

Fig. IV *Examples of ostraka found in the Athenian agora. The names scratched upon them are those of prominent political figures—Aristides, Pericles and Themistocles.*

acknowledged that the normal number must have been well exceeded at special votes of this kind, in particular at ostracisms, which were always timed for the autumn, when the farming population might be expected already to have gathered in the harvest and to be concerned with selling it in the city markets. Nevertheless an attendance so far in excess of six thousand as to permit of a positive vote of at least that number against a single individual is difficult to accept.

If any further support is needed for the quorum theory, as opposed to the consensus theory, it is to be found in the details of the political background to the final ostracism, which took place in 417 BC. In that year the two leading figures, Nicias and Alcibiades, each had reason to fear that he would be the victim of the vote, and as a consequence, we are told, their supporters formed a mutual pact of neutrality which resulted in the Assembly's voting for the expulsion of a third party.[160] The fact that the two statesmen considered such an arrangement politically expedient must suggest that both anticipated a very close vote, and therefore that the hostility of the Athenians towards them was fairly evenly apportioned. Yet, had a minimum of six thousand votes cast against one individual been necessary to secure his ostracism, neither man could have had much to worry about. Both would have found comfort in the prospect of an almost fifty-fifty split in the vote and would have deemed their disreputable manœuvre totally unnecessary.

If Plutarch's theory of the quorum is to be accepted, it is perfectly logical also to accept his reference to a preliminary count. To conduct a detailed breakdown of the number of votes cast against each individual must undoubtedly have been an arduous task, rendered no easier by the discrepancy in the shapes and sizes of the voting tokens and perhaps by the near illegibility of some of the scratchings made upon them. If, therefore, there was any doubt as to whether as many as six thousand had voted, it would have been very reasonable to make a quick check of the total number of *ostraka* deposited in the receptacles without reading them before embarking on what might prove to be a fruitless task.

The essential and perhaps the only significant difference between an ostracism and a vote in another plenary Assembly lay in the form of balloting itself. The clearest clue to the voting procedure adopted comes from Xenophon's account of the arrangements made by the Athenians at the famous trial of the Arginusan generals in 406 BC. These proceedings, which involved the constitution of the Assembly as a special criminal court, were most unusual; but the voting called for a straight 'yes' or 'no' decision and almost certainly followed the pattern established for decisions on immunity. The *probouleuma* of the Council called for a vote of the citizens by tribes, as in the case of ostracisms, and provided that two voting receptacles should be set up for each tribe. Before the vote the herald was to make a public announcement that those who considered the accused guilty should place their ballots in the foremost receptacle and those who considered them innocent in the rearmost.[161] The ballots used were simple *psephoi* or pebbles, but it is probable that they bore an official marking and that they were handed out to the voters by the archon in charge as they entered the voting enclosure through their tribal entrance.

The sources make it very clear that the chief purpose behind the use of the ballot at these Assemblies was not to facilitate counting but to ensure secrecy. The difficulties of devising a form of secret ballot for elections, when so many officers had to be named at once by a semi-literate body, were obviously regarded as unsurmountable; but the democracy clearly subscribed to the principle that, when the fate of an individual citizen was in the balance, secrecy should be observed wherever possible. Whether this ideal was ever satisfactorily achieved is another matter. In the sense that the voter could effectively conceal the way he was voting if he himself made the effort, it probably was. It was possible for him to turn over his *ostrakon* face down, when he indicated to the presiding archon that he held only one in his hand, and, in the case of the other ballots, it is notable that reasonably effective means were devised of enabling the voter to choose between the two receptacles undetected. But if the voter wished to advertise the sense of his vote there were apparently few difficulties put in his way. There was clearly nothing to stop a citizen showing his *ostrakon* to all and sundry before he entered the voting arena, and, unless very strict precautions were taken, it is likely that he would find it easy, if he so wished, to indicate publicly the receptacle into which he cast his pebble.

THE ATHENIAN COUNCIL

The principles underlying voting procedure in the Council of Five Hundred were similar to those which applied in the Athenian Assembly. In voting upon resolutions and appointing the various annual officials whom it was their peculiar responsibility to elect, the councillors gave their decision by a show of hands. In all cases where the rights and status of an individual were involved they employed a ballot.

The attested forms of balloting are two. At a formal judicial trial they employed *psephoi*, and the proceedings were very similar to those in the Assembly as described by Xenophon.[162]

But the Council also exercised a disciplinary authority over its own members, and it could at any time take a vote on the provisional expulsion of any councillor whom it judged to be unworthy. For this purpose the councillors used not pebbles but olive leaves, with the result that the vote itself was given the name *ekphyllophoria*, 'the casting out by means of the leaf'.[163] We cannot be sure either how these leaves were used, or indeed why they were used, in such votes; but, in view of the fact that the *ekphyllophoria* was customarily followed by a formal trial for misconduct, which finally determined the fate of the councillor in question, it should perhaps be supposed that these proceedings were regarded as very much more informal than any which involved the use of *psephoi*. Clearly, there was no official distribution of voting tokens if the councillors used olive leaves, and there may have been no elaborate checks to ensure that each person cast only one vote.

Aristotle conveys the impression that the arrangements for supervising all voting and for counting and determining results were identical for Council and Assembly. In other words, before 380 the ruling prytany under its president of the day enjoyed collective responsibility; after 380 the charge fell to the nine *proedroi*, each representing a different tribe. This change was almost certainly effected in the interests of impartiality. While proceedings were exclusively in the charge of a single tribe some form of collusion was theoretically feasible; but when responsibility was transferred to a random group drawn from the entire body the chances of such collusion were virtually eliminated.

Another change which may have been influenced by considerations of voting was that made in the Council's seating arrangements. Before 410 the councillors appear to have sat wherever they chose, with the result that those who shared a common viewpoint tended to congregate in groups. In a show of hands, of course, such local concentration of votes was not conducive to the maximum independence of judgment, for the neutral and indifferent would naturally be inclined to follow a solid lead. There was therefore a strong case for regulating the seating. In the Assembly, which was a body of large and indeterminate size, such a solution to the problem would have been impracticable. But not so in a stable body of five hundred members. A system was devised for allotting seats to councillors by lettered section, and in 410 a clause was introduced into the Council oath of office by which each councillor swore that he would sit in his allocated place.[164] It has sometimes been assumed that the seats were allotted on a tribal basis, but the unearthing of allotment machines which appear to have had as many as fifty horizontal rows of slots on the face and as many vertical rows as there were tribes suggests that the random break-up of the Council membership may have been much more thorough. If these machines were used for the Council, as seems likely,[165] they imply the use of a process of double sortition similar to that which was employed for the selection of jurymen. Each vertical row of slots would have been filled with the tickets of the councillors of a single tribe drawn in a random order. The resulting complete horizontal rows would thus have contained the tickets of one councillor from each tribe, and each of these groups of ten would have been assigned by the operation of the lot mechanism to a specific lettered section of ten seats in the Council chamber.

THE ATHENIAN COURTS

The most frequent experience of voting for the average Athenian was probably in the popular courts. Even in the fifth century there existed a permanent panel of no less than six thousand jurors, which was selected once a year by lot from among those who offered themselves for service.[166] Later, in the fourth century, any citizen who was over thirty and was not debarred by reason of indebtedness or loss of rights was at liberty to have himself registered on the panel, and the jurors for particular cases were selected by lot from among all those registered who presented themselves for service on the day.[167] The frequency with which each individual was called upon cannot, of course, be exactly determined. It is known that the courts were in session on most days of the year except for feast days and the days of the Assemblies, and, when Aristophanes estimates the total as three hundred, he may not be guilty of too gross an exaggeration. Naturally, the numbers of jurors required on any one day varied with the amount of business to be done as well as with the type of cases to be heard, for the complement of any one court could be as high as 1,500 or as low as 200; but it is significant that in Aristotle's day provision was made for as many as ten courts to sit simultaneously. At a conservative estimate, it may be deduced that most registered jurors were called upon to serve at least one day in seven, and probably with greater regularity in the fifth century, when the panel was smaller and the courts had to cope with the extra lawsuits brought to Athens by her overseas allies.

Throughout the history of the courts voting was by ballot. During the fifth century the token used was a common mussel shell or, perhaps later, an imitation shell made of bronze. When the vote was called, each juror supposedly received one such token and was required to cast it in one of two vessels positioned one behind the other, probably at the rear of the president's tribunal. The foremost vessel was the receptacle for ballots in favour of condemnation, and the rearmost for those cast in favour of acquittal.[168] The voting procedure was thus very similar to that observed in the plenary Assemblies. It was clearly considered to provide some degree of secrecy, and is contrasted by Lysias with the method of placing the ballots on open tables, which he says was introduced by the Thirty deliberately in order to render court proceedings more susceptible to influence.[169] How this element of secrecy was achieved, however, is less certain. A few cryptic words in Aeschylus' *Agamemnon* might be taken to suggest that the voters could readily be observed as they cast their votes, but that their hand movements in fact gave little away. When the gods voted to determine the fate of Troy, says the poet, they cast their ballots by placing them in the urn of blood 'while the mere unfulfilled hope of a hand approached the other urn'.[170] There are two possibilities. One is simply that the voters aimed to conceal their vote by extending one of their hands over each of the two vessels so that no onlooker could discern from which hand and into which vessel the ballot dropped. The other is that the two vessels were covered at the top by a single convex lid containing an opening large enough for the insertion of an arm, and that the choice between the two urns was thus made while the hand itself was concealed from view.[171] In either case there would be reason in placing the vessels one behind the other rather than alongside each other; for hand or arm movements would thus have been much more difficult for those standing behind to distinguish.

The methods followed in Aristotle's day were very much more foolproof, and, thanks to the detailed account given in the *Constitution of Athens*, they can be reconstructed in much greater detail. The tokens then used, of which several well-preserved examples have been unearthed, were discs of bronze with a short shaft passing through the centre. When all the speeches were over, two such discs were distributed in full public view to each juror by four tellers, who had been appointed by lot before the start of the proceedings. One of these had a solid shaft, while that of the other was hollow (Fig. V). The two discs were placed in a special stand, in front of each juror. Then, after enquiring whether there were any outstanding objections to the evidence from the litigants, the herald called for the vote, announcing, 'The hollow token for the plaintiff (or "for condemnation"); the solid token for the defendant (or "for acquittal")'. At this point the jurors took their tokens from the stands, holding them by the ends of the shafts in such a way as not to reveal which hand held the hollow token and which the solid one, and proceeded to the front of the court, where there stood two vessels, one of bronze and one of wood. Into the bronze urn, which had a slot in its top just wide enough to permit the insertion of a single disc, they deposited the token which represented the sense of their verdict; into the wooden urn, which was wide open at the top, they deposited the other.

The use of two tokens of a different type not only ensured greater secrecy; it also undoubtedly made the count more simple and rendered it virtually proof against manipulation. In the fifth century, presumably, the contents of the two urns were emptied out and counted independently by the tellers. Given a degree of connivance, therefore, there was some scope for falsification. Under Aristotle's procedure, however, only the contents of the bronze urn were emptied out and counted, and, to facilitate the counting operation, use was made of a large reckoning board, rather like a cribbage board, which contained holes into which the shafts of the voting discs could be slotted. The normal procedure was to slot in all the hollow-shafted discs at one end of the board and all the solid-shafted ones at the other. This had three positive advantages. First, since the rows of slots on the board were of equal length, it was possible to make and check the count of solid and hollow discs in a matter of seconds. Second, it was a simple matter to verify at a glance that the number of votes cast corresponded to the total number of jurors who had voted.

Fig. V *Voting tokens used in the Athenian public courts during the fourth century BC. The inscription reads* ψηφος δημοσια (= *official ballot*).

Third, it was an easy matter for anyone in the courtroom to satisfy himself concerning the accuracy of the count and the correctness of the verdict by making a cursory inspection of the reckoning board, in which the hollow and solid shafts of the tokens at either end were exposed to view.

The result of the voting in court was given out in the name of the president by a herald, a tie on votes always being regarded as a decision in favour of the defendant or accused. This, however, was not necessarily the end of the proceedings. In cases where a penalty was not determined by law or where damages had to be assessed, it was sometimes necessary to have a second vote to decide between different penalties or damages proposed. In Aristotle's day this vote seems to have been conducted on similar lines to the first. The official discs were presumably restored to the jurors, who then deposited the one with the hollow shaft in the sealed bronze urn if they agreed with the proposal of the plaintiff. In the fifth century, however, when shells were used for the main vote, an altogether different method was used for voting on the penalty. Waxed tablets were distributed, and the jurors were required to draw upon them a long line if they favoured the proposals of the plaintiff, or a short line if they favoured the proposals of the defendant.[172] No explanation is provided of the use of two such different voting procedures in the one court; but it certainly appears that the Athenians were prepared to go to more trouble to ensure an accurate count and an entirely secret vote when the jurors were required to determine penalties than when they were called on to decide upon guilt or liability. The need to provide waxed tablets and the extra work of sorting and reading which was necessarily involved in the determination of the result must have been disadvantages which were considered to be more than outweighed by the elimination of any possibility of error on the part of the voters, and by the greater secrecy resulting from the use of a single voting urn.

The Athenians do not appear to have devised any particularly sophisticated method of dealing with voting in cases where the interests of more than two parties were involved. Demosthenes suggests that in his day the procedure amounted to no more than calling upon jurors to deposit a single ballot in one of a number of vessels each of which represented the claims of a different party in the dispute.[173] In such cases, obviously, the element of secrecy must have been extremely limited.

Whether voting in the Athenian courts was compulsory is debatable. Since it was the custom to enrol an odd number of jurors for each case,[174] the existence of a provision for the possibility of a tied vote would appear to imply that it was not. Nevertheless, the very insistence on having the odd number suggests that a hundred per cent vote was accepted as the norm; and in later times at least it is probable that it was virtually guaranteed by the sanction of withholding state payment from those who abstained. As each juror presented himself to vote, he handed in his official identity staff and received in exchange a voucher on which he could draw his pay. Furthermore, if a second vote was to be taken, he was required first to reverse the process, taking his staff once more in return for the voucher, and then, after the completion of all the arguments in court, to collect his voucher yet again before casting his further vote. It should be supposed that great care was taken to ensure that the number of vouchers handed out and the number of staffs handed in corresponded in each case with the total number of votes which were cast.

CHAPTER V

MANIPULATION AND FRAUD

THE ELECTORAL CANVASS AND THE DELIVERY OF THE VOTE

OF ALL THE ASPECTS of Greek elections the conduct of the canvass is perhaps the one on which our information is the most sparse. In the case of Sparta this is neither remarkable nor significant, for Aristotle, who is the chief source of information on the Spartan system, is more concerned with constitutional theory than with practical politics. It is not unlikely that, as at Rome and in other oligarchies, the elections were regarded as little more than opportunities for a trial of strength between representatives of a comparatively small number of families who saw the tenure of office as their birthright. In the case of the *gerousia* Aristotle certainly confirms that this was so. The councillors, he says, were traditionally chosen from among the 'best men', and their rule was a *dynasteia*, a form of government in which office was confined in practice to the few and handed down from father to son. Nevertheless, the electoral contest was very much a reality, for, as Aristotle notes with disapproval, the Spartan lawgiver regarded ambition for distinction as no less essential an ingredient in the good ruler than intrinsic worth. It is probable, therefore, that while members of distinguished families had a reasonable chance of acquiring the status of councillor at some stage in their later life, their success at any particular election depended not a little upon the assiduity with which they cultivated their various friends and dependants. The ephors, of course, were in a somewhat different category, for, according to Aristotle, they could be drawn from any section of the Spartan community and were occasionally men of meagre means. But, as it is not even certain who constituted the electoral body, it would be idle to speculate overmuch on the conduct of their canvassing. If there is justification for the view that they were appointed by the *gerousia*, and if Aristotle is right in conveying the impression that they were more commonly the recipients than the givers of bribes,[175] it is perhaps not unreasonable to suggest that those of the ephors who were not themselves members of the 'best' families were inclined for the most part to be their protégés and pawns. In this case it is possible that the annual elections to the ephorate were commonly stage-managed by those who belonged to the governing class, and that they too, like the less regular elections to the *gerousia*, provided opportunities for trials of strength between prominent individuals or factions.

The absence of more than a few passing references to electoral candidature in the Athenian tradition is very much more remarkable, particularly when it is considered how much the Athenians prided themselves on their democratic institutions and how much contemporary information on the working of Athenian society has survived in the late fifth- and fourth-century writers. Indeed, so little is recorded that it cannot be said either how an aspirant to elective office contrived to get his name on to an official list of candidates or how soon before the day of the election itself such an official list was published. There might be some justification for deducing from this silence that candidature and the canvass played a comparatively insignificant role in Athenian public life; and indeed this impression is to some extent confirmed by the only extended reference to the subject which has survived, namely Plutarch's account of the electoral successes of the late fourth-century statesman, Phocion. 'This man', he writes, 'was elected general more times not only than any of his contemporaries but also than any of his predecessors; yet he never canvassed his fellow-countrymen or made any effort to obtain the office, accepting it only because he was asked to do so. All historians admit that he was elected forty-five times and that he never once missed being elected, since, even when he was away, the Athenians used to send for him. As a consequence his enemies used to wonder that Phocion, who always thwarted the Athenians and never flattered them by word or deed, should be favoured by them, and they were wont to remark that the Athenians in their hours of relaxation used to amuse themselves by listening to the speeches of the more lively and brilliant orators, but that they made their appointments to public office in a serious and sober vein, choosing for that purpose the most severe and sensible man in Athens and the one too who alone—or at any rate more than anyone else— was in the habit of opposing their impulses and wishes.'[176]

Although Phocion was of late date and could be regarded as an exceptional case, there is little reason to doubt the truth of this suggestion that, all other things being equal, the Athenians were inclined at an election to pay more attention to a candidate's worth than to his immediate external appeal. After all, the offices to which appointment was made by direct vote at Athens were comparatively few, and the reason that they were not thrown open to the lot along with the rest was quite simply that there was demanded of their incumbents a measure of skill and expertise which was to be found only in a select few. On their own tacit admission, therefore, the Athenians regarded an election as an opportunity to assess the relative worth of the candidates; and it is unlikely that they allowed themselves readily to be bribed, cajoled, or otherwise persuaded to reject a candidate of outstanding merit in favour of one whose qualifications were manifestly poorer.[177]

That the Athenians elected their generals at least with an eye principally to merit is strongly suggested by the history of ostracism in the fifth century. The most notable victims of ostracism were prominent statesmen who had themselves been frequently elected to the office of general and who were in some cases probably members of the board at the very time that the vote was taken.[178] This apparent contradiction between the actions of the Assembly in first electing a man to office and then expelling him from Athens can only be understood if it be accepted that the two decisions were reached on each occasion on the basis of fundamentally different considerations. At the vote for an ostracism and in the subsequent ostracism itself the Athenians were concerned to break a serious deadlock which had resulted or was in danger of resulting from a clash of attitudes among their leading magistrates. At an election, on the other hand, their primary concern was to assess the relative merit of the candidates put forward by each of the ten tribes.

What little is known about the rules of candidature points to the same conclusion. It would seem that they were framed so as to impose the least possible discipline upon the candidates and allow the greatest possible freedom of action to the electorate. Thus, election in absence is well attested during the period of the Peloponnesian War in the cases of such generals as Demosthenes, Nicias and Alcibiades;[179] and there seems to be little ground for the contention that this represented an exceptional wartime concession to those who were away from Athens in the service of the state, and that in normal circumstances the presence of the candidate was required by law. Indeed, a statement of Theophrastus to the effect that anyone appointed to an elective office could renounce the appointment on oath so long as he had reasonable grounds for doing so has cast some doubts on whether inclusion in the official list of candidates even required the candidate's consent.[180] Unfortunately, the only attested examples of 'swearing out' relate to the appointment of citizens to special commissions or embassies,[181] when there is unlikely to have been sufficient time for the preparation of an official list of candidates, and when nominations were probably accepted from the floor of the Assembly to be voted upon forthwith, rather than to regular magistracies. But it is clear that in principle the Athenians wished themselves to be free to call upon the services of those whom they thought could serve them best. It is possible that, in order to expedite electoral business and to bring some sort of order into the proceedings, they insisted on the preparation of an official list of candidates for the regular annual magistracies, and that, as Plato indicates, they allowed, but severely restricted, last-minute additions to that list; but, in view of the fact that they frequently elected persons who were too far away to submit a personal application, it must be considered doubtful whether even in normal times they allowed themselves to be limited to the choice of those who had submitted their own names or signified their consent to stand.

Elections at Athens, then, were probably very much more the direct concern of the electorate and very much less the concern of a ruling class than was the case in more oligarchically based communities such as Sparta or Rome. And this is one reason why competition for office, while not altogether lacking, was considerably less intense. When the electoral body has a keen eye for intrinsic merit the number of those who can hope to succeed must of necessity be limited. It should be remembered too that the boards of elected magistrates were larger than they were in many other states, one representative normally being chosen from each of ten tribes, and that in some ways the holding of office at Athens was considerably less attractive than it was elsewhere. Thus, each magistrate had to undergo a most thorough scrutiny of his private life and political outlook at the *dokimasia* and was called on to pass muster no less than nine times during the year. The consequences of using an excess of initiative in an emergency could also be dire, as the successful generals after Arginusae learnt to their cost. A further valid point is made by Pseudo-Xenophon, when he contrasts the elective positions with those which carried state pay as being offices which conferred great responsibility without complementary financial reward.[182] This point, reinforced as it is by the story of the poverty-stricken Phocion in Plutarch, can be countered, of course, by citing the cases of less scrupulous generals such as Alcibiades, who enriched themselves at the allies' expense; but as a general principle it should be accepted that in normal circumstances the elected officers had far less opportunity for deriving great financial benefit from office than, for example, their Roman counterparts.

Although these considerations go far to explain why the theme of candidature and the canvass does not feature more prominently in Athenian literature, it would be very misleading to suggest that electoral contests at Athens were not sometimes very much alive. The Greeks had their word—*spoudarchia*—for political ambition, which was in current use in the fifth century;[183] and despite the apparent unattractiveness of certain offices there were undoubtedly those who sought them.[184] When there was no obvious candidate and two or three contestants for a place were fairly evenly matched there may well have been considerable activity prior to the voting. To judge from the limited evidence available, any one of three factors may have contributed in large measure to the election of a candidate whose ability did not make him an automatic choice—the championship of his cause by a popular leader and demagogue, the active support of the *hetaeriae* or political clubs, or some form of direct personal canvass.

The first of these is likely to have been the most effective and perhaps the most common, at least as far as the major offices were concerned. It has commonly been recognized that the friends of Pericles were prominent among his colleagues at the time of his ascendancy and absent from the board of generals when he was in disfavour. Later Demosthenes spoke of favours in offices which were at the disposal of the leaders of the people[185] and was himself accused by Aeschines of having promised to secure election to the generalship for another.[186] For years at a time the Athenian people would allow themselves to be guided in their decisions by one man whose hold upon them rested largely upon his mastery of the art of rhetoric. Occasionally, as in the case of Pericles, such a man was talented in other ways and held office himself. More commonly he had no other useful attributes and did not even aspire to offices which he knew that he could not competently discharge. But, whether or not the Athenians were willing to entrust him with responsibility himself, they were often ready to act upon his electoral recommendations when they had little else to guide them. This form of direct approach to the mass electorate must clearly have been an invaluable asset to a candidate, and given the complete ascendancy of the people's champion of the day the tactics must have been virtually impossible to counter.

It was at times when such a person was not active that the political clubs are likely to have gone into action.[187] These basically aristocratic associations are alleged by Thucydides to have been largely instrumental in placing those who were opposed to democracy on the board of generals immediately prior to the oligarchic revolution of 411 BC.[188] They were officially banned on the restoration of democracy at the end of the fifth century, but they clearly continued to work underground.[189] Their mode of operation is obscure. Rather than working in competition one with another on behalf of rival candidates, they possibly only became active when they were united in support of a candidate or candidates who were intolerant of the excesses of radical democracy. Their chief strength, it should be supposed, lay in the fact that they were the sole organized and disciplined groups on the Athenian political scene. By using their forces to the maximum efficiency they could no doubt arrange for contingents of voters in suitable numbers to come in from the outlying areas, and they could ensure that groups of sympathizers placed themselves strategically in the voting arena so as to be able to exert the maximum influence upon the hesitant and indifferent voters around them. It should be remembered that the method of voting by show of hands lent itself particularly to the influencing of the mass by example. It is possible, too, that other less savoury ways were employed of delivering the vote, but, if they were, the clubs must have been at great pains to cover their tracks. There is little doubt that even the most inoffensive organized attempts to pre-determine the outcome of the voting in Roman style were frowned upon as unacceptable. The attitudes current even in the mid-fifth century are made clear by Sophocles' representation of the efforts of Menelaus in preparing for the contest between Ajax and Odysseus over the possession of Achilles' arms.[190] The audience of the day were obviously expected to treat it as a serious charge that Menelaus had 'made votes' for Odysseus by conducting a canvass of the chiefs. The objectionable element in the behaviour of Menelaus, and presumably also in the operations of the political clubs, was that they delivered blocks of votes by secretly deploying an organization to prepare the ground prior to the day of the vote.

It is probable that there were many who could call on the services of neither a popular leader nor the oligarchic clubs, in which case their only resort was a personal canvass. In view of the fact that the Assembly was normally attended by perhaps three to four thousand people drawn largely from the urban population, assiduous self-advertisement could presumably have been a fruitful exercise, and Demosthenes assures us that those who aspired to

elective office often went round from one citizen to another,
promoting their own cause.[191] Since, as we have seen, the Athenians were more inclined than some to insist upon the candidate's
suitability to perform his task, the emphasis in this canvass is
likely to have been less upon the general qualities of character
which the Romans so much admired than upon the possession of
an adequate technical skill. Generals, said Isocrates in a satirical
moment, were frequently chosen for the size of their muscles and
their bodily strength.[192] In other words, the people may have had
rather the wrong conception of the qualities which were of paramount importance in their generals, but they at least insisted that
they should possess them. This point is confirmed by Xenophon's
story of the defeated candidate in the elections to the generalship
who complained bitterly that he had been passed over in favour
of one who could not, like himself, evidence his experience of war
by his battle scars.[193] On this occasion the electorate had clearly
not been convinced; but there is an implication that in his canvass
the rejected candidate had looked to his own scars to win him the
votes he needed.

BRIBERY

To assess the part played by bribery in Athenian public life is
difficult. Reference is made to the subject by the fourth-century
orators and political propagandists on a number of occasions. Thus,
Isocrates complains of the populace that it flouts its own laws by
electing to the generalship those who are themselves guilty of offer-
ing bribes;[194] Aeschines refers to charges brought against a group of
persons for bribing the law-courts and the Assembly;[195] and Lysias
speaks of the mass of candidates who distribute largesse freely in the
knowledge that they will later be in a position to recover their losses
twofold.[196] Again, as evidence for a somewhat earlier period can be
cited Euripides' story of an Agamemnon who ordered his slaves to
go out among the poor and to slip silver into their hands in the
market-place. Clearly, these allusions and allegations must have
had some factual basis, and it would be idle to deny that there was
scope for corruption in connection both with the appointment of
magistrates and with voting generally in the Assembly and the

law-courts. But it is none the less questionable whether it can have been particularly widespread, especially in cases where the votes of large numbers of people were involved. The average upper-class citizen of Athens could not himself dispose of the sort of wealth which would be required to rig a vote in an open Assembly attended by upwards of three thousand people. Unlike the second-century Roman *nobilis*, who was enriched beyond measure by booty and could perhaps look forward to a profitable provincial governorship as a means of recovering a heavy debt, the Athenian aristocrat was impoverished by war and paralysed by the burden of the liturgy, and he normally had little prospect of future wealth on which to call. The sort of exercise in mass corruption—by the staging of elaborate games or the provision of open banquets—that Roman aspirants to office were wont to promote in an effort to enhance their *clientelae* would have been quite impracticable, and, since the Athenians did not share the Roman attitude to *beneficium* and *gratia*, perhaps much less effective. Distributions of cash to individuals, on the other hand, if they were to be meaningful, would have involved an outlay far larger than any one candidate could afford. It is therefore likely that the only occasions when a serious attempt was made to bribe a mass body of voters were those on which the operation was organized by a consortium. When, for example, the political clubs intervened at the elections—and this may not have been very often—bribery may well have proved for them an effective instrument. They could call upon the pooled resources of all their members; they could avail themselves of methodically kept records in order to determine where money might most profitably be distributed; they could organize groups to keep a careful check upon the way in which those who had accepted bribes in fact cast their votes; and they could organize the means to take corporate reprisals against those who refused to submit to pressure. It should be taken as significant that, when Aeschines refers to the attempted bribery of the Assembly, he distinctly conveys the impression that this was not an everyday occurrence, and speaks in terms of the activities of a group rather than of an individual.

More common, no doubt, than any mass bribery of the voters

were attempts to bribe individuals or small groups who were in a position of influence. Demosthenes, for example, accused Aeschines of accepting bribes in respect of his conduct on an embassy to Philip;[197] while Aeschines in his turn accused Demosthenes' associate, Timarchus, of accepting bribes and even of indulging in blackmail when he held the office of auditor. Perhaps more germane to this study, he accused the same Timarchus of having acquired every one of his public offices to date 'not by the exercise of the lot or by direct election but by purchase in contravention of the laws'.[198] Exactly what is implied by this charge is by no means clear, particularly as Aeschines cites only one major Athenian office which Timarchus had held—that of auditor, appointment to which was regularly made by lot. But there would appear to be two possible interpretations. One is that the accused bribed the official or officials responsible for conducting the sortition to falsify the process and commit a fraud. The other is that he used the power of bribery in order to bypass the process of sortition. It is difficult to believe that repeated falsification of the lot was a practical proposition; and the second interpretation is perhaps more acceptable. If anything, it is confirmed by two other references in the fourth-century tradition to alleged irregularities in the appointment process—the statement of Aristotle that the allocation of minor magistracies to the demes was abandoned owing to the tendency of the demes to sell the offices assigned to them (*cf.* pp. 49 f.), and the assertion of Aeschines that Demosthenes had been appointed to the Council not by the process of the lot but by bribery and intrigue.[199] In all these cases the suggestion is that money changed hands with a view to ensuring that no contest took place. Exactly how this object was achieved is a matter for speculation. In the case of Demosthenes, the significant point is probably that he belonged to one of the smaller demes in which the number of politically active citizens was very limited, and that he may therefore have found it relatively easy to buy off potential rival candidates for a place on the Council and thus to ensure that the number who actually submitted themselves for appointment did not exceed the deme's annual allocation. In elections to the minor magistracies, on the other hand, at which the deme organizations themselves are alleged to have indulged in corrupt practices, the manœuvres are likely to have been more complex. It is unlikely that the deme officers could regularly and openly have auctioned off the magistracies at their disposal to the highest bidder, when the standard procedure laid down by law was to invite applications and submit all these names to the process of the lot. What the demes are more likely to have 'sold' were their good services in discouraging multiple applications. Such services offered by deme officials in return for a cash payment from an ambitious demesman could well have been effective. Most of those applying for minor office are likely to have been more concerned to win a year's change of occupation at state expense than to further their political careers, and it is not difficult to imagine the type of concession at the hands of local government which could have induced them to defer their application for office to a later year. By the same token, of course, it could be argued that for a candidate to bribe his way into office in this manner was more the exception than the rule. Clearly, anyone who was prepared to pay out a large sum for a minor office or a seat on the Council must have had his reasons. Either, therefore, he must have been sufficiently unscrupulous to hope to use the office for personal aggrandizement, as is alleged of Timarchus, or, like Demosthenes, he must have been confident enough in his powers of persuasion to regard the tenure of a magistracy or a seat on the Council as an effective aid to the influencing of public policy.

In view of the important role played by the popular courts at Athens, it is not surprising that the sources give some prominence to the bribery of jurors. According to Aristotle, bribery first reared its head when Pericles introduced payment for jury service, thereby debasing the character of the juries and ensuring that thereafter it was invariably the common people rather than the upper classes who offered their services in this capacity.[200] The story that the first offender was a certain Anytus, who was prosecuted in 427 BC after his loss of Pylos, is a little difficult to accept;[201] but the prevalence of judicial corruption after this date is confirmed not only by the fourth-century orators but also by the attested lengths to which the Athenians were apparently prepared to go in an effort to stamp it out. The maximum penalty on conviction was no less than death; and the procedure which was used daily in Aristotle's time to determine the selection and allocation of jurymen and magistrates to particular courts was so elaborate as to appear almost ludicrous. The processes of sortition employed before any court was finally constituted were no fewer than nine. That part of the procedure by which the jurors for the day were selected from among those who offered themselves for service has already been detailed in an earlier chapter. It involved three sortitions—the selection by a draw of one person in each section to be responsible for drawing the tickets of those who in that section had submitted their names, the actual draw of the tickets to be placed in the allotment machines, and the acceptance or rejection of names by the operation of the machine itself. But this was only the start of the proceedings. Next it was necessary to allocate each of the jurors who had been picked for service to a particular court. First, lots were drawn to assign letters and identifying colours to each courtroom, and an appropriate plaque was placed over the several entrances. Then each juror drew a lettered ballot-ball from an urn, which indicated the court to which he was assigned. This he showed both to the presiding magistrate, who placed his ticket in a container bearing the same letter, and, as an additional check, to an attendant who handed him a staff bearing the colour appropriate to his courtroom letter, which he was thenceforward required to carry. When all this was done, there followed the allocation of magistrates to the particular courts over which they were to preside; and this involved two further processes of sortition—the simultaneous drawing of counters from two containers, which resulted in the matching of an indicated magistrate with an indicated courtroom, and, prior to this, the appointment by lot of two officials who were to be responsible for making this draw. Finally, when the composition of each court had been determined, the presiding magistrate drew at random the tickets of ten jurors, one from each of the juristic sections represented in the court, and then again drew from out of these ten a further five in order to decide which jurors should act as tellers and time-keepers.[202]

It is evident enough that none of these elaborate precautions could have availed to thwart a mass operation designed to suborn at least fifty per cent of the jurors who might find themselves assigned to any one particular court. But such tactics, involving heavy expense, could have been made possible only through the combined efforts of the political clubs, and they are unlikely to have been employed except on the rarest of occasions. Indeed, Aristotle's explanation of the various stages of the procedure which he outlines suggests that in the past bribery had been effectively directed at small groups or at a few key men. Thus, the person who was assigned the task of drawing the tickets of the applicants and slotting them into the machine was drawn by lot 'because, if the same man were repeatedly employed in this duty, he might tamper with the results'. The letter of the courtroom assigned to each juror was duly recorded 'to make sure that the juror took his seat in the court assigned to him, and to make it impossible for him to arrange to sit in the same court with certain others'. The magistrates were allotted to their courtrooms 'so that they would have no prior knowledge of the cases over which they would preside', and the tellers were appointed by sortition 'as a precaution against their being intimidated beforehand and as a guarantee that there would be no advance jobbery'. By such comments Aristotle leaves us in little doubt as to the methods which had at one time been used to predetermine a jury's verdict. What we cannot say is how long it was before the procedure detailed by Aristotle was perfected, or whether in fact it was as altogether foolproof as it was designed to be.

FRAUD

It is likely that the opportunities for deliberate fraud in connection with both the voting and the allotment procedures of the Greeks were numerous, and, although there is a minimum of concrete evidence on the subject, it would be naïve to suppose that they were not frequently exploited.

At direct elections the essential weakness of the Spartan system, apart from the very crude method of voting employed, lay in the fact that ways could so easily be devised of illegally conveying information to the closeted judges concerning the order in which the candidates were to present themselves to the Assembly. The weakness of the Athenian system lay simply in the inevitable imprecision of the count, when large numbers of people voted in the mass by the raising of hands. Exactly how the count was conducted and whether more than one official acted as a teller for each section of the Assembly is not known; but it is reasonable to suppose that the transfer of this responsibility from the councillors of the ruling prytany to a board of *proedroi* in the early fourth century reflects suspicions about the former's reliability. A group of individuals who were members of the same tribe and whose identity was known well in advance of the voting might well have conspired either freely or under persuasion to produce a false result. The *proedroi*, on the other hand, being representative of all the tribes, and being selected by lot only on the day of assembly itself, would obviously have been less likely to connive at a fraud, unless of course the process of sortition by which they were appointed was itself rigged.

When voting was by ballot, it was no doubt easier to take proper precautions both to protect against the possibility of double voting and to ensure the accuracy of the count. In the courts, for example, the voting tokens were carefully distributed and bore an official marking. Furthermore, the count was conducted by tellers appointed by lot, and some care was taken to check that the number of tokens deposited in the urns corresponded exactly with the number of jurors who had voted. But elsewhere, if not in the courts, there was clearly scope for abuse. The discovery of numbers of *ostraka* clearly written in the same hand suggests that at an ostracism interested parties handed out pre-prepared ballots to the citizens, and perhaps in particular to those of them who were illiterate.[203] And in one of the few detailed references to fraudulent voting in the tradition Demosthenes reveals that balloting at the deme level was very far from being well-ordered. Complaining bitterly of a recent ballot in his own deme, when the demesmen had been called upon to confirm the citizen standing of each of their fellows in turn, he claims that his enemies deliberately delayed the presentation of his own name until it was dark and until the majority of the demesmen had left the Assembly to return home. Only thirty people remained; but, when the votes were counted, no fewer than sixty were found to have been cast.[204] The key to this incident may well lie in a statement of Pollux that olive leaves, and not official tokens, were used as ballots in votes of this kind.[205] In this case there could have been no means of distinguishing valid and invalid votes, and a voter who wished to cast a double ballot could either have accepted two or more leaves from an accomplice, if indeed they were issued at all, or supplemented the one which he was given with one or more others which he already had on his person. It is, of course, difficult to believe that the Athenians would commonly have tolerated such laxity when binding decisions were to be taken; and it is perhaps noteworthy that the use of olive leaves is only attested for cases where the decisions taken were of a preliminary character and subject to revocation or confirmation on appeal in a properly ordered court of law. It is probable that the majority of such votes, whether in the demes or in the Council, were regarded as a matter of routine. The use of official tokens, and the imposition of careful checks over the voting and the count, would have been unduly time-consuming and might only have been considered necessary if fraudulent proceedings had been commonplace. As it was, such tactics as Demosthenes describes are likely to have been successful only on the rare occasions when a man was sufficiently well known to have many enemies and when as a consequence he was the victim of a large-scale conspiracy. It is possible that the Athenians were prepared to take the view that this in itself constituted a sufficient reason for requiring a citizen to undergo an official scrutiny in the courts.

Attempts to tamper with the operation of the lot in Athenian public life must have been common, and that they were initially successful appears to be suggested by the increasingly sophisticated methods which the Athenians felt themselves obliged to adopt. It is possible to conceive of several ways in which the lot in its more primitive form could have been fraudulently manipulated. An applicant, for example, might well have contrived to present himself twice to take part in the draw, or he might have been sufficiently accomplished in sleight of hand to escape notice while discarding one lot and substituting another which he had concealed on his own person. Such tactics would have presented less difficulty, of course, if there had been some measure of collusion on the part of the presiding official; had two or three persons in authority been brought into the conspiracy it would have been perfectly feasible for one or more of the lots to have been so marked as to be discernible to the touch of those in the know. Admittedly, the sources preserve no concrete examples of the use of methods such as these, but for proof that it was common there is no need to look further than those provisions in the jury selection procedure which were specifically designed to ensure that the person who made each particular draw was not himself an interested party.[206]

Most of these opportunities for manipulation were no doubt eliminated by the introduction of the allotment machine, and in particular by the tube mechanism, which both precluded all forms of prestidigitation in the allotment process itself and enabled the order in which the lots were drawn to be exposed to full public view. In order to rig the election of any individual in a sortition involving the use of an allotment machine it would have been necessary both for the official appointed to slot the tickets into the face of the machine to arrange for the ticket of the favoured candidate to be set in a predetermined slot, and for the magistrate who was in charge of pouring in the counters to arrange that a white counter entered the tube in a predetermined position. Neither feat can have been easy to achieve; and when it is considered that the two officials concerned in such a manœuvre would themselves have been chosen by lot it is hard to escape the conclusion that the difficulties to be overcome by any who sought to tamper with the more sophisticated allotment processes of the fourth century were formidable, if not insuperable.

There are only two passages in fourth-century literature which can conceivably be construed as suggesting some fraudulent interference with the allotment procedures of the day. One comes from Aeschines' preamble to his speech against Ctesiphon, where he refers in general terms to 'those who have secured the

presidency of the Council not by lawful allotment but by trickery'.
This might appear to suggest that the allotment process by which
councillors were in turn chosen to preside for a single day during
their year of service was in some way fraudulently rigged. But,
significantly, when Aeschines develops the theme later in his
speech with specific reference to Demosthenes, he makes it clear that
what he regards as having been procured by trickery was not the
presidency, but simply the seat on the Council, which of course
made appointment to the presidency at some time during the
year an odds-on chance.[207] The other passage appears in a speech
of Demosthenes, where reference is made without accompanying
detail to the practice of 'having the name of the same man
entered on two tickets'.[208] There is here a specific allusion to some
form of fraud; and perhaps the simplest explanation of the words
is that they apply to a process of sortition, and in particular to the
insertion of two tickets bearing the same name in different slots on
the face of an allotment machine. There is no means of knowing
whether this was a gambit which was commonly or successfully
employed, but at best it is likely to have been of strictly limited
value. It would obviously have had most advantage at an allotment, such as that for the selection of jurors, at which more than
one applicant was to be chosen and the chances of success were
reasonably high. But this was precisely the type of allotment at
which the use of such a manœuvre would have carried with it the
greatest risk; for it would have required only that both tickets
should be drawn for the fraud to be exposed. In the interests of
non-detection, therefore, the use of this tactic is likely to have
been restricted to those occasions on which only one candidate
was to be selected from a group. By arranging for the surreptitious
removal of a ticket bearing the name of another candidate and
the substitution of one bearing his own, a candidate could of
course have doubled his chances; but, except perhaps at deme
level, where the number of applicants for any one position may
have been very small, the manœuvre could have offered only
something very far short of guaranteed selection.

PART TWO

ROME

CHAPTER VI

VOTING ASSEMBLIES AT ROME

ROME DURING THE REPUBLICAN ERA was governed in practice by an oligarchy. Yet in her public life the part played by the voting masses was in some respects as vital as it was in democratic Athens. In one or other of their voting assemblies the Romans elected all of their annual magistrates—well over fifty of them in the Ciceronian age—appointed most of the supernumerary officials who were required from time to time, approved or rejected all legislation which the magistrates saw fit to initiate, and until well into the second century BC sat in judgment as a court of appeal on those charged with criminal offences.

There was one basic and essential difference between voting in the Greek city-states and voting at Rome. In Greece, as we have seen, it was the vote of the individual which mattered and which contributed to the final count. In Rome it was the vote of an artificial social unit. In the Assembly at Athens the vote of each individual counted for as much as that of his neighbour; and even in oligarchic Sparta the principle which underlay the vote by acclamation was that each man had a voice of equal strength and an equal will to use it when the vote was called. Greek society, of course, had its administrative units, and such units were at times used to facilitate the ordering and the counting of the vote; but as a general rule the fact that an individual was a member of one particular unit rather than another did not give him a greater or lesser influence on the outcome of the vote. At Rome the reverse was true. In all her assemblies it was the artificial subdivision of society, and not the individual, which served as the unit of vote in the final count. Certainly, the vote returned by each voting unit was determined by the individual votes of the majority within it, but for a number of reasons which we shall consider later the influence of any one voter often depended very considerably on the voting unit to which he was assigned.

The origin and effects of this principle of voting, frequently referred to as the principle of the 'group vote', will be discussed in the next chapter. But first it is necessary to look at the nature of the voting groups themselves, and also at the structure and competence of the voting bodies of which they were constituents. Whereas in most city-states of Greece there was but one popular Assembly, there were at Rome from quite early times no fewer than three—the *comitia curiata*, in which the unit of vote was the *curia*, the *comitia centuriata*, in which it was the century, and the *comitia tributa*, in which it was the local tribe. Furthermore, the last category embraced two distinct assemblies, the tribal assembly of the whole people (*comitia populi tributa*) and the tribal assembly of the *plebs*, from which patricians were technically excluded (*concilium plebis*).

COMITIA CURIATA

The Roman *curiae* belonged to the feudal structure of the early aristocratic state. They were thirty in number and, according to the tradition, were sub-divisions of the three clans or kinship tribes, the Ramnes, Luceres and Tities.[209] The origin of assemblies of the people by *curiae* was therefore clearly pre-Republican. Indeed, the Roman sources would have us believe that the people exercised voting rights by *curiae* in regal times.[210] This, however, is less credible. When the assembled people attended the *inauguratio* of their king, for example, which we are told they did, they might conceivably have given expression to their approval by shouts of acclamation, but it is highly improbable that they registered a formal vote. The king was almost certainly viewed as one whose selection was ratified by Jupiter, in which case any vote of the people would have been inappropriate.[211] The role played by curiate assemblies even in Republican times is obscure, and it has very possibly been afforded exaggerated emphasis. That they did meet and conduct a formal vote in which the individual *curiae* served as voting units is suggested by the fact that in the latter part of the Republican era the residual functions of the curiate assembly were performed by thirty lictors, who as a pure formality were summoned by a magistrate to register a vote;[212] but it is likely that the scope of the curiate assembly's powers was very limited. There is little evidence that this gathering was ever used for elections or routine legislation, and, in view of the close associations of the *curiae* with the old organization into clans, there is little to recommend the suggestion that the dissident plebeian body may have used a curiate formation for its deliberations.[213] The most well-attested function of the assembly was to carry a law in favour of newly elected consuls and praetors. Sometimes loosely called the *lex de imperio*, this law probably had no essential connection with the *imperium* (the power of command), which was surely conferred by the electing body, but merely served to confirm the right of the magistrates in question to take auspices in their official capacity and on behalf of the Roman people.[214] Other responsibilities included those of ratifying wills, of effecting adoptions, and of authorizing the transfer of patricians to the *plebs*.

It is not likely that the people continued to assemble in any numbers to vote in the *comitia curiata* for long. The voting function of these assemblies can rarely have had more than formal significance, and with the decline of close aristocratic control over the populace the substitution for the people of thirty lictors must have been an early development. Indeed, by 443 BC curiate assemblies appear already to have lost much of their importance; for when the office of censor was first created in that year the responsibility for conferring the right of auspices upon the new magistrates was given not to the *curiae*, as it had been for the consuls, but to the centuries.[215]

COMITIA CENTURIATA

Whereas the *curiae* were units of primitive Roman society, the centuries and the territorial tribes were creations of the late monarchy. According to the tradition it was the penultimate king, Servius Tullius, who in the mid-sixth century both assigned the population to tribes on the basis of domicile and effected a complete remodelling of the Roman military structure. The new army is described in detail by Livy. It was made up of 193 units of one hundred men known as *centuriae*. Eighteen of these were provided by the cavalry (*equites*), who represented the aristocratic *élite*, five more by non-combatant contingents, and the remaining 170 by the infantry. These last were divided in the census into five classes according to their property, and were further divided into an equal number of juniors—between the ages of 18 and 46—who were fit for active service and seniors—over the age of 46—who constituted a reserve to guard the city in an emergency. The full scheme handed down to us by Livy and Dionysius of Halicarnassus[216] may be tabulated as follows:

	Juniors	Seniors	
Cavalry			18
Non-combatants			5
Infantry	Juniors	Seniors	
Class I	40	40	80
Class II	10	10	20
Class III	10	10	20
Class IV	10	10	20
Class V	15	15	30
			193

Part of this scheme is undoubtedly of Servian origin. There are good grounds for believing that the legion of six thousand men was a feature of the later part of the regal age; and, since Livy's description of the armament carried by the various classes of infantry enables us to identify the legionary troops as those drawn from the first three property groups, the total given of sixty centuries of juniors from these three groups (40 + 10 + 10) wears the appearance of being authentic.[217] Nevertheless, it is clearly impossible that the population of regal Rome should have been able to sustain an armed force of over nineteen thousand men.

Many of the figures in this scheme must relate to a later date; and indeed many of its elements probably relate not to the structure of the Roman army at any stage, but to the structure of the political assembly of the Roman people which was modelled upon it.

Despite the contrary view of the later Roman writers, it is virtually certain that the adaptation of the centuries for political use was of post-regal origin. The vacuum left by the collapse of the monarchy must have been felt most keenly in the military sphere, and not surprisingly, therefore, those who assumed executive authority in the place of the kings were men experienced primarily in military command. Known later as *consules*, they were originally called *praetores* (leaders), and their association was with the centuriate army. It is here that must lie the explanation for the transformation of tactical units in the army into units of vote in a political assembly. At the outset the military personnel alone will have gathered in their centuries, if not to choose their commanders, at least to give formal sanction to their appointment. But, as and when these commanders assumed more of the civil functions of the kings, the restriction of the vote to those actually enrolled in the legions would have become inappropriate; and room would have had to be found within the existing centuriate system for three classes of citizen previously not represented— those who were ineligible for legionary service owing to their low property census, those who were over military age, and those who possessed the proper qualifications of age and property but were not at the moment enrolled. It is very possible, therefore, that the centuries of classes IV and V and the entire group of senior centuries were political creations of an age when centuriate voting was already in being.

It is not our concern in what is primarily a study of voting to consider the dates of such modifications in the original Servian structure, or to determine whether the final total of voting units and the distribution of centuries among the seniors and in the lower property classes was fixed by any one section of society with an eye to political advantage. It must suffice to illustrate the essentially timocratic structure of the assembly which finally emerged. There were 193 units of vote in all, of which no fewer than eighty were from the first property class and a further eighteen comprised the equestrian *élite*, the centuries of *equites equo publico* who constituted an aristocracy of birth. These two groups could therefore produce between them one more than a majority of the total possible number of votes cast. It should be noted, further, that these privileged centuries were considerably smaller than those of the lower property classes. Unlike the original military centuries of one hundred men, the political centuries were not of uniform size; and even in the early Republic the complement of a century of the fifth class must have been many times greater than that of a century of the first. In the later Republic, of course, following the vast increase in the citizen population, this variation became very much more pronounced; and indeed Cicero could report that in his day there were more people enrolled in the one supernumerary century of the *proletarii* than in all the centuries of the first property class put together.[218] A further bias in favour of the wealthier voters was created by the actual order in which the units voted; for, as we shall see in a later chapter, precedence in the order of voting, and more particularly in the order in which voting results were declared, conferred no small advantage under the rules of Roman voting procedure.

At some date between 241 and 220 BC the structure of the centuriate assembly was changed. Unfortunately, full details of the reform are not known, as it fell within the period not covered by Livy's extant narrative; but from a passage in the *De Republica*, in which Cicero is commonly supposed to be outlining the structure of the assembly in his own day, two essential features of the reformed body become clear—first, that the total number of voting units remained at 193, and, second, that the number of centuries included in the first class was reduced from 80 to 70.[219] Furthermore, from a chance allusion to the later system in Livy's account of the Servian institution,[220] as well as from numerous references from a later period to the units of vote in the centuriate assembly as 'tribes',[221] it becomes evident that in the upper classes at least the centuries were composed by reference to the tribal division of the population. This means in effect that, whereas before the third-century reform the members of a common property class and age group were assigned to centuries at random or at the discretion of the censor, they were thereafter assigned to them by reference to the tribe in which they were registered. All members of a single tribe who belonged to a particular property class were therefore enrolled in one of two centuries reserved respectively for seniors and juniors; and, as the number of tribes after 241 BC stood at thirty-five, the complement of any class was of necessity restricted to seventy. That this co-ordination of tribes and centuries extended throughout all the classes of the reformed centuriate system is questionable. Mommsen believed that it did; he reconciled his view that the total number of centuries in the five classes was thus 350 with Cicero's total of 170 (193 less 23 centuries of *equites* and non-combatants) by suggesting that the 280 centuries of classes II, III, IV and V were grouped by lot in twos and threes on each voting occasion so as to produce between them 100 units of vote.[222] This hypothesis, little heeded at the time, has since been thought to derive some support from the knowledge recently gained that a similar system of grouping permanent units by lot into a smaller number of units of vote was in fact employed in a special electoral assembly set up by Augustus in AD 5.[223] But it is still far from proven, and many prefer to believe that only the centuries of the first or the first two property classes were co-ordinated with the tribes in this way, and that the numbers of centuries allocated to the lower classes were adjusted in such a way as to leave the total complement of all five classes at 170 as before.[224] Wherever the truth may lie, there is no reason to suppose that the fundamentally timocratic bias of the assembly was disturbed, or that the reform was inspired by a democratic ideal. As we shall see (p. 198), there were those in governing circles who saw considerable advantages to be gained from the co-ordination of centuries with the tribes in at least the more influential upper property classes, and, if this change could only be effected by reducing the complement of the first class to seventy centuries, so making it impossible for any final decision to be reached without calling upon some of the votes of the second class, this was in their view but a small and insignificant price to pay.

The weighty influence enjoyed by the *equites* and by those enrolled in the upper property classes in the centuriate assembly is to be explained in the first instance in terms of the nature of the Servian army. Here the burden of cavalry and infantry service fell upon those in the upper property bracket. Thus, when for the reasons given an essentially military structure came to be adapted for political use, the strong voice given to the equestrian and legionary personnel was accepted as being the due reward for service and responsibility. Later, in more sophisticated times, the timocratic principle was openly embraced as a political ideal. Even after legionary service had been thrown open to the proletariat at the end of the second century BC it was ardently defended by Cicero. 'Servius', he wrote, 'so disposed the centuries in the classes that the votes were under the control of the rich and not of the masses. He accepted the principle, to which we must for ever adhere in the Republic, that the majority should not have the strongest voice. . . . No one was deprived of the right of suffrage, and yet he who had most to gain from the well-being of the state could use his vote to the greatest effect.'[225]

The principal and by far the most important function of the centuriate assembly was to appoint the major magistrates of the Republic—the consuls, who were Rome's chief executive officers, the praetors, of whom the first was created in 366 BC and whose numbers grew progressively to meet the increasing demands of jurisdictive service and provincial government, and the two censors, who were first created in 443 BC to shoulder some of the administrative responsibilities which had previously fallen to the consuls. In the earliest days, and very possibly at all times when elections were conducted by an *interrex*, the assembly merely gave or withheld its assent from nominated candidates equal in number to the vacant offices to be filled, but probably from the middle of the fifth century onwards it exercised an effective right of choice.[226] In theory, the assembly also held wide legislative and judicial powers. It was from the outset a vehicle for magisterial legislation, and it is clear from an extant extract of the Twelve Tables that it must have been recognized as early as 450 BC as the body competent to hear not only cases brought before it by plebeian tribunes but also capital cases submitted on appeal from the sentence of a magistrate.[227] In practice, these functions were very largely performed by other bodies, and this tendency increased with the advance of the Republic, the reason being that the voting procedure in the *comitia centuriata* was extremely cumbersome and time-consuming. The centuries continued to be employed, however, whenever tradition or political expediency demanded. Thus, since the centuriate assembly traditionally represented the people at arms, it was always called upon to vote a declaration of war; and when, for example, in 57 BC Pompey wished to marshal support for recalling Cicero from exile, it was this assembly, where Cicero's equestrian friends exercised the greatest influence, that he chose to use for his purpose.[228]

Despite a number of unsuccessful attempts to have the assembly reformed in a democratic sense by arranging for the centuries to vote in an order determined by lot rather than according to the strict rotation of classes,[229] its structure remained unscathed until after the death of Caesar. Only after the Civil Wars, in the dying days of popular suffrage, did the organization and the procedure become less rigid, and then no doubt only as a result of the apathy among voters which was induced by the new Augustan regime.[230] For as long as the popular election of consuls and praetors remained anything of a reality, however, Augustus found means to perpetuate their timocratic basis; for, as we now know from the Tabula Hebana which came to light as recently as 1947, he conferred what appears to have been almost a determining influence on their outcome upon a select body of senators and senior men of equestrian rank—in other words, upon a small-scale but representative replica of the centuries of the first property class and the *equites* in Republican times.[231]

COMITIA TRIBUTA

The youngest of Rome's assemblies were those in which the units of vote were the territorial tribes; of these there were two—the tribal assembly of the plebeian body (*concilium plebis*) and the tribal assembly of the whole people (never specifically entitled in the tradition, but commonly known as the *comitia populi tributa*). The first of these to emerge was almost certainly the former. In 494 BC, at the time of the first secession, the poorer elements at Rome had already begun to meet together unofficially, to deliberate on the policy to be adopted, and indeed to appoint representatives— *tribuni*—who might present their grievances and demands to the governing oligarchy. Suggestions that voting was conducted in an orderly manner at this early stage, and even that *curiae* or centuries were used as voting units, may be discounted. It is far more probable that decisions were taken by general acclamation. In 471 BC, however, an attempt was made to order proceedings. On a proposal presented by L. Publilius Volero it was resolved to establish a permanent assembly from which all patricians would be excluded, and in which voting would be conducted, as in the existing curiate and centuriate assemblies, by groups. The groups were to be the regional areas, or tribes, into which Servius Tullius had divided the *ager Romanus* and which now possibly numbered twenty-one, four in the urban area and seventeen in the rural area outside the city.[232]

The process of voting by tribes was, of course, very much more simple than that of voting by centuries, since the voters were not divided according to age or property census and the total number of voting units was only 21 as compared to 193. It is therefore unlikely to have been long before the example of tribal voting was followed in the official sector. There is indeed some evidence that the people as a whole began to gather and vote by tribes under the presidency of an official magistrate as early as the fifth century. Livy has isolated references to voting by tribes in 446, 383, and 357 BC, and it is not impossible that tribal assemblies had always been used to elect quaestors, first chosen by the people in 447 BC, as well as those officers who frequently replaced the consuls as chief magistrates between 445 and 367—the so-called consular tribunes. The adoption of some form of tribal voting for legislation of an uncontroversial nature and for minor elections may well have accompanied the granting of official recognition to the plebeian *concilium* and to its presiding officers in or about 449 BC.[233]

The existence of these tribal assemblies of the whole people is decisively established by the text of an extant consular law of

9 BC.[234] As has been mentioned, the name by which the Romans themselves knew them is never mentioned in the tradition, and the reason for this omission may well be that in the later Republican age the formal distinction between the two types of tribal assembly had little but historical significance. During the Struggle of the Orders in the fifth and fourth centuries, the *concilium plebis* and the tribal assembly of the people differed appreciably in terms both of composition and of authority. The patricians, at that time excluded from the *concilium plebis*, were an influential section of the population, and the resolutions of the *concilium plebis* ranked, for a time at least, as inferior to those of the tribal assembly of the whole people in that they required patrician sanction (*auctoritas patrum*) to attain the force of law. In 287, however, with the class struggle at an end, the *concilium plebis* was given authority to legislate without restriction on behalf of the whole people. Technically, patricians were still excluded; but, as the extension of the franchise reduced them to a tiny minority of the total citizen population, their presence or absence can have made little difference to the vote, and it is very questionable whether any formal attempt was made to exclude them. The conduct of an official check would have necessitated much administrative effort to little purpose, and indeed the non-existence of such a check is strongly suggested by the use of language in extant official documents which expresses genuine doubt on the part of the scribes as to whether the measures concerned qualified as *leges* (acts of the whole people) or as *plebiscita* (acts of a body from which patricians were excluded).[235]

The essential difference between the two tribal assemblies lay in the presidency. Whereas the *comitia tributa populi* could be summoned only by a curule magistrate, the *concilium plebis* could be summoned only by a plebeian official, normally a tribune. The functions of the two bodies, however, were very similar. Both conducted regular elections, the plebeian assembly those of the plebeian officers, the popular assembly those of all minor official magistrates. Both on occasions exercised judicial functions, although these activities declined with the growth of the standing courts in the second century BC. Both were also responsible for carrying legislation. Almost certainly the more active body was the *concilium plebis*. There was a simple reason for this: except during the early and closing years of the Republic, when the tribunes were at loggerheads with the governing class, the magistrates and the Senate found it convenient to delegate responsibility for conducting routine comitial activity to the tribunes, who by the nature of their office were confined to Rome and therefore had fewer rival commitments.

CHAPTER VII

THE PRINCIPLE OF THE GROUP VOTE

THE PRINCIPLE OF VOTING by groups, which was universally adopted in Roman assemblies, is one which has no known exact parallel. Voting by groups to appoint delegates to a representative body is of course common. It was employed by the Athenians in electing members of the Council of Five Hundred, and it is frequently employed today in the election of modern parliaments. Voting by groups is found in certain federal assemblies of the Hellenistic age, where the vote was taken by cities rather than by heads;[236] it is found also in the American presidential elections, where the President is nominated by an electoral college which is itself chosen by the various states of the Union. In all these cases, however, the group vote is the product of a sophisticated political system, and its avowed object is to secure fair representation for all those entitled to a voice. At Rome, on the other hand, the group vote was a primitive institution, and it is to be found employed from the outset in primary assemblies which in those early days were easily accessible to all who cared to attend.

In view of the abuses which attended group voting during the Republic, it is tempting to suppose that the principle was deliberately embraced by the governing class as one which lent itself to greater political manipulation and might well serve to delay the advance of popular sovereignty. This, however, is undoubtedly to mistake effects for causes. The tribal assembly, where most of Rome's voting took place, was not even the creation of the governing class; and it is unlikely that the group vote there conferred any appreciable advantage on political organizers until such time as a sizable section of the enfranchised public lived too far from Rome to permit of regular attendance. The centuriate assembly was, of course, an official creation, but here the development of the full centuriate organization, which guaranteed a preponderant influence to the wealthier classes under the group vote system, almost certainly post-dated the institution of voting. The explanation of the group vote in Rome's assemblies is therefore more probably to be found elsewhere—in the peculiar structure of early Roman society, and in the comparative suddenness with which voting at Rome developed after the fall of the monarchy and the institution of the Republic.[237]

Something was said in the previous chapter of the important role played by the *curiae* in regal society. Indeed, as particular *gentes* were assigned to particular *curiae*, it is very possible that the curiate division of the people was of earlier origin than the state itself, and belonged to the primitive gentile society which preceded its establishment in the eighth century. The presence of the *curiae* at such important happenings as the inauguration of a king may well have served not only to add dignity and solemnity to the occasion but also to signify the acquiescence of the *gentes* as a whole. When with the establishment of the Republic it was considered necessary to endow the new magistrates with the right of taking auspices—which the king by reason of his *inauguratio* had not required—it was very natural that the Romans should look to the *curiae* with their strong gentile and religious associations to perform this function. A vote was necessary, but by the very nature of things it was a vote of the *curiae*, and not of the individuals who composed them, which was required.

The centuriate assembly, of course, did not have the same feudal roots, and there is a good case for arguing that some form of centuriate vote was at least as old as the vote in the *comitia curiata*. But the process by which a full political assembly evolved out of an army was also peculiar to Rome. If, as has been suggested, the electoral activity of the centuriate body was a development from the show of allegiance at one time made by the soldiery to its commanders, it is very understandable that the votes should have come to be counted by centuries rather than by heads. The army would almost certainly have expressed its feelings by acclamation rather than by any formal vote, and the existing division of the army into tactical units known as centuries would have lent itself to a very much more orderly sounding of opinion than would otherwise have been possible.

Group voting in the two oldest forms of Roman assembly, curiate and centuriate, can reasonably be explained, therefore, in terms of the nature of early Roman society and the origins of voting itself. Tribal voting, of course, came later, when in 471 BC the plebeians decided to conduct their business in a more orderly fashion than they had done hitherto. But by this time voting by groups had presumably become accepted practice at Rome. It had obvious administrative advantages, and, if we may judge from the fact that the principle was voluntarily embraced by the plebeian body, it cannot at this time have been viewed as unduly undemocratic.

Whatever may be said of the original adoption of group voting at Rome, however, there can be little question that it was later consciously upheld for the reason that it could be adapted so much more easily than individual voting by heads to serve the interests of a class or group. Elsewhere where there was timocratic government, this was normally achieved by some form of restriction of the franchise. In Rome, thanks to the group vote, it was achieved without any violation of the principle of full adult male suffrage. It was sufficient to ensure that in the major electoral assembly the voting units containing the wealthier citizens had a smaller complement than the rest, that they were themselves more numerous, and—what was also of some importance—that they enjoyed precedence in the voting. Again, in other communities where voters were counted by heads, a candidate or would-be legislator required the support of over fifty per cent of the actual voters present to ensure success. At Rome, in theory at least, he could succeed with the backing of a fraction over twenty-five per cent. Thus anyone who was assured of a bare majority of voters in just 97 of the 193 centuries or 18 of the 35 tribes could win the day even if he captured not a single individual vote in the remaining centuries or tribes. In the later Republican age, when the canvass of votes became a highly organized affair, this was a factor which political managers were quick to appreciate.

From the third century BC onwards the unit of vote in all Rome's active assemblies was the tribe. The complete tribe was the voting unit in the *concilium plebis* and the *comitia populi tributa*, while in the *comitia centuriata* each individual century—at least in the first property class—was composed solely of members of the same tribe, albeit only those who fell within the same class and age group. Tribal membership depended upon place of domicile, and, although in several cases a single tribe contained pockets of citizens from widely separated geographical areas, most tribes came to be predominantly associated with particular regions of Italy.[238] This fact has led many modern scholars to lay stress upon the representative element which the tribal vote introduced into the Republican *comitia*. It is urged that the group vote system did much to ensure fair representation for those in outlying areas at a time when a great majority of Roman citizens lived at more than a normal day's travelling distance from the centre of comitial activity; for, as votes were counted by units rather than by heads, a mere handful of visitors from a distant corner of Italy who happened to be present when an assembly was held and who belonged to the same tribe would have been in as strong a position to influence the outcome of the vote as several thousands of city dwellers who were constantly at hand to record their vote in one of the urban tribes. This was undoubtedly the case for at least part of the time; but it would be a mistake to assume without question that the Romans recognized this representative element to be more than a contingent consequence of the operation of tribal voting, or that they ever cherished the group vote principle on this account. Their lack of concern is perhaps illustrated by the failure of the nobility to take any steps to cater for the constitutional consequences of the depopulation of the rural areas in the second century BC. Those who migrated to Rome at this time appear to have retained their membership of the particular rural tribe in which they had been registered while they were still farming the land. Consequently, as their numbers grew, they found themselves in a position to outvote any fellow-tribesmen who happened to be present from their home areas, with the result that the *comitia* gradually came to be dominated by urban interests. This trend could very readily have been checked if the censors had taken the simple step of reassigning the immigrant urban population to one of the four city tribes; but there is no suggestion that they ever attempted to do this, or that the idea was ever seriously mooted.[239] Indeed, it may well be that it was not until the last days of the Republic, when Caesar and subsequently Octavian chose to advance their cause by posing as champions of *tota Italia*, that the demand for fair representation of the outlying citizenry became a live political issue; and it was not until the *comitia* were already in their death throes that Augustus sought consciously to tackle the problem by experimenting with the idea of a postal vote.[240]

To say, however, that the principle of the tribal vote was not embraced for its representational advantages is not to deny that it was welcomed, and often used, as a means of securing a greater or lesser influence for specific groups or classes. At the outset, of course, the tribal division was of no political consequence, for the *ager Romanus* did not extend so far from Rome as to affect attendance at the assemblies, and there was no obvious distinction between the interests of those registered in one tribe and those registered in another. By the second half of the fourth century, however, this was no longer true. The extension of the franchise on a large scale and the successive creation of new tribes had put many citizens beyond convenient travelling distance from Rome, and a resurgence of commercial and manufacturing activity, spurred on by the establishment of contacts between Rome and Campania, had resulted in the emergence in the city of a group whose interests differed from those of the rural citizens, wedded to the traditional agrarian economy. In the year 312 BC the censor Appius Claudius proposed that the strict allocation of tribe by reference to place of domicile or location of property should be abandoned, and that the city population should be given the right to register in the tribe of their choice.[241] Although his motives have been variously interpreted, it is not unlikely that his chief purpose was deliberately to give more weight in the voting at tribal assemblies to the embryonic trading community, which under the existing system was denied all effective influence by reason of its being confined to but four of what was at that time a total of thirty-one tribes.[242] The plan was not a success, for only eight years later, in 304, the censors Fabius Rullianus and Decius Mus repealed the measure and took steps to restrict the city-dwellers once again to the four urban tribes.[243] Nothing, therefore, was effectively changed. But the political tussle of these years was not without significance for constitutional theory. Whereas the exclusion of the urban voters from a position of influence in the assemblies had previously been a mere accident of the tribal system, it appears now for the first time to have been consciously accepted as desirable. Firm control over tribal registration and a strict adherence to the principle of tribal group voting were to be its guarantees.

A similar attempt to achieve the same end by invoking the principle of the tribal group vote was almost certainly made by the reform of the centuriate system some sixty or seventy years later. As explained in the previous chapter, the essence of this reform lay in the fact that it related the composition of the centuries of at least the first property class to tribal membership by providing that all members of a single century should also be members of a single tribe. The object, therefore, was clearly to achieve for the centuriate assembly what had already been achieved for the tribal assembly in 304, namely the built-in predominance of the rural voters. Under the Servian system the centuries of the first property class, whose composition was determined by the censors without the necessity of any reference to tribal membership, could easily have come to be dominated by wealthy urban voters more readily able to turn out to vote. After the reform, however, these wealthy urban voters were confined to eight of the seventy centuries of the first class, there being two such centuries for each of the four urban tribes.

There is reason to believe that the intended diminution of the influence of the city-dwellers was originally linked to a particular stand on general policy. Whereas Appius Claudius may well have wished to prepare Rome for expansion into the world of Mediterranean commerce, his opponents in the late fourth century, and perhaps also the authors of the later centuriate reform, were concerned to preserve the essentially agrarian economy of Rome, and were consequently opposed to the extension of Roman interests to the south of the peninsula and, later, overseas. In their eyes, therefore, an increase in the voting strength of those who had urban employment was both unnecessary and undesirable. By the end of the third century, however, when Rome was already committed to becoming an imperial power, the great majority of the nobility came to accept the predominance of the rural voters as a basic principle of official policy. This they undoubtedly did for selfish reasons. For one thing, so long as the outcome of a vote was determined by the few who travelled to Rome from a distance, the control which the individual noble families and the Senate as a whole could exercise was more complete. For another, the Roman institution of *clientela* operated more effectively in the rural areas, where the population was more static and the influence of the large landowning families could make itself felt.[244]

Other examples of the deliberate use which the nobility made of the tribal group vote principle to serve its own purposes are to be found in the restrictions which it sought to impose upon the voting strength of the newly enfranchised Italians after the Social War in 89 BC and in the repeated attempts which were made to control the votes of freed slaves.

The *lex Julia*, which ended the Social War by accepting the principle of Italian enfranchisement, provided for the enrolment of the new citizens exclusively in a limited number of tribes, probably all of new creation.[245] The fear, perhaps more imaginary than real, was that the new citizens, who of course far outnumbered the old and who were still smarting from the treatment they had received before the war, would attend the assemblies in sufficient numbers to upset the calculations of the political manipulators and so interfere with the nobility's control over elections. In the event the plan did not succeed. The new tribes were never created, and within five years provision was made for the distribution of the Italians among the existing thirty-one rural tribes.[246]

The case of the freedman vote is more complex, for attempts

were made from time to time both to extend and to limit the voting strength of freedmen. There is little doubt, however, that the official policy was restrictive, and that it was represented by the action of the censors of 220, who confined this class to the four urban tribes,[247] and later by that of the censors of 169, who, after considering depriving freedmen of their vote altogether, finally decided to allow them registration in *one* of the four urban tribes to be determined by lot.[248] Cicero, who was a staunch supporter of the official oligarchic line in most things, speaks in laudatory terms of Gracchus, the censor of 169. 'By transferring the freedmen into the urban tribes', he remarks, 'the censor saved the Republican constitution from collapse.' That he could thus express himself suggests that Mommsen and his school were very much mistaken in representing the majority of freedmen as clients of the nobility who maintained a steady allegiance to the interests of their past masters. This may have been to some extent the case in the earlier Republic; but from at least the second century onwards those who were dependent upon members or friends of the ruling aristocracy can only have been a small proportion of the total number. A large number, when emancipated, must have taken up residence in the city, where according to their subsequent success they would either have acquired wealth and independence in the world of business or have submerged in the urban proletariat. In either case it was very much in the interests of the nobility as a whole that these men, who might otherwise have been enrolled in the rural tribe of the area where they had been employed before manumission, should be prevented from unduly influencing the outcome of the vote at Rome.

It is noteworthy that the more liberal attitude to freedmen displayed by certain censors in the early second century appears to have extended only to that small part of the freedmen class which had already become integrated with the landowning community. Livy writes of the censors of 179 BC that 'they changed the arrangements for voting and ordered citizens in tribes on a regional basis according to their social class, their conditions, and the source of their income', and it is probable that he here refers to the concession, withdrawn ten years later, whereby freedmen with sons over five years of age and with landed property which qualified them for inclusion in the second class of the census were allowed to register in the rural tribes.[249] As has sometimes been suggested, the censors of 179 may well have taken this step in an attempt to promote their own factional interest by swelling the numbers of their potential supporters in the electoral assembly; but, in so far as the influential freedmen concerned would be enrolled in one of the traditional *clientelae* of the nobility and the effect of their vote could therefore be readily calculated, the concession did not seriously violate the basic principles of official policy.

We have seen that although group voting was not introduced at Rome for any ulterior political motives it was later embraced and revered by the nobility for the help which it afforded in enabling them to organize the vote and so maintain control. When, therefore, in the last hundred years of the Republic an attack was mounted against the traditional oligarchic form of government, it was the group vote among other things which its opponents strove to undermine. In the centuriate assembly, of course, it was difficult to make any effective impact, since the wealthy voters, who were for the most part still representative of the interests of the tribes in which they were registered, had an inbuilt control. Unsuccessful attempts appear to have been made to abolish the order of precedence in voting which favoured the centuries of the upper classes, and in the disordered days of the first century BC there was some interference with the activity of the censors which may well have impeded the allocation of the citizens to their proper classes; but on the whole the effectiveness of control exercised over elections by the nobility cannot have been seriously diminished. In the tribal assemblies, however, the authority of the collective nobility was less secure. The more extreme efforts of its opponents, typified by the proposals of such men as P. Sulpicius and C. Manilius in 88 and 67 to effect the free registration of all freedmen in the rural tribes, were successfully resisted.[250] But, thanks to the active or passive cooperation of the many individual nobles who were prepared to sacrifice the traditions and interests of their own class to their own more immediate advantage, the retention of a prior registration in a rural tribe by those who took up residence in the city of Rome went unchecked. In legislative assemblies at least, therefore, where attendance from the rural areas was small, group voting ceased to be an instrument of senatorial control. The assemblies came to be dominated no longer by those who could regulate the attendance of the rural voter, but by those who, by direct appeal and the employment of demagogy, were in a position to build up the largest following from among the urban proletariat.[251]

CHAPTER VIII

PRELIMINARIES OF THE VOTE

PRIOR NOTICE AND DEBATE

THERE WAS AT ROME an established procedure to be followed before an assembly was called to register a vote. The first move was always the publication of an edict, either by the magistrate or by the tribune of the *plebs*, in which was set out the proposed subject for the vote. This was normally pronounced by word of mouth in the first instance at a gathering of the people (*contio*) specially called for the purpose and was subsequently published in written form on a whitened wooden tablet or more exceptionally, in the case of laws which were considered certain to be carried, on more durable material such as bronze.[252] The form of this edict, of course, varied according to the nature of the proposed vote. In the case of an election, it possibly listed some, if not all, of the candidates; in the case of judicial proceedings, it gave details of the identity of the accused, the nature of his crime, and the penalty prescribed; and in the case of legislation, it gave the full text of the proposed law, which, since the *lex Junia* of 56 BC at least, had to be deposited in the *aerarium* and could not legally be altered in any detail.[253]

Apart from indicating the subject of the vote the edict also named the day for the voting; and here the magistrate or tribune concerned was considerably restricted in his choice. He could not call a voting assembly on any of the *dies nefasti*, which were set aside for religious acts, on any of the *dies fasti*, which were reserved for the administration of justice, or on the *nundinae*, or eighth day of the Roman week, when the rural population commonly came to the city to conduct business.[254] This left only 195 *dies comitiales* on which the voting assemblies could legally meet. Furthermore, as two votes could not be conducted on the same day, it was often necessary for a junior magistrate to defer to a senior who had staked a prior claim. Finally, at least in the last century of the Republic, he was compelled by law to fix the vote at least twenty-three days after the promulgation of his edict. This mandatory interval between promulgation and vote, which was known as the *trinum nundinum*, was prescribed for legislation by the *lex Caecilia Didia* of 98 BC.[255] In Mommsen's view it had been required very much earlier, and there are indeed references in the historical sources to the *trinum nundinum* in connection with legislation and elections as far back as the fifth century.[256] On the other hand, the more reliable tradition for the middle Republican period does cite examples of magistrates holding elections in a hurry and on the advice of the Senate calling the assemblies for the 'first possible comitial day',[257] and it is perhaps to be noted that the only known cases of votes being disallowed on the grounds that the *trinum nundinum* rule had been broken fall within the first century.[258] The truth is probably that the interval had been established by custom both for legislation and for elections as early as the late third century, but that it was not embodied in law until this, along with so many other established customs, came to be flouted for personal advantage in the unsettled conditions of the post-Gracchan years. This view gains support from consideration of the probable purpose of the *trinum nundinum*. As soon as a large percentage of Roman citizens found themselves domiciled at an appreciable distance from the city, it will have become necessary in the interests of equity to provide them with sufficient warning of a vote to enable them to make arrangements to travel to Rome, if they so desired. What is perhaps more important in a society where the delivery of the vote depended to such a great extent on the activity of the noble factions, the three-week warning period will have ensured that the presiding magistrate and his confidants did not enjoy the exceptional advantages which exclusive foreknowledge of the date of the vote would have conferred upon them.

Although the voting would normally take place on the day named in the edict, it is unlikely that a fresh edict had invariably to be issued and a second *trinum nundinum* observed when for any reason a vote on the nominated day proved impracticable. We have examples of elections which were held a day or two late, and in one passage Cicero appears to suggest that there were some five days on which he could legally have conducted a vote.[259] There can be no certainty in this matter, but it would not have been unreasonable if the edict had guaranteed that the vote would take place either on the nominated day or on one of the four *dies comitiales* directly following it. In the event of a deferment those who had travelled to vote could then have been sure of an opportunity to cast their vote within a reasonably limited period.

Although the voting public may from at least the third century have been given three weeks' notice of the content of proposed legislation and of the intent to hold elections, it is very questionable whether they had for so long been guaranteed notice of a full list of the candidates from which they were to be called upon to choose. It should be remembered that in the early days of the Republic it had not been customary in official elections to allow the electorate any real freedom of choice whatever. Centuriate assemblies had simply been summoned either to accept or to reject the names put before them by the presiding magistrate, and it is extremely unlikely that he published the names of his intended nominees before the day on which the assembly gathered. Indeed, the nature of early procedure is almost certainly reflected in the elections of later days which were occasionally conducted by an *interrex* at times when no magistrates were in office or were available to conduct them themselves. In these cases, too, it is all but certain that no freedom of choice was allowed to the voters, and that each successive *interrex* presented the assembly with the names of two nominees for the consulship which he called upon the voters to accept or reject. The fact that each *interrex* held office for only five days and that each produced his own pair of nominees suggests that the assembly can have been given little, if any, prior notice of names in these circumstances. This, then, was the traditional procedure; and, when at an early date the presiding magistrate at normal elections accepted the principle of nominating more candidates than there were places to be filled and so providing the electorate with an opportunity to exercise a real choice, there would have been no immediate reason for departing from the original practice of notifying the voters of names at the electoral assembly.

The trend towards early publication of candidates' names must inevitably have begun when individuals started to take the initiative by professing to the magistrate their desire to stand and so seeking his nomination. Once this practice, known as *professio*, became established, the candidates clearly made it their business to advertise their aspirations to office and to conduct their own canvass. But even then there may have been no official list, or at least no complete one, published before the day of the elections. There were instances in 211 and 169 BC of a candidate securing election after announcing his candidature at the very last minute, and there were many more occasions when an individual appears to have been elected without his having declared himself a candidate at all.[260] It is tempting to interpret such elections in terms of what in the USA is called the 'write-in' vote, that is, the unprompted decision of the voters to cast their votes in favour of someone who is not an official candidate; but such an explanation is entirely inconsistent with the essential nature of the Roman election, in which the function of the voters was to give an answer to a question put by the presiding magistrate. It is further ruled out by our knowledge that in collecting the returns from the various voting units the presiding magistrate enquired in turn about the number of votes cast in favour of specific candidates, and can therefore have taken no cognizance of votes cast in favour of individuals whom he did not recognize.[261] It follows that, if elections sometimes resulted in the success of men who had not professed their candidature, this can only have been because the presiding magistrate had exercised his traditional right to nominate the individual concerned immediately prior to the vote.[262]

During the last century of the Republic hard and fast rules were laid down regulating the profession of candidature, very possibly for the first time. It is clear that *professio* had to be made before a certain set date, and that, probably from 62 BC, it had to be made within the city and in person. Thus, when Caesar approached Rome in 60 BC after his praetorship in Spain, he was forced to forgo his hopes of celebrating a triumph and to enter the city to present his candidature by a certain date, if he was to realize his object of attaining the consulship for 59;[263] and ten years later the chief bone of contention between Caesar and the Senate concerned the requirement that Caesar should appear at Rome in person to stand for a second term of office. It would appear to have been feasible to secure exemption from this rule through special legislation or senatorial decree until 52, but by Pompey's law of that year even this loophole was effectively stopped.[264] The period of time which was required to elapse between the profession of candidature and the day of the elections is commonly believed to have been the *trinum nundinum*. In fact, however, it is likely to have been somewhat shorter. As we have seen, the *trinum nundinum* was essentially related to the edict which in the first century gave due notice of the intention to hold a vote. If, as our sources suggest, there was a set period— *legitimum tempus*—during which intending candidates were required officially to profess their candidature,[265] this will almost certainly have followed the publication of the edict and so have made an incursion into the *trinum nundinum* itself. Despite the contrary views of Mommsen, the events of 60 BC are most satisfactorily explained on the assumption that Caesar arrived in Rome when the edict for the consular elections had just been published. That he could be frustrated in his effort to secure exemption from the requirement to profess his candidature in person by Cato's single filibuster in the Senate indicates that the time allowed for *professio* was comparatively short, possibly no more than three or four days.

The passing of firm legislation relating to the *trinum nundinum* and electoral candidacy must inevitably have detracted in some measure from the autonomy of the magistrates, which in the earlier Republic had been absolute. It is a fair assumption, for example, that with the advent of compulsory *professio* the magistrate lost his time-honoured right to nominate anyone of his choosing. Although the legislation may not have been directed against magisterial authority in the first instance, it would have lost all effectiveness if those who were not willing to conform had been able to achieve their purpose none the less through the agency of a single friendly consul. There are indications also that *professio* became a sufficient, as well as a necessary, condition of nomination, except in cases where the intending candidate was clearly disqualified under the law. This, however, did not constitute such a serious diminution of the presiding magistrate's authority; for, although he may no longer have been competent to refuse to nominate, he could still, and on occasions perhaps did, refuse to take any note of the votes cast in favour of a particular candidate when announcing the result of the election.[266]

The extent of the preliminary debate which took place during the *trinum nundinum* varied considerably according to whether the projected vote was elective or legislative. Where elections were involved, the official view was that persuasion in the form of oratory should for the most part be excluded, and that the 'party' machinery for delivering the vote should be allowed to operate unimpeded. Unofficial meetings of the people (known as *contiones*) specifically summoned to discuss the merits or demerits of a candidate were unknown, and, although the presiding magistrate may sometimes have advocated the choice of a particular candidate at the *contio* held on the day of the elections itself, even this may have been the exception rather than the rule. Furthermore, from the mid-second century onwards there was a rule that no new bill should be promulgated during the *trinum nundinum* immediately prior to an election. The principal object of this regulation was possibly to prevent a legislative vote being taken when the population of Rome was unduly swollen on account of the elections, but the Romans may also have been concerned to ensure that candidates would not have an opportunity to win votes through the advertisement of their policies in informal discussions on projected legislation.[267]

During the period between the promulgation of a bill and the vote upon it discussion was by comparison very much more free, although it was of course discussion in which the masses of the *populus* were themselves not allowed to participate. The author of the measure himself normally played the most prominent part in this debate. He summoned a series of meetings both to explain the content of his bill, which, as we know from extant texts, could be far from simple, and to allow for the expression of views both by himself and his supporters and on occasions by notable adversaries. Only those invited were permitted to speak, but by custom these frequently included private citizens of note as well as colleagues, other magistrates, and tribunes.[268] Their chairmanship of such gatherings provided magistrates with the right not only to select speakers but also to cross-examine them; and it was therefore not uncommon in the case of controversial legislation for tribunes and other magistrates not directly concerned with the bill's authorship to convene *contiones* of their own. Such was the *contio* called by the consul, Cicero, in early 63 BC, which presented him with the opportunity to deliver his well-known speech *De Lege Agraria* against the proposed Rullan bill. Discussion of this kind clearly served a useful purpose, although it was possibly more effective in securing or preventing the interposition of a tribunician veto than in swinging many votes; on occasions it resulted in the withdrawal of the proposed measure and even in its reintroduction at a later date in an amended form.[269]

THE SUMMONING OF THE VOTERS AND THE PLACE OF ASSEMBLY

When the day which had been fixed by edict for the vote arrived, the presiding magistrate customarily proceeded to the place of assembly between midnight and sunrise. There he set up his tribunal and began to watch the heavens for a sign that Jupiter looked with favour on the conduct of comitial business.[270] This ritual, known as the taking of auspices, was, except perhaps in the earliest days, largely a formality; it is probably fair to say that in the latter part of the Republic, when religion was very much a pawn in the hands of the politicians, the desired sign only failed to appear when postponement of the assembly was deemed politically expedient. There followed the summoning of the voters, normally at first light, the early hour being dictated by the need to contain what were often very protracted proceedings between the hours of sunrise and sunset.[271] In the case of the centuriate assemblies, in particular, where there were as many as 193 separate units of vote, a very early start must have been essential if proceedings were to be completed in a single day.

Both the nature of the summons and the place of assembly differed with the form of *comitia* which was to be employed. The curiate assembly had necessarily to meet within the city boundary (the *pomerium*), and it commonly assembled in the Comitium, an enclosed area close to the steps of the Senate House. In its case the summons was given by a herald, or occasionally a lictor, who used a *tuba* or *lituus* and made his announcement first at the place of assembly, and then at various points round the walls of the city.[272] By contrast, the centuriate assembly historically represented the people of Rome in arms—the *exercitus urbanus*—and it was consequently illegal for the voters to assemble inside the city, where no command could be given to the soldiery. The normal meeting-place, therefore, was the army's one-time training ground, the Campus Martius, which lay outside the city walls.[273] Because of the antiquity of the centuriate system and its traditional military associations, the process of summoning such an assembly was a complicated ritual. An announcement was first made from the *rostra* in the Forum. Then a red flag was hoisted on the Janiculum, indicating that the citadel was garrisoned against surprise attack while the 'army' was without. Finally the military signal for departure was sounded by trumpet both on the Capitol and around the city walls.[274]

Procedure prior to the holding of a tribal vote was less standardized. In the case of the *comitia populi tributa* it is reasonable to suppose that use was made of a herald to summon the voters, as with the *comitia curiata*. Plebeian officers, however, were bound by no law or tradition, and as they dispensed with the taking of auspices so too they probably dispensed with any formality in the calling of the tribes. With the tribal assemblies there were also fewer, if any, restrictions on the place of meeting. One of the earliest tribal votes, we are told, was taken at Sutrium and was accepted as valid;[275] and, although this was a very exceptional case, the fact that tribal assemblies were never confined to within the *pomerium* is proved by the established custom of holding all electoral assemblies, at least in the last century of the Republic, on the Campus Martius.[276] How early this practice developed is not easy to determine and is a matter of some dispute. Mommsen views with suspicion even Plutarch's testimony that an election was conducted on the Campus Martius in 124 BC and prefers to date the move to the Campus to as late as the Ciceronian age, when, as he points out, the more frequent use of the Campus is attested by the plans that were then afoot to build permanent voting enclosures (*saepta*) on the spot.[277] Fraccaro, on the other hand, prefers to associate the beginnings of tribal voting in the Campus with the institution of a voting procedure whereby voting units cast their votes simultaneously rather than in succession—a procedure which, while being speedier, must have made considerably more demands on space. This in turn he dates to the middle of the second century, although, as we shall see (p. 171), there is a strong possibility that it should be dated not a little earlier.[278]

For legislative and judicial voting the tribes appear to have assembled in a variety of places. The Flaminian meadows were occasionally the site of the plebeian gatherings of the fifth century;[279] and it is not improbable that the first official tribal assemblies summoned by magistrates were commonly held in the Comitium, the traditional meeting place of the *comitia curiata*.[280] In the later Republic, however, at least two other sites feature prominently in the sources—the open space on the Capitoline hill[281] and the Forum.[282] Lily Ross Taylor has recently pointed out that all recorded assemblies on the Capitol were plebeian and belong to the period before 121 BC, and she has very reasonably suggested that the tribunes may have chosen this particular meeting place as a matter of policy, either because, having no auspices, they wished to claim the protection of Capitoline Jupiter from whom the auspices came, or because they sought to separate themselves from the vicinity of the Senate House. This custom may well have grown up at a time when the magistrates proper were commonly using the Comitium. In the last century of the Republic, however, there is little doubt that the Forum was

universally used by tribunes and magistrates alike. The evidence
from the Ciceronian age is extensive; and it is noteworthy that
the historian Livy, in what may well be an anachronistic allusion
to fourth-century conditions, reflects the situation in his own times
by using the words *forum et campus* to designate the entire field
of tribal comitial activity, legislative and electoral.[283]

The move to the Forum is dated fairly accurately by Varro
and Cicero to the third quarter of the second century, for both
ascribe it to the action of C. Licinius Crassus, who was a tribune
in 145 BC. 'He was the first man', says Varro specifically, 'to bring
the people out from the Comitium to the Forum to vote on
legislation.'[284] It is thus tempting to associate the move with the
need for more space which must have accompanied both the
swelling of the population in these years and the change-over
from the oral to the written vote (pp. 158f). Tribunician assemblies
on the Capitol continued for a short while after this, but, as Livy
repeatedly remarks, the congestion in this confined area was
particularly acute.[285] The advantages of using the Forum, where
the intending voters could be conveniently addressed from the
rostra and where there was considerably more freedom of movement, cannot have been ignored for long. By the first century its
use was probably regarded as essential, if only because the various
items of equipment required for the conduct of an orderly written
vote could not readily be duplicated or transported from place
to place. Furthermore, although no permanent voting enclosures
were ever constructed in the Forum as they were in the Campus
Martius, there is evidence that in Cicero's time the ropes used for
dividing off the members of the various tribes one from another
had been displaced by light wooden barriers.[286] These presumably
were easily dismantled and erected, and must have been kept at
hand for use whenever they should be required.

THE PREPARATIONS FOR THE VOTE

The casting of the vote in Roman *comitia* was necessarily preceded
both by the formal putting of the question to the voters and by the
reading aloud of either the full text of the proposed bill or, in the
case of an electoral assembly, the complete list of nominated

candidates for office. The first function was performed by the presiding magistrate himself, who used a set form of words which reflected the tradition—no longer observed at elections—that the voting public was simply required to answer 'yes' or 'no' to a straight question.[287] The second was performed by a herald, who was prompted by one of the magistrate's scribes standing at his side.[288] In the case of tribal legislative and judicial assemblies there was frequently also a limited amount of debate, though not, it seems, at elections or in centuriate assemblies, where the process of voting was considerably more time-consuming. Exactly when the putting of the question took place is not very clear, although our knowledge that a tribunician veto could be interposed at any time during the course of the herald's *recitatio* and 'during the period in which private persons were having their say' might well be taken to suggest that the question itself was put at the very start of the proceedings.[289]

All this happened in what was still technically regarded as a *contio*, an unsorted gathering of the people which could legally be attended by all and sundry, whether or not they were entitled to participate in the actual vote.[290] The transformation of *contio* into voting assembly was signalled by the issue of an instruction from the presiding magistrate which must have resulted in the withdrawal of those not entitled to vote and a considerable reshuffling of those that remained. In the Campus Martius the formula appears appropriately to have been a simple *ite in suffragium*—'proceed to the vote'. Here, where the voting of the units was conducted simultaneously, there were permanent voting enclosures and ample space for the *contio* outside.[291] It was therefore a simple matter for those who were due to vote immediately—the entire company in tribal assemblies, the first-class centuries in centuriate—to proceed direct to the appropriate enclosure and for the remainder to wait their turn outside, no doubt still in an unsorted state. In the Forum and at other sites the instruction given was commonly *discedite* (literally 'depart'), and it is less clear what was actually involved. The scholiast Asconius explains that the word *discedere* does not here bear its normal meaning but signifies the sorting out of the people into the respective tribal units in which they were entitled to record their vote.[292] In a relatively confined space this cannot have been a very orderly proceeding. In the Forum, it is true, it is just possible that an area could have been marked out by ropes, or in later days wooden barriers, in preparation for the separation of the gathering into voting groups, while the *contio* was still in progress. This is to suppose that the *contio* could have been held in a different part of the arena from that later occupied by the waiting voters. On the Capitol, however, or even in the Comitium, where conditions were much more cramped, this would have been out of the question. Here there can only have been a temporary withdrawal while the area was hastily roped off and the voters sorted themselves out; this is indeed confirmed by Livy, who, in describing an assembly on the Capitol, refers to the empty space in the centre of the arena which was vacated as the process of sorting got under way.[293]

Before the commencement of the voting process itself there was one last thing to be done. Lots had to be drawn between the tribes for two different purposes. The first of these was to select the tribe in which should vote those Latins who happened to be present at Rome at the time of the vote.[294] The Latins (before their enfranchisement in 90 BC) were non-citizens who, among their other special privileges, enjoyed the right of casting their vote in one single voting group at tribal legislative assemblies and very possibly at tribal electoral assemblies also. This was, of course, of no practical value to the Latins, for the influence of the few voters present, confined as they were to but one of the thirty-five voting units, will have been negligible. It was, however, a matter of some concern to the particular tribe to which these Latins were assigned; for it was at least conceivable that the voice of the citizen tribesmen, if attendance was poor, would be nullified by that of the Latins temporarily added to their ranks. To assign the Latins permanently to any one tribe would therefore have been unfair to the tribe in question; and resort to the lot on each occasion that a voting assembly was called was an obvious and reasonable alternative.

The second purpose of the lot was to select the voting unit

which should be called upon to vote first. In the centuriate assemblies after the reform of the third century BC this unit was probably invariably drawn from one of the thirty-five centuries of juniors which belonged to the first property class. In view of the fact that centuries were co-ordinated with tribes in this class, it was therefore identifiable by the name of a tribe.[295] This *centuria praerogativa* not only voted before the rest of the assembly; it also had the result of its vote announced before the remainder of the centuries were called. It was therefore in a position to set a pattern for the voting and to exercise not a little influence on the uncommitted members of later centuries. Cicero indeed speaks of it as the 'omen of the elections' and makes the somewhat extravagant claim that the consular candidate who was put in first place by the prerogative century invariably secured election.[296] The reason for the institution of the practice of conferring a prerogative vote upon one unit remains a matter for conjecture; but as it dated from the latter part of the third century, when the number of candidates at elections was probably on the increase and the verdict of an ever-growing electorate was becoming less predictable, there is much to be said for the view that it was designed to ensure a speedy and decisive result to electoral contests by discouraging too great a spread of votes among the several candidates. That the Romans should have decided upon sortition as a method of selecting the prerogative century is more easily explained. For one thing, the election campaign would have been reduced to a mockery if the identity of such an influential voting unit had been predetermined in any way. For another, the influence which it did exert was likely to be more effective if its selection could be represented to the more superstitious among the voters as a manifestation of divine will.

In the tribal assemblies—except, of course, in the electoral assemblies of the later Republic, when the voting of all the units was simultaneous and no sortition therefore took place—the tribe singled out by the lot was known not as the *praerogativa*, but as the *principium*.[297] And, as the name given to the selected voting unit was different, so also was the purpose of the selection. With the votes taking the form of a simple 'yes' or 'no', there was certainly not the same case as at elections for establishing an early voting pattern. As we shall see later, it is far from certain that the result of the vote of the *principium* was announced before the other tribes were called; and what evidence we have in the sources on the course of tribal voting suggests that any prediction of the final outcome was normally based on the results from the first few tribes rather than on that from the first tribe alone. The object of selecting the *principium* by lot was therefore probably simply to ensure that there was a constant variation in the order in which the tribes were called to the vote. The alternative would have been to adhere on each occasion to the established order of precedence among the tribes, known as the *ordo tribuum*, but this would have had the marked disadvantage of virtually disfranchising the tribes at the bottom of the list, who would rarely have been called to vote until a majority had already been reached and the issue decided. It is conceivable that the lot was used to determine the entire order on each occasion; but since there is no mention of this in the sources it is more probable that the selected *principium* simply indicated the point in the *ordo tribuum* at which the presiding magistrate should begin to call the tribes, and that the remaining tribes then voted in sequence, beginning with that immediately below the *principium* in the list and ending (if the voting went that far) with that immediately above it.[298]

This entire process of sortition appears to have taken place at a slightly different stage of the preliminary proceedings according to where the voting assembly was held. On the Campus, both in tribal and centuriate assemblies, the dismissal of the *contio* was tantamount to the actual summons to the vote, for the voters proceeded immediately to the voting enclosures. It follows that the lots to determine the tribe of the Latin vote, and, in the case of the centuriate assembly, the prerogative century, must have been drawn before the end of the *contio*. Elsewhere, on the other hand, where there was but one voting enclosure, and where the dismissal merely resulted in the sorting out of the voters into groups preparatory to their being summoned to the vote, the lots would have been drawn as the redistribution of the voters into their several tribes was taking place.

CHAPTER IX

THE CASTING OF THE VOTE

METHODS OF VOTING

THE METHOD USED TO record the vote in Roman Republican assemblies changed on at least two occasions. In the first and most primitive stage voting was undoubtedly by acclamation. Apart from the fact that the Latin word for 'vote' was *suffragium*, which was almost certainly derived from the same root as *fragor*, meaning 'a breaking', and hence 'a breaking into sound', 'a loud noise',[299] the very development of the Roman practice of counting votes by groups suggests, as we have seen, that the concept of the individual vote was not original. When the Romans gathered in their *curiae* to witness the inauguration of their king, they no doubt greeted the appointment with shouts of approval,[300] and it is likely that a similar method was used both by the units of the early centuriate army to signify their acceptance of their commander and by the plebeian masses of the early fifth century to voice their approval of particular courses of action which their leaders suggested.

The inadequacies of this system are likely first to have been keenly felt with the development of the electoral vote into a free choice between rival candidates, though, of course, the example of Sparta proves that it may not even then have been altogether unworkable. The exact date of its abandonment is impossible to determine, but the first half of the fifth century is strongly indicated. It is difficult to imagine that the plebeians could effectively have excluded patricians from their voting processes, as they did in 471, if voting was still conducted by acclamation; and it is therefore likely that the introduction of an individual vote accompanied the establishment of an ordered plebeian

Fig. VI *Three coins depicting different forms of voting receptacle. The vessels shown left are vases* (urnae). *The vessel on the coin above—which also illustrates a legislative ballot marked with a 'U'* (*for* U[ti Rogas])*—is a wicker basket* (cista).

assembly. The example so set will almost certainly have been quickly followed by the magistrates in the official centuriate and tribal assemblies of the whole people.

The second stage in Roman voting procedure, then, was that of the oral vote, and this lasted until the third quarter of the second century BC. The basic process was simple. The individual members of each voting unit filed past an official known as the *rogator* (questioner), who was appointed by the presiding magistrate. As they did so, they announced their answer to the question put, or, in the case of an election, named the candidates of their choice. The *rogator* in turn recorded the votes by making a mark (*punctum*) with a sharp instrument on a large waxed tablet against the appropriate verdict or name.[301]

The obvious opportunities which this oral vote provided for electoral abuse led in the second century to its replacement by a form of written ballot. The three main ballot laws were the *lex Gabinia* of 139, which introduced the ballot for elections, the *lex Cassia* of 137, which introduced it for most judicial decisions, and the *lex Papiria* of 130, which introduced it for legislative votes.[202] With the aid of scattered literary references and of the portrayal of some features of the voting act on extant coins of the late Republican period it has fortunately been possible to construct some sort of picture, albeit a far from complete one, of the voting process in the days of the written ballot.[303] The Roman ballot-box was a large urn (*cista*) which was variously made of wicker or stone (Fig. VI). Numismatic evidence suggests that this rested on a stand so that its opening was at a level with the average voter's shoulder, and that it was positioned on a raised platform— possibly on a level with the magistrate's tribunal, possibly some-what lower—which in turn was approached from the floor of the voting enclosure by a sloping wooden ramp. This ramp, known at Rome as the *pons*, was a well-established feature of voting assemblies and goes back to the days of the oral vote.[304] It is pictured on coins as little more than a narrow plank which in width would not hold more than a single person; but, as Marius carried a law in 119 designed to make these *pontes* narrower,[305] there is reason to believe that they may at one time have been considerably wider and may have accommodated canvassers who stationed themselves there with a view to overlooking the vote and, possibly, intimidating the voters.

In the Campus Martius, where units voted simultaneously, and where, as we have noted, there stood, at least in the late Republic, permanent separate voting enclosures, the number of voting urns and of *pontes* leading to them may be supposed to have equalled the number of units customarily called upon to vote at any one time—certainly thirty-five, and possibly seventy. The tribunal must have been of considerable length, and it is not impossible that each *pons* led to an independent stairway at the rear by which the voters filed out after recording their votes.[306] In accounts of other assemblies reference is sometimes made to *pontes* in the plural; and it is therefore reasonable to assume that, even where units voted one at a time, there were at least two *pontes* leading from the one enclosure, and that the voters filed in two parallel lines past two voting urns, positioned perhaps one on either side of the magistrate's tribunal. Here too the voters will have descended by stairs, although these may often have formed part of the permanent construction—the *rostra* or the steps of a temple—on which the tribunal was temporarily established.[307]

The ballots used at Rome were small wooden tablets covered with wax, which varied in size according to the needs of the occasion.[308] At electoral assemblies these were provided blank, and the voters entered upon them the names, or at least the initials, of the candidates of their choice.[309] In judicial assemblies it is clear from the coins that voters were provided with a single tablet on which were inscribed two letters, normally on the same side—L for *libero* (I acquit) and D for *damno* (I condemn) (Fig. VII).[310] They had then simply to cross out the letter which did not represent their verdict. The procedure at legislative votes is slightly less certain. In one of his letters Cicero speaks of an occasion when the militant tribune, P. Clodius, deliberately refrained from distributing tablets marked with the letter U, which signified an affirmative vote;[311] and this has been taken by some to indicate that at legislative assemblies voters were commonly provided with two voting tablets, one inscribed with the letter U (for *uti rogas* or 'yes'), the other with A (for *antiquo* or 'no'), and that they then placed one in the voting urn and discarded the other. It is very difficult to understand, however, why the procedure in legislative assemblies should have differed from that in others. Furthermore, there is no mention or portrayal anywhere of a second container for discards, which would have been necessary if voters were not to be left with the second tablet on their person at considerable risk to the secrecy of the ballot. It is tempting, therefore, to suppose that here too only one tablet was issued, and that the extent of Clodius' gerrymandering lay in his having distributed tablets on which the letter U had not been marked.[312]

THE DISTRIBUTION OF BALLOTS AND THE IDENTITY CHECK

Two matters which have received comparatively little attention in past discussions of Roman voting procedure are the timing of the distribution of ballots, and the nature of the check, if any, which

was made on the voters' credentials. Both are essential features
in any normal voting process; and, although we have no direct
information on these points, it is worth considering the possibilities.

It is a common assumption that the Roman voter received his
ballot either as he was actually mounting the *pons* leading to the
voting urn or as he was just about to mount it. One basis for this
assumption is the prescription in an Augustan electoral law that
the ballots should be set out at the beginning of proceedings
'alongside the voting urns',[313] although the original positioning
of the ballots surely has little direct bearing on the time, place, or
method of their subsequent distribution. Another is the voting
scene depicted on a coin of the late second-century moneyer,
P. Licinius Nerva. This coin portrays three persons. One is
depositing his ballot in the voting urn, while a second is standing
some way behind him on the *pons* and extending his hand to a
third, who is positioned below the level of the *pons* and alongside
it (Fig. VIII).[314] The traditional interpretation of the scene is that
the second person on the *pons* is a *custos*—one of the officials
who replaced the *rogatores* after the introduction of the written
vote—and that he is handing an unused ballot to the next voter
on the floor of the enclosure. This, however, has three major
flaws. Firstly, voters did not approach the foot of the *pons* from
the rear, that is, by passing alongside it; secondly, if one man was
already voting before the next had set foot on the *pons*, the time

Fig. VII *Left, a voting tablet with ring attached
(see also Fig. VI for the obverse of this coin) and
right, a coin commemorating the* lex Coelia *of
107 BC and showing a ballot such as was used
in judicial assemblies (see also Fig. VI for the
obverse of this coin).*

taken by the whole voting process must have been excessively long; and thirdly, if the coin was minted after Marius' law which narrowed the *pontes*—and there is some suggestion that it was actually intended to commemorate it[315]—there would hardly have been enough room on the *pons* for the *custos*. The alternative is to identify the second man on the *pons* as the next voter and the man stationed below as the *custos*. This removes all the difficulties we have mentioned and is clearly the more attractive interpretation. But, if we go along with the further suggestion that the second voter is depicted receiving his unused ballot from the *custos*—which is far from certain—we must surely accept that the coin portrays a scene peculiar to the legislative and judicial vote; for, whereas it would have been feasible for a voter to erase a single letter on his ballot in the short time which elapsed between his receiving it on the *pons* and depositing it in the urn, it would have been completely impossible for him in the same short space of time to have inscribed upon it the names or initials of all the candidates in an election for whom he wished to vote. In certain multiple elections, as for the tribunate or quaestorship, each voter had as many as ten or twenty votes at his disposal, and the recording of these votes must have been a lengthy business.

At electoral assemblies, therefore, it is all but certain that the voters received their ballots well before they approached the voting urn. The likelihood is that they were distributed by *custodes* or tribal officials either as they stood in the enclosure awaiting their turn to vote or possibly as they actually filed into the enclosure. The voters would therefore have been in a position to mark their ballots as they stood on the floor of the enclosure, from where, incidentally, they could see the very large tablet listing the names of all the candidates which was set up for their convenience in front of the tribunal.[316] As we have noted, this may not have been the procedure adopted at legislative and judicial votes, but, if the coin in question can possibly stand another interpretation, there is little reason to suppose that the practice adopted in the various forms of assembly was so essentially different.

The second problem concerns the nature of the check, if any, which was conducted on the voters' credentials. It is a curious fact

Fig. VIII *Voting scene depicted on a coin of P. Licinius Nerva.*

that our sources nowhere provide any clear reference to the existence of such a check in any of Rome's assemblies, electoral or legislative; yet it is difficult to see how it could have been dispensed with. At most times during the Republic there were strong political motives for controlling the exercise of the franchise. In the first two centuries it was of considerable concern to the plebeian body that patricians should be excluded from the votes of the *concilium plebis*; from the middle Republic onwards there were repeated efforts on the part of the nobility to restrict by law the voting rights of freedmen; and in the second and early first centuries BC, when the issue of Italian enfranchisement was a live one, the Romans must have had some means of preventing the usurpation of voting rights by unauthorized immigrants. Furthermore, it is impossible that the Romans, who were so jealous of their group voting machinery and of the timocratic class structure of the centuriate assembly, should not have taken some precautions to ensure that a citizen did not cast his vote in the wrong tribe or century nor cast it more than once.

It has sometimes been suggested that the check was entirely informal, and that the Romans relied upon the familiarity of the tribal officials with their own membership and upon their ability readily to recognize a cuckoo in the nest at sight. But, while this might conceivably have been a fairly effective safeguard in early years, when the franchise was limited, it is difficult to believe that it could in any sense have been a workable arrangement after the fourth century. The alternatives are two. The name of each voter could have been checked against a censorial list at some time between his entering the enclosure and casting his vote. This, however, is an unattractive suggestion. The sheer bulk and weight of the list, presumably inscribed on wax, would have rendered it unportable and would have necessitated its being positioned at a set point—either at the entrance to the enclosure or at the foot of the *pons*. Wherever it was placed, the process of checking names against a list which contained many times more names than those who actually presented themselves to vote would have been a time-consuming process which would have delayed the succession of voters passing up to the voting urns by twenty seconds per voter at the very least. Such a delay would have been intolerable, particularly when the voting of the units was successive. Furthermore, this form of check would not necessarily have been particularly effective; for, in the absence of the great majority of tribesmen on each occasion, it would have been a comparatively simple matter for an unauthorized person to present himself under the name of a citizen known to be absent and in this way to cast his vote on several occasions in different units. The other and more attractive alternative is that all Roman citizens were provided with some form of identity token on which was inscribed name, tribe, and property qualification, and that they were required to display this to a *custos* at some point along the line. The natural place to make such a check would, of course, have been by the voting urn itself; and, in view of what has already been said about the distribution of the ballots, there is perhaps a good case to be made out for the suggestion that the scene on the coin of Licinius Nerva represents not the transference of a voting tablet but the display of an identity disc by the voter on the *pons* to the *custos* standing below. Unfortunately, there is no additional evidence to corroborate this theory, and it should be mentioned that the existence of such identity tokens is never referred to in the sources. The most that can be said is that it provides a perfectly feasible explanation of what must surely have been an essential part of the voting process, and one which pays due regard to that vital element of time which, perhaps most of all, influenced the development of Roman voting practice.

THE FIRST VOTER

It may reasonably be assumed that for the most part the voters in any one voting unit went up to the vote at random—in other words, that the order in which they recorded their vote coincided roughly with the order in which they had chanced to enter the voting enclosure. There appears, however, to have been one notable exception to this rule; and it is worth dwelling upon this exception and upon its implications for the outcome of the vote.[317]

In the prescripts of laws carried in the tribal assemblies mention by name was made not only of the tribe which had been the first to be called—the *principium*—but also of the individual voter in that tribe who had been the first to record his vote.[318] It is almost certain that the identity of this man, and very possibly of the first voters in other tribes as well, was predetermined. The literary evidence on this matter, although meagre, is fairly conclusive. The most important item is an extract from Cicero's speech in defence of Plancius, at the point where the orator is commenting upon the charge of the prosecution that Plancius senior had been the first to cast his vote in favour of one of Caesar's laws in 59 BC: if the essence of the prosecution's complaint is simply that Plancius voted in favour, he argues, then he can surely hardly be blamed; for, being a *publicanus*, he could not have been expected to do otherwise. Nor, however, can he be blamed for more precisely being the first to cast his vote—a role which may be understood to have been assigned to him by the lot or by Caesar himself; for no one can be held responsible for the outcome of the lot, and the fact of his being selected by so great a man as Caesar can only be to his credit![319] It is perhaps not immediately apparent from this what were the precise roles which Cicero supposed had been played by the lot and by Caesar in determining that Plancius should be the first to vote; and those who have commented upon the passage have commonly made the mistake of supposing that the use of the lot and of direct selection by the presiding magistrate are cited as alternative methods of determining the identity not of the individual who would vote first, but of the *principium* to which he would necessarily belong.[320]

This view, however, is wholly untenable. In the first instance, all our other evidence indicates that the identity of the *principium* was invariably determined by lot;[321] and the general tone of the passage rules out the possibility that Cicero is here admitting unconstitutional or unethical behaviour on the part of Caesar. Secondly, it is impossible to reconcile the view that Cicero is throughout alluding simply to the selection of the *principium* tribe with his remarks about Caesar's personal assessment of Plancius' standing, which imply that he played, or could have played, some part in assigning to him the role of first voter. In my view, the passage will stand only one interpretation. It is that Caesar was responsible on the occasion in question not for the choice of the *principium*, which, as always, was left to the lot, but, as Cicero's words most naturally imply, for the choice of Plancius to cast the first vote within it. The lot and direct selection by the consul are introduced into the argument by Cicero not as alternative methods for making the same choice, but as successive agents for making two independent choices, both of which contributed in some sense to Plancius' being the first person to cast his vote at the *comitia*. The lot determined that the tribe to which Plancius belonged should be the *principium*, whereas Caesar chose Plancius to vote first in it.

Since Cicero does not suggest in this passage that Caesar's behaviour was in any way abnormal, it is reasonable to assume that direct selection of the first voter by the presiding magistrate in legislative assemblies was common, if not regular, practice. This impression is confirmed by the only other literary reference to the first voter—a passage from Cicero's speech *De Domo* in which he taunts P. Clodius with having had to rely upon the services of a good-for-nothing slave leader named Fidulius to act as first voter on the measure which led to his exile.[322] It is also a necessary corollary to the fact that the first voter was invariably one who cast his vote in favour of the magistrate's motion. Not only does the verb *sciscere*, used in the official texts of laws, mean 'to cast an affirmative vote', but Cicero makes it clear both in the *Pro Plancio* and the *De Domo* that the charge of having supported the measures in question was implicit in the complaints that the individuals concerned had been cited as first voters. Clearly, the identity of the first voter could not in this case have been determined at random or by the will of his assembled fellow-tribesmen. He could only have been one who was pledged to support the motion and who was thus assigned his role for that very purpose.

Of course, the mere fact that the first to vote in the *principium* tribe is alone cited in the prescripts of laws should not blind us to the very real possibility that individuals were selected to cast the first vote in each and every tribe; indeed it may well be thought that, if the *principium* itself enjoyed no particular influence in the voting, the right of the presiding magistrate to appoint a first voter in that tribe alone could have had very little meaning or purpose. It is worth noting that if the magistrate's right to appoint a first voter had been restricted to the *principium* the selection would presumably have been made at the *comitia* itself, after the *principium* had been determined by lot, and from among those seen to be present at the vote, whereas if he had been entitled to select first voters for every tribe the choice could obviously have been made well in advance of the comitial proceedings and could have fallen on any members of the citizen body who were prepared to pledge their support and guarantee their presence at the vote. It hardly needs saying that the latter would have been the easier and the more natural arrangement. Furthermore, it accords more satisfactorily with the *De Domo* extract, in which Cicero not only implies that Fidulius was Clodius' choice but also acknowledges the real doubt as to whether the slave leader was actually present at the vote at all.

It is self-evident that this right of the presiding magistrate to nominate first voters, particularly if it extended to all the voting units and not to the *principium* alone, must have furnished him with the means of influencing substantially the outcome of the vote.[323] As the first voter was invariably a supporter of the motion before the assembly, it follows that, even after the introduction of the secret ballot, the sense in which he voted must somehow have been made public knowledge. The exact procedure is a matter for conjecture. In the days of oral voting, perhaps, the *rogator* or his herald may have made a public announcement to the assembled tribesmen, giving the name of the first voter and indicating his favourable vote. Later, too, when voting was by written ballot, much the same procedure could have been followed, the first voter voluntarily showing his ballot to the *custos* before depositing it in the voting urn. Alternatively, precedence in voting and support for the motion may have become so inseparably associated in the public mind from early times that formal announcements of this kind were regarded as unnecessary. In other words, the mere identification of the individual who went up first to cast his vote may have become in itself a sufficient indication to the other voters that he had voted in favour of the motion. In any event, it is beyond question that the either witnessed or publicized support of a prominent and respected individual will often have done much to influence indifferent or uncommitted voters, particularly from his own tribe, and thus that the chance of a magistrate's being successful in carrying a measure through the *comitia* may well frequently have depended to a large extent upon his ability to secure the open and avowed support of persons who enjoyed the esteem and respect of their fellow-voters.

As we have seen, the evidence for the part played by first voters relates solely to legislative votes in tribal assemblies. Whether a similar practice was observed elsewhere must remain a matter for conjecture. That first voters were selected in the centuries of the *comitia centuriata* is perhaps unlikely in so far as an effective lead was given to the mass of voters here by the *centuria praerogativa*, the result of whose vote was declared before any further voting took place. But in the judicial assemblies of the tribes, where voting appears to have been successive, the nomination of first voters may well have been a regular feature; and, if it be accepted that individuals were selected to be first voters for all the tribes in legislative assemblies, there is no logical reason why the same procedure should not have been followed in electoral assemblies, where the tribes voted simultaneously and where there was no *principium*. Such a practice would certainly go some way towards explaining the apparent influence exercised by presiding magistrates over elections which they conducted; but, in the absence of any confirmation in the tradition, it would be unwise to regard the nomination of first voters at tribal elections as anything more than a remote possibility.

THE VOTING ORDER OF THE UNITS

Some of the problems relating to the order in which the voting groups cast their vote have already been touched upon. Reference has been made, for example, to the role of the *centuria praerogativa*, which cast its vote prior to the rest of the assembly in the *comitia centuriata* (p. 155), and to the process of sortition by which the order of voting in the tribal assembly was determined (p. 156); also, certain basic assumptions have inevitably been made about the order of proceedings in different voting arenas. But, at the risk of some repetition, it will be useful here to assemble in one place most of what is known on the subject of successive and simultaneous voting, and in particular to consider how and why Roman practice developed as it did.

Turning first to the centuriate assembly, it is beyond dispute that there was always an element of succession here, in the sense that the various property classes voted in strict rotation. Details of the procedure in the original Servian organization are provided by Livy and Dionysius. First were called the centuries of *equites*, and then came the first, second, third, fourth and fifth classes in their turn.[324] After the reform there were minor changes in the upper centuries; but a strict order was still observed, with the calling of each successive class being preceded by an announcement of the results of the voting of the class which had cast its votes immediately before it. First came the prerogative century, chosen, as we have seen, by lot; then the centuries of the first class, voting together with twelve of the equestrian centuries; next, the six most aristocratic centuries of *equites*, known as the *sex suffragia*, so positioned perhaps in order to set an example in the voting to the less predictable centuries of the lower classes; and finally, the second, third, fourth and fifth classes in rotation. In the last years of the Republic several radical attempts were made to secure the abandonment of the procedure of calling the centuries by their classes, but to the best of our knowledge these plans were never brought to fruition, and Cicero's detailed description of an election held in 44 BC establishes that the normal order of calling the centuries was still observed at the very end of the Republic.[325]

By contrast, it is equally unquestionable that, at least in the first century, the individual units in these classes voted at one and the same time. This is confirmed by the simple fact that in the late Republic there was available in the Campus Martius a commodious building, known as the *saepta*, in which a large number of centuries could be separately housed and could cast their votes simultaneously. It is strongly suggested too by the text of the municipal charter of Malaga, which, like other colonial charters of the period, was closely modelled upon Roman constitutional procedure. Here explicit provision is made for simultaneous voting in separate compartments. 'Let the presiding magistrate call the citizens to vote by *curiae*,' says the charter. 'Let him summon all the *curiae* to the vote at the same time, and let all the *curiae* cast their votes by ballot in their several compartments.'[326] That this system of voting was original, however, as Mommsen insisted, is extremely improbable. There are indeed two strong arguments for the view that at one time voting in all the assemblies, both centuriate and tribal, was successive. One is that, as we have seen, the original manner of recording the vote was by acclamation. It stands to reason that at this stage the principle of succession must of necessity have been observed; and it is hardly likely that succession gave way to simultaneity as soon as the voting units began to be sounded by oral individual vote rather than in the mass. The other is that throughout the Republic the Romans observed the practice, to be discussed more fully in the next chapter, of terminating proceedings as soon as a number of candidates equal to the number of places to be filled had secured an absolute majority of possible votes. This strange attachment to precedence in attaining an absolute majority rather than to the more equitable principle of relative majority must clearly have had its roots in established tradition; and the practice can most naturally be explained as a time-saving device dating from a period when all 193 centuries voted in succession.

The actual date of the change to simultaneous voting in centuriate assemblies is not easy to determine. It will certainly have been after the introduction of a genuine free choice between candidates at elections, but, in view of the fact that the votes of as many as 193 centuries had in theory to be cast and counted, it is unlikely that the successive vote long survived the very appreciable extension of the franchise which took place in the late fourth and early third centuries. Perhaps Livy is to be believed when he writes of the centuries being summoned one by one at an election held in 298 BC,[327] but, if so, the change cannot have come very much later. It is notable that the same author refers in his account of the year 211 to a private enclosure (*secretum ovile*) in which two centuries of the same tribe held consultations.[328] This tends to confirm what we should expect—that by the close of the third century the Campus Martius was divided off into compartments of some sort, which were sufficient in number to house as many centuries as voted at any one time. Very possibly this number was thirty-five, in which case the seventy units of the first class, the only class whose complement exceeded thirty-five, will have voted in two instalments.

In the tribal assembly the voting of the units was undoubtedly successive throughout the Republic in all cases where the vote was legislative or judicial. This was firmly established in 1915 by Fraccaro, who produced a long list of passages relating to the entire period from the fourth to the first centuries in which the sources refer fairly explicitly to the successive vote.[329] Two of the most telling of these are Valerius Maximus' description of a trial in 329 BC in which an ill-advised outburst by the prosecutor influenced the voting in mid-course 'after fourteen tribes had already cast their votes', and an allusion in Asconius to the successive calling of the tribes during the vote on the Gabinian plebiscite in 67 BC.[330] Evidence that this continued to be the normal procedure is provided by the text of one of the last pieces of tribal legislation, the *lex Quinctia* of 9 BC; for this indicates both that the vote was taken in the Forum, where in the confined space available it would surely have been impossible to arrange for the erection of thirty-five separate *pontes*, and that the practice was observed of appointing a *principium* and so determining an order in which the tribes were to be called to the vote.[331]

At tribal elections, however, both those of the junior magistrates conducted in the *comitia tributa* and those of the plebeian officials conducted in the *concilium plebis*, the voting of the units was simultaneous in the later Republic. This is established by the detailed descriptions of first-century aedilician elections which are provided by Cicero and Varro, and also by the knowledge that elections were held in the Campus Martius, where use could have been made, and according to Cicero was made, of the wooden enclosures and of the apparatus placed there for the use of the centuries of the *comitia centuriata*.[332] Unfortunately, firm details of electoral procedure in tribal assemblies before the first century are not available. If we discount the last assembly of Tiberius Gracchus, which is now commonly regarded as having been legislative rather than elective in character,[333] the earliest election of which we have any details is that of Gaius Gracchus in 122; and this Plutarch in a somewhat garbled account places in the Campus Martius. The date of the adoption of simultaneous voting is therefore a matter for speculation. In Fraccaro's view, the change was connected with the introduction of the written ballot in the middle of the second century,[334] but the contention which underlies this view—that the introduction of the written vote led to a considerable protraction of proceedings—is open to challenge. It could even be argued that in multiple elections in particular, which were the order of the day in tribal assemblies, the use of the ballot actually speeded up the voting process (*cf.* p. 188).When voting was oral, each voter must have spent an appreciable time listing the candidates of his choice to the *rogator* by word of mouth, but, with the coming of the ballot, the rate at which voters passed over the *pontes* must have been considerably quickened, if, as we have supposed, the voters could fill in their ballots at leisure as they waited their turn in the voting enclosure. Certainly, the counting of the votes will have been more time-consuming after the introduction of the ballot than before, for the counters will have been faced with the task of compiling the lists of votes for each candidate which under the oral system the *rogator* had before him the moment that voting ceased. This, however, would have resulted in a serious lengthening of proceedings only if it had been thought necessary to complete the count of the votes cast by one tribe before the next tribe was called to vote. If, as would have been the more sensible course, the count continued while further tribes voted, the extra time involved in the more complicated counting process would have been negligible.

Although the introduction of the ballot was not one of them, there were a number of factors which made a change to simultaneous voting more urgent at elections than at legislative and judicial votes. Firstly, there is reason to believe that electoral *comitia* were very much better attended. Rural voters who could not hope to visit Rome for every legislative vote would have been canvassed and encouraged to attend for the elections. The crowds may well have proved too great for the Forum to accommodate them, and of course the time taken for each tribe to cast its vote must have been considerable. Secondly, as we have just noted, the actual recording of the individual vote would have taken very much longer at an election conducted by oral voting than at an oral vote on legislation, where the voter was required to answer the *rogator* with a simple 'yes' or 'no'. And thirdly, it is certain that an electoral vote would normally have demanded the consultation of a greater number of tribes than a legislative or judicial vote; for, whereas the first eighteen tribes called may frequently have been enough to pass a non-controversial law or pronounce a clear-cut verdict, they will most certainly not have been enough in most cases to provide the required number of candidates with the minimum of eighteen votes which they each needed to secure election.

It is very likely that these factors made themselves felt in the tribal assemblies well before the second half of the second century, when the written vote was introduced; and indeed, once the centuriate assembly had provided itself with the apparatus necessary for conducting a simultaneous vote of its individual units (p. 171), it is improbable that the tribal assemblies delayed long in availing themselves of the facilities which were at hand in the Campus.

It has been suggested that the use of the Campus by the tribal assemblies must have dated from at least 312 BC, on the strength of Livy's comment that in that year the censor, Appius Claudius, 'corrupted the Forum and the Campus' by changing the composition of the Roman tribes. Nevertheless, while these words are significant in that they confirm Livy's own association of the Forum and the Campus with the legislative and elective functions of the tribal assemblies respectively, they could easily be used here in an anachronistic context. If, as Livy himself suggests, the centuries were themselves still voting successively in 298, the most likely date for a change to simultaneous voting both in centuriate assemblies and in the electoral assemblies of the tribes would appear to be some time in the third century. Indeed, it is not impossible that there was some connection between the change in procedure in one or both of these forms of assembly and the famous reform of the centuriate organization which was effected in the latter part of that century. This reform resulted in the identification of the centuries of at least the upper classes with sections of tribes and must as a consequence have necessitated the provision of voting enclosures and platforms, whether collapsible or fixed, equal in number to the total of Roman tribes; it may well have suggested, and will certainly have facilitated, the use of the Campus and its equipment by the tribal assemblies themselves.[335]

CHAPTER X

THE DETERMINATION OF THE RESULTS

SOME OF THE MOST interesting and most vital features of Roman voting procedure are associated with the determination of the results of the voting, and in particular with the formal declaration of returns from the various groups. It is, for example, an accepted fact that where the voting of the units was successive the timing of the declaration of results could have a marked effect upon the course of subsequent voting, and that where it was simultaneous, as at elections, the eventual outcome could be materially affected by the order in which such a declaration of results was made. In this chapter it is proposed to consider the known facts about the procedure followed from the moment that the first group or groups completed the voting process, and to examine some of the more controversial issues to which these facts give rise.

THE COUNTING OF THE VOTES

In the days of the oral vote the process of counting the votes cast in each voting unit was a comparatively simple one. As we have seen, the *rogator* recorded the individual votes on a large waxed tablet by inscribing dots against the names of the candidates whom the voters had chosen (or, at a legislative or judicial vote, against the particular affirmative or negative verdict for which they had opted). No sooner, therefore, had all the voters of the tribe or century filed past him over the *pontes* than he was in a position to add up the number of dots in each line and to arrive fairly speedily at an overall result. With the introduction of the written ballot, however, the counting process naturally became more complex. The voting urns were first removed to a convenient open space behind the voting area, which was presumably suitably prepared and equipped in advance for the conduct of the count, though in Republican days there was nothing comparable to the later covered building (the *diribitorium*) which was completed too late to be of any material service. The ballots were then removed one by one from the urns, duly read by all concerned, and deposited finally in another container known as a *loculus*. The votes marked on them were translated into dots on a waxed tablet similar to that which had previously been used by the *rogatores* at oral votes; and these dots were then added up in the same manner to obtain a result.[336]

The number of people involved in this procedure appears to have been considerable. The count was conducted by the officials known as *custodes* (guardians), who had replaced the *rogatores* with the introduction of the ballot, and who were also responsible for supervising the actual voting and possibly, as we have seen, for checking the voters' identity.[337] These were men of some note, being chosen from a select body of nine hundred senators and knights on the official jury lists, and they of necessity came from a group other than that to which they were assigned.[338] There were at least three of them officially appointed for each group by the presiding magistrate, but at electoral votes it was permissible for each candidate to appoint at least one, and possibly in certain cases more than one, in addition, in order to watch over his particular interests.[339] It would appear that all of these *custodes* had access to the ballots, and that each had the right, even if perhaps he did not use it, to conduct an individual count on a tablet of his own. Presumably, the three official *custodes* were required to keep independent counts, and the returns could only be sent in when they had agreed their figures and these had been passed by those responsible for looking after particular interests.

THE REPORTING OF RESULTS TO THE PRESIDING MAGISTRATE

The report prepared by the *custodes* for the presiding magistrate was a simple one. As the choice of a voting unit was determined on the basis of a relative majority among the individual votes, the returning officer was concerned only to know the numbers of votes cast in favour or against a resolution or in favour of each candidate; and it is likely that a tablet providing these details was taken to him by one of the *custodes* who acted as spokesman as soon as possible after the completion of the count. It was Mommsen's belief that this communication of results from the voting units to the magistrate was made in public, and that, even when the units voted simultaneously, the order in which the returns were publicized was determined by the speed at which the various officials could produce their figures. There are, however, serious objections to this view, which has been shown to have been based upon a misreading of a vital section in the charter of Malaga.[340] For one thing, it is at variance with an account given by Varro of an aedilician election in the last century of the Republic, when the interested parties are represented as retiring from the scene after the end of the voting to hold a philosophical discourse, returning to hear the results declared only after an interval of at least two hours. For another, for reasons which will be explained in the next section, the publication of the returns from all the voting units in a chance order would not only have been unnecessary but could well have been both misleading and embarrassing.

It should be assumed, then, that the returns from the various tribes or centuries were communicated to the presiding magistrate, at least at electoral *comitia*, in private. This, of course, means that the presiding magistrate could easily have formed a rough assessment of the probable outcome of the vote before he embarked upon his official declaration of the results.

THE DECLARATION OF RESULTS

The form of the official declaration of results, or *renuntiatio*, as it was called, may be reconstructed from details given in the Malagan charter, and from a humorous anecdote related in Cicero's *De Oratore*.[341] A herald acted as the mouthpiece of the presiding magistrate throughout. He first addressed himself to the spokesman for a particular voting group and enquired of him

the details of the individual votes cast. At a legislative vote he
would ask in turn for the number of votes cast in favour of the
motion and then for the number cast against it. At an electoral
vote he would name each of the candidates in turn and enquire
about the size of his vote. When these figures had been given
he formally proclaimed the verdict of the voting group in question. At an electoral vote this involved listing as chosen by the
tribe or century as many candidates as there were places to be
filled in an order of precedence which corresponded to the size
of the vote which each had secured. In the event of a tie in
individual votes there was a set procedure at Malaga which was
almost certainly modelled upon that at Rome. At a legislative or
judicial vote a tie was interpreted as a negative: in other words, the
unit concerned was announced to have voted for the rejection of
a bill or for acquittal. At an election the procedure was simply
for the presiding magistrate to put the matter to the lot and to
afford precedence to whichever of the two tying candidates was
first drawn.[342]

In considering the timing of the *renuntiatio* and the order in
which the results were proclaimed it will be convenient to deal
independently with those assemblies where the voting of the
units was successive and those where it was simultaneous. As we
have seen, this distinction corresponds, at least as far as the second
half of the Republic is concerned, with the distinction between
legislative and judicial assemblies on the one hand and electoral
assemblies on the other.

The evidence leaves no room for doubt that, where voting
was successive, the results from individual tribes were made
known progressively, and that the verdict of certain tribes was
therefore already known before others were called in to vote.
Furthermore, the order in which the results were announced was
clearly determined by the order in which the tribes were called
in to vote; and, as we have seen, this order was itself fixed by the
process of sortition resulting in the nomination of the tribe known
as the *principium*. Indeed, the very appointment of a *principium*,
and the consequent observance of a different voting order on each
occasion, can only have been designed to ensure that the tribes whose

returns were *declared* first, and who therefore effectively decided the result, were not the same at each assembly. Although, however, the results were declared progressively in the same order as that in which the tribes voted, there is no good reason to assume that there was a delay after the voting of each tribe, and before the next tribe was called, while the votes were counted and the result announced. When voting was oral, such a delay might have been feasible, but not surely after the introduction of the ballot. It is noteworthy that the *principium* is nowhere claimed to have played precisely the same influential role in the tribal assembly as did the *centuria praerogativa* in the centuriate; and, although the early returns must obviously have set a voting pattern which the uncommitted would be prone to follow, the sources significantly refer at times to the trend set by the first two or three tribes rather than by the *principium* alone.[343] It is probable, therefore, that results were declared as and when they were determined, possibly at the next convenient interval in the subsequent voting. As the voting was of the straight 'yes' or 'no' variety, it is unlikely that the declarations would normally have been more than one tribe in arrears; but the time-saving over the whole proceedings must have been considerable.

At assemblies where some or all of the voting groups voted simultaneously, the results from all such groups were declared together. It was, however, a curious feature of Roman voting practice, dating presumably from the time of the successive vote in elections, that an absolute majority was viewed as not only a necessary but also a sufficient condition of election. This meant that the declaration of results continued until, and only until, as many candidates as there were places to be filled had received $\frac{1}{2} + 1$ of the possible votes—in the tribal assembly, the votes of 18 out of the 35 tribes, in the centuriate assembly the votes of 97 out of the 193 centuries.[344] The actual outcome of an election could therefore well be affected by the order in which the results from the various units were announced; and it was possible for offices to go to men who either did not carry the largest number of groups, or at least would not have done so if every group had been permitted to vote. This seeming anomaly can be simply illustrated. Let it be supposed that at an election held in a tribal assembly there were three candidates for two offices, A, B and C. After results from 24 of the 35 tribes had been announced, two of these candidates, A and B, had secured the required minimum of 18 votes necessary for election. With a total of 48 votes declared at this stage, A and B had 18 each, and C 12: in other words, twelve of the tribes had voted for A and B, six for A and C, and six for B and C. At this point, according to Roman practice, A and B were declared elected. Yet, if the results from the remaining eleven tribes had been taken into account, and if by chance nine out of those eleven had cast their votes for A and C, C would have been shown to have accumulated 21 votes as against only 20 for B. Of course, when the number of places to be filled was small and the number of candidates was not considerably larger, the chances that the successful candidates would not also have been elected on the basis of relative majorities were slim; but the greater the number of places and the larger the number of candidates, the more likely was this system to produce what by modern standards would be regarded as a distorted result. In a tribunician election, for example, when ten places had to be filled, it would have been statistically possible for as many as 19 candidates to secure an absolute majority of 18 votes, if returns had been made from all the tribes.[345]

In view of the significant effect which the order of announcing results could have upon the outcome of an election, the Romans had recourse to the lot to determine what that order should be. The procedure attested in the literary tradition is fully detailed in the text of the Malagan charter. 'When the returns from all the voting groups have been brought in, the presiding magistrate shall throw the names of the groups into the lot, and, as each name is drawn out, he shall order a declaration to be made of the candidates whom that particular group has chosen. As candidates in turn secure the votes of a majority of the voting groups, he shall declare them duly elected, and he shall continue doing this until as many magistrates have been declared elected as there are places to be filled.' Provision is even made here for the eventuality of two candidates securing the absolute majority with the declaration of results from one and the same group. Rather than continuing the count until one of the two secured a lead, the presiding magistrate was to draw lots and to give precedence to the individual whose name came out first.[346]

At an election held in a tribal assembly lots were drawn to determine the order in which results were declared throughout the entire list and until such time as all the required places had been filled. At the major elections held in the centuriate assembly, on the other hand, where the groups in any one class voted simultaneously but the classes themselves voted in succession, it is unlikely that the lot was used to determine the order of results in the early stages. After the reform of the third century the combined votes of the equestrian centuries and those of the first class still fell nine short of the absolute majority of ninety-seven; and it is therefore probable that the results from these centuries, all of which necessarily counted, were read out in an established order. In this case use of the lot will first have been made with the declaration of results from the second class.

PROCEDURE AFTER THE DETERMINATION OF EARLY RESULTS

The fact that the Romans determined the result of a vote in the manner outlined gives rise to a number of questions relating to the procedure adopted after a majority decision had been reached, or, in an electoral vote, after one or more of the candidates had attained an absolute majority.

It is known that in the centuriate assembly both the voting of the units and the progressive declaration of results stopped as soon as the required number of places had been filled. Did the same thing happen in the tribal assemblies? Fraccaro argued that it did not, but that the tribes continued to vote and further results were made public.[347] He suggested both that the tribal assembly was in origin a more democratic institution than the centuriate, and that the influential citizens in the various tribes would have wished the sense in which their tribes voted to be put on record; and he attempted to find support for his view in the several references in the authorities to decisions taken by 'all thirty-five tribes'. In particular, he cited Plutarch's comment on the resolution of the *concilium plebis* to deprive the tribune

Octavius of his office in 133 BC: 'If it was equitable that the tribunate should be given to him on the vote of a majority of tribes, surely it is more equitable that it should be taken from him by the vote of them all'.[348] These passages, however, do not provide the proof which Fraccaro suggests. The phrase 'all thirty-five tribes' could well be merely a collective formula for the tribal assembly as a whole; and the comment of Plutarch is consistent with a distinction between a majority vote and a unanimous vote of the tribes *whose results were actually declared*. Furthermore, even if it be accepted that the tribal vote was developed to offset the timocratic centuriate structure rather than for its greater convenience, the democratic principle was inherent in the system itself and surely did not require the extension of proceedings after the determination of a result. As the Romans were clearly concerned with the time element in developing their voting procedures, it is preferable to assume that in the tribal assemblies as well as in the centuriate both voting and declarations ceased as soon as the outcome of the vote was determined. This view accords better with the retention of the principle of the absolute majority at elections, for publication of the full results might well have been expected to give rise to protests against manifest injustice and demands for a change of procedure.[349] It also accords better with the practice of appointing a *principium* at legislative assemblies; for, as we have seen (p. 156), the determination of a different order of voting at each assembly can most satisfactorily be interpreted as a move designed to ensure that certain tribes should not be permanently disfranchised by reason of their being at the bottom of a regular order and so finding the result decided and the assembly disbanded before being called upon to cast their votes.[350]

A more difficult problem is raised by consideration of the effect of the early election of one or more candidates upon the subsequent voting and upon the form of further declarations by the presiding magistrate. This is a matter of some complexity. In both tribal and centuriate assemblies, when a candidate obtained his absolute majority and was consequently declared elected there will almost invariably have been several groups which had already voted but whose results were yet to be declared. In such cases, did the presiding magistrate continue to take note of the votes cast in favour of the already elected candidate and to announce that candidate as the choice of further units, or did he concern himself only with the votes cast in favour of the remaining candidates? And, if the latter, did he return for each unit only as many candidates as there were places still to be filled, or did he return as many as there were places originally to be filled? With regard to centuriate assemblies, of course, there is a further question, for in such assemblies candidates will frequently have been declared elected not only when there were some results from groups that had already voted still to be announced, but when there were still entire classes of centuries yet to be called to the vote. What was the position of these subsequent voters? Did they have one vote less at their disposal than those who had voted before them, or did they retain as many votes as there were places originally to be filled?

The first reaction of the present-day observer to these questions is perhaps to dismiss out of hand the possibility of a subsequent vote and declaration of results which altogether ignored the earlier filling of one or more of the places. But it should be borne in mind that there are several features of Roman voting practice which do not in the least conform to the standards of modern democracy. Let us then consider first the case of the later voters in the centuriate assembly. The entire structure of the assembly was designed to confer the greatest influence upon the centuries of the upper classes, which were the first to vote, and we should not therefore expect procedures to be such that a voter in a lower class enjoyed any greater individual influence than one in a higher. Strange as it may at first appear, this is in fact an argument for the view that the later voters had as many votes at their disposal as their earlier counterparts rather than fewer; for, as any student of voting knows, the individual who in a multiple election uses all his votes exerts considerably less influence than one who uses only a few. In other words, a restriction of the votes at the disposal of the later voters could only have forced them to play the more influential role normally reserved for the knowledgeable expert.

If, on the other hand, they had returned their full quota of votes, the chances that a candidate who had won substantial support in early voting would quickly attain his absolute majority would have been very much greater. Some positive support for this view that later voters were able to dispose of the full number of votes is perhaps to be found in the suggestion of Cicero that an already elected candidate was in a strong position to ensure that votes which would otherwise have been cast for him were cast for a political associate instead. Speaking of the praetorian elections for 66 BC, he clearly implies that Antonius owed his election to his own (Cicero's) early success in the voting returns and to the consequent switching of votes in Antonius' favour by his supporters.[351] If such manœuvres were common, it would certainly help to explain the frequent association of political allies in office at Rome.

If it was indeed the case that the later voters in the *comitia centuriata* retained their full quota of votes even after one or more of the candidates had secured election, it must surely have followed that the presiding magistrate himself continued to return in respect of each voting unit as many candidates as there were places originally to be filled. What cannot be said, of course, is whether in this event he took note of further returns from the voting units which favoured candidates who had already obtained their absolute majority, or whether alternatively he ignored such returns and determined the results from each unit solely on the basis of the votes cast for the remaining candidates. If he had adopted the former course, the as yet undeclared results from all the units which had already voted—namely, *all* the units at a tribal election, and all the remaining units from a single class at a centuriate election—would, of course, have been unaffected. If, on the other hand, he had adopted the latter, then every result subsequently declared, whether in a tribal or a centuriate election, could have been affected. In either case, of course, the procedure followed would have been one which can only be judged somewhat odd by modern standards; but it is worth noting that it would have yielded two very important advantages in the context of Roman elections. In the first place, it would have lessened the chances,

presumably quite high when there was a large number of candidates in the field, that all results would be declared before an
adequate number of candidates had obtained the required
absolute majority of votes. This point can be very simply illustrated. Let it be supposed that in a four-cornered contest to fill two
consular places one candidate (A) secured the votes of all the first
97 centuries to have their results declared (an absolute majority),
while the remaining three (B, C and D) won 32, 32 and 33 votes
respectively. If those who were enrolled in the other 96 centuries
could dispose of only one vote each and so return only one
candidate, it would have been perfectly possible for none of the
other three candidates to obtain 97 votes and conceivable that
D would end up as top scorer with as few as 65. If, on the other
hand, the remaining centuries continued to dispose of two
votes (192 in all), it would have been mathematically inevitable
that one of the three candidates would end with a minimum of
97. Clearly, with more candidates in the field an indecisive result
could still have been perfectly possible, but it would have been
very much less likely.

A second advantage of this procedure is that it would have
tended to produce a decisive result at an earlier stage, and so cut
short what must at best have been extremely protracted proceedings. Indeed, as soon as the number of as yet unsuccessful candi-
cates had been reduced to the number of places originally to be
filled, the count and the declaration of results could reasonably
have been halted and the total votes of the candidates duly
calculated. Thus, when two candidates had been elected in a six-
cornered contest for four praetorian places, the remaining two
places could automatically have been awarded to the two of the
remaining four candidates who at the time had the largest number
of votes to their credit, on the ground that with only four candidates
left in the field each one was bound to be returned by all of
the remaining centuries. This, of course, is always provided
that the votes which the candidates had already secured plus the
number of units whose returns were yet to be declared added
up to ninety-seven. If they did not, the election could have been
declared indecisive without further ado.

There is one further point which lends some force to the suggestion that as many candidates were returned for each unit as there were places originally to be filled. It is that in the centuriate assembly such a procedure would have guaranteed much greater influence to the wealthy members of the centuries which voted earliest. So long as multiple returns were ensured from the centuries of the lower classes, there was a virtual certainty that any candidate who had secured even as many as 40 or 50 votes from the centuries of the first property class would obtain his majority of 97 votes before another who first began to attract any appreciable support from among the voters of the second or a lower class.

THE TIME ELEMENT IN VOTING PROCEDURE

Both in this and in the preceding chapter the interpretation given of particular procedures has on several occasions been dictated by consideration of the time element in Roman voting. Before we end this survey of the actual voting process, therefore, it would perhaps be well to look at this matter of the length of comitial proceedings in a little more detail.

Let us first consider the case of the oral vote. The rate at which the individual voters filed over the *pontes* will naturally have been determined by the most time-consuming element in the voting process. At a legislative vote this will almost certainly have been the conduct of the check, if any, which was made on the voters' credentials (*cf.* p. 162); and, as such a check may reasonably be supposed to have taken some three to four seconds, it is a fair assumption that voters in a single file could have passed over the *pontes* at the rate of approximately fifteen per minute. At an electoral vote, on the other hand, the longest part of the process will undoubtedly have been the reciting of the names of candidates by the voter to the *rogator*, and as a consequence the rate of movement will have depended upon the total number of candidates to be elected. It could have varied from something like twelve per minute when a college of two was being elected, to as few as three per minute when, as at tribunician elections, ten places were to be filled.

These figures underline the strength of the case for the view that simultaneous voting was introduced for electoral votes at an early stage. If it be assumed that at a successive vote the voters filed over the *pontes* in two lines rather than one, it would have been feasible at a legislative vote for ten thousand persons to pass over in a little under six hours. At a tribunician election, however, little more than two thousand could have passed over in the same period; and even from quite early times it is reasonable to suppose that at an electoral assembly the average attendance was considerably larger than that. In the centuriate assembly, of course, and therefore at the elections of the major magistrates, there was a further time-consuming factor, which in tribal assemblies was less serious because of the very much smaller number of voting units involved. This was the declaration of results. As we have noted (pp. 180f), the actual order in which the results were announced was determined by the drawing of lots between the centuries. For each unit, therefore, a lot had to be drawn, the spokesman of the appropriate voting unit had to be summoned, the herald had to question him formally concerning the votes cast for each of the candidates in turn, and the presiding magistrate had finally to declare the result on the basis of the figures given. It is extremely difficult to imagine how this could all have been accomplished in under three minutes at a minimum; and in this case it will have taken in the region of four hours to complete the declaration for the centuries of the *equites* and the first property class alone. At a successive vote, even if they passed over the *pontes* in two files and had on average their nominal complement of one hundred, these centuries would have taken over five hours to cast their votes. Thus nine hours would have elapsed before even the second class centuries were called in to vote.[352] It is a reasonable assumption, therefore, that successive voting can only have been practicable at a time when either attendances were very small or the issue was almost invariably decided by the centuries of *equites* and the first class.

The change to the written ballot in the second century had a varied effect upon the length of time taken by the voting process. In the legislative and judicial assemblies, where the voting of the units was successive (pp. 171f), there was no appreciable change. The rate at which the voters filed over the *pontes* was the same as before, and, provided always that the count of the votes cast by one unit was conducted while another was voting, the extra time taken over the count can have been of little consequence. As before, an assembly of some ten thousand voters could have cast its vote in approximately six hours, and the whole proceedings could have been completed in seven.

At an electoral assembly the actual casting of the vote must have been speeded up by the introduction of the ballot. Provided always, of course, that the voters ascended the *pons* with a ballot already marked, and that they did not have to hold up proceedings by writing names upon it at a late stage, the actual time taken in voting must have been the same as at legislative assemblies, and an amount of time saved over the oral vote in proportion to the number of candidates to be elected. This saving in the actual casting of votes, however, would naturally have been offset, and more than offset, by the additional time taken in the count. At the oral vote the count could have been conducted within a matter of minutes by reference to the master tablet of the *rogator*. At a written ballot it must have taken very much longer. As the units voted simultaneously, the actual time spent over the count at an election conducted in a tribal assembly depended upon the size of the representation from the largest tribe, which, to judge from the size of the enclosures in the Augustan *saepta*, could well have been in the region of two thousand in the late Republic.[353] For a number of independent *custodes* to transfer even two names from as many as two thousand ballots on to a master tablet and mutually to agree the final figures can have been no small task. The only light cast by the tradition on this point comes from a story of Varro which suggests that at an election of two aediles a discussion lasting at least two hours could have taken place between the end of voting and the start of the declaration of results.[354] Even this seems a conservative estimate; and it should of course be noted that, if a count took two hours to complete when only two magistrates were being elected, it could well have taken ten hours at a tribunician election. At elections in the centuriate assembly the voting units were of course much smaller, and the time taken to count the votes of the largest unit will therefore have been correspondingly less; but against that one has to remember both that the declaration of results took far longer in a centuriate assembly, and that, with the classes of centuries voting successively, there were theoretically five periods during which

	LEGISLATION *successive voting*	TRIBAL ELECTIONS *simultaneous voting*	CENTURIATE ELECTIONS *simultaneous voting within classes*
Voting Rate	30 per minute (in two files)	15 per minute	15 per minute
Voting Time	6 hours	2 hours	Class I & *equites* 15 minutes Class II–III 30 minutes Class IV–V 1 hour
Time for Count	Simultaneous with vote-casting Overlap of 30 minutes	2 hours (college of two) 10 hours (college of ten)	Class I & *equites* 15 minutes (college of two) 1 hour (college of eight) Class II–III 30 minutes (college of two) 2 hours (college of eight) Class IV–V 1 hour (college of two) 4 hours (college of eight)
Declaration Time	30 minutes	1 hour	Class I & *equites* 4 hours Other Classes 1 hour each
TOTAL	7 hours	5 hours (college of two) 13 hours (college of ten)	Minimum of 6½ hours (college of two) 8¾ hours (college of eight) Maximum[355] of 14½ hours (college of two) 24½ hours (college of eight)

the actual casting of votes was held up while the votes of previous units were counted and the results declared.[356]

In the foregoing table an attempt is made to present estimates of the total time taken by the voting process in the days of the written ballot for the various types of assembly. The calculations are based upon the assumption that the average attendance at a legislative vote was in the region of ten thousand, that the largest single unit at a tribal election was approximately two thousand, and that the largest single unit at a centuriate election varied from, say, two hundred in the first class to something more like a thousand in the fifth. These figures, of course, cannot be verified, and the estimates of time consumed can only be extremely approximate. Nevertheless, even if allowance is made for a considerable margin of error, they are sufficiently striking both to make it apparent that any further serious delays at any stage in the procedure would have been intolerable, and to lend support to the contention that the Romans may well have been influenced by the time element in framing electoral rules which by modern standards are judged eccentric.

CHAPTER XI

THE MANIPULATION OF THE VOTE

No SURVEY OF ROMAN voting procedures would be complete without some reference to the various methods which were employed by those concerned to influence the outcome of the voting. The subject is, of course, a vast one, and a full treatment of it would be well beyond the scope of a general study of voting practice such as this; but it is none the less desirable that something should be said both of the legitimate means which were used to deliver the vote and of the many malpractices and frauds to which the Romans not infrequently resorted when all other efforts failed.

THE DELIVERY OF THE VOTE AT MAJOR ELECTIONS

It is a commonplace that the concept of the modern political party was entirely foreign to the Roman political scene. The Roman candidate did not represent the interests of a large group embracing a sizable proportion of the population, he was not pledged to the support of specific policies, and normally he did not even attempt to associate himself in the eyes of the electorate with a particular political creed. The Roman electoral campaign was therefore an essentially personal one.[357] There is, of course, a danger here of overstatement. The portrayal of the Roman *nobilis* as one who held no strong views on important issues, and thus no political principles, is an altogether distorted one, as also is the suggestion that the composition of the associations into which he entered with his fellow nobles was not at least to some extent determined by the sharing of common political attitudes. The scant evidence available for the third century BC, for example, is sufficient to prove beyond all reasonable doubt that the Senate at that time was divided into two main camps clearly distinguishable by the diametrically opposed views which their members held on the vital issues of foreign policy.[358] It was inevitable, therefore, that the backing which a candidate received from his noble colleagues should frequently have come from those who were in agreement with his policies; and it is very conceivable that on some occasions at least, when particularly vital issues were involved, the known political stand of a candidate may have affected the measure of his support at the polls. But here any remote parallel between a Roman election and an election in a modern democratic state ends. Political differences were rarely, if ever, introduced into a candidate's campaign. Indeed, if we are to trust the advice supposedly given by Quintus Cicero to his brother in the pamphlet known as the *Commentariolum Petitionis*, the taking of any political stand during the campaign was to be studiously avoided for fear of making enemies.[359] Whereas the modern candidate is primarily concerned to sway the floating voter by convincing him of the justice of his cause, the Roman had but one principal object in his canvass—to ensure that those committed to his personal following attended the *comitia* in sufficient numbers to ensure him victory.

There are several reasons for this essential difference between the Roman electoral campaign and that of a modern democratic state. A very simple one is that in Roman times there were very few opportunities for communication and no media of propaganda. Except possibly in very early times, when Roman territory did not extend far beyond the city walls, it would have been quite impossible for a candidate to present himself before anything approximating to a majority of the voters during his campaign, or in normal years to find a cause which would appeal equally to all those whom he might be able to contact. A second reason is that the distance to Rome from the outlying areas of the *ager Romanus* was so great that voters could not be relied upon to make the journey unless they felt some obligation to do so or had some other more direct form of inducement. Except perhaps in times of crisis, the mere propagation of a political programme could not have been enough to inspire the necessary fervour. But possibly the most fundamental explanation of Roman campaigning practice is simply that it was moulded as early as the fifth century BC in days when any direct personal appeal by a member of the governing class to the electorate in the mass would certainly have been regarded as a form of treachery. In the early days of Republican government, when the depressed economy and the constant threat of external interference made the over-throw of the aristocracy and the establishment of one-man rule a very real possibility, the governing class sought strength in its solidarity. The attempts of such men as Spurius Cassius and Marcus Manlius to secure power by making a direct political appeal to the electorate in the mass served as a warning to the nobility of the dangers of the direct canvass,[360] and it is significant that the two earliest known laws on electoral matters actually forbade candidates to draw attention to themselves by whitening their togas and debarred them from travelling to the local market towns to address public meetings.[361] Offices were to be filled by popular election, but elections were to be conducted and fought according to a code of rules devised for the protection of the entire governing class. Success at the polls, therefore, testified not so much to the candidate's own personal appeal or to the popularity of his policies as to the extent of his patronal influence and the size of his *clientela*.

It follows from this that a Roman noble's campaign for office was very far from being confined to the year of his candidacy. However wide the circle of friends and dependants which he inherited from his family, considerable efforts had to be made in his early years to establish new and lasting contacts with those who could greatly influence the voting. Such in particular were the wealthier men from the municipalities who went to make up the first class in the electoral assembly, and who were in a position not only to travel to Rome to vote themselves but also to bring many others with them from among their own circle of friends and dependants. The ideal contact for the Roman candidate was the municipal magistrate or a leading member of a local equestrian company or trade guild who was himself in a position

to confer benefits on many people from a similar walk of life
and so in return to command their loyalty and their support for
the candidates whom he endorsed. The Roman noble had ample
opportunity to establish contacts of this kind, and to confer
benefits for which he could later demand a fitting return. He could
travel widely; he normally served in his youth as a junior officer
in the army, when he possibly had considerable influence with
those in higher authority;[262] he could practise in the law-courts,
where he could uphold the cause of the very men whose services
he later hoped to enlist; he could cultivate friendships with
men of great influence in the financial world, as Cicero did
with Atticus; he could make use of his house at Rome to extend
hospitality to men of note from the municipalities when they
visited the city; he could use his influence with political friends in
high office to secure the conferment of political benefits; and he
could hold many in his debt by the simple process of writing
testimonials. The bond established by the conferment of a
beneficium transcended all others in the Roman code, and any
budding politician might reasonably hope to reap a worthwhile
return for the extension of such favours.

Needless to say, a candidate could rarely have hoped to secure
election by the votes of his own influential municipal friends and
their respective dependants alone. He will normally have had to
rely also upon the support given to him by other members of
his class who were willing to marshal their own *clientelae* in
his interest. It was also his particular concern, therefore, not only
to nurture long-established political associations with his fellow
nobles, but even to forge new ones. This was frequently achieved
by arranging for a marriage alliance between families, and the
primarily political significance of such marriages is attested by
the fact that the resulting new relationships and associations were
frequently unimpaired by subsequent divorce and remarriage.

At all times, but more particularly in the last century of
Republican government, there were certain men who by reason
of their position were able to command a considerably larger
proportion of electoral votes than their colleagues. These were
men whom few candidates could afford to number among their

enemies and whom many, if only for reasons of expediency, would have liked to enlist among their friends. There had always been the men of censorial rank who had been able to use their high office to confer sizable favours in the form of a grant of citizenship, a favourable allocation of tribe, or even a lucrative contract. There were the financial kings, such as Crassus, who claimed to have most of the Senate in his pocket, and who could probably have damaged the interests of many hundreds through the companies he controlled. There were the great military commanders, like Pompey and Marius, who could call upon a substantial following among their disbanded soldiery. And finally there were the less reputable political managers who devoted themselves to gaining control over the assemblies more by corruption and blackmail than by any other means. Such was Cethegus, of whom it was said in the seventies that no noble could attain office without first winning his favour.[363] Clearly these men could not be ignored in an electoral campaign; if a candidate could not secure their support he was at least concerned to ensure their neutrality.

Although the assistance of political associates was essential to any electoral campaign, it should not be supposed that they applied themselves to the process of bringing in the voters with the same enthusiasm and thoroughness as did the candidates themselves. Indeed, had they done so, it would hardly have been necessary for the candidate to go to such pains to extend his own personal retinue of friends and clients. Their support frequently took the form of a written commendation (*commendatio*) which was sent to the candidate to be used as he saw fit,[364] and it was common for such commendations to be painted on signs along the roads and on the walls of properties owned by the clients of the candidate and his supporters in the municipal towns.[365] There can hardly have been the same pressure upon the friends of a noble associate to organize a large attendance of voters from among their dependants as there was upon the friends of the candidate himself; but a noble's *commendatio* will surely have been enough to ensure that any of his clients who were disposed to come to Rome for the elections did not cast their votes in favour of another.

As it was the tribe which was the basic unit of vote even in the centuriate assembly, it was naturally with an eye to the division of the people by tribes that the canvass was conducted. It is noteworthy that Cicero is advised by Quintus to study carefully the map of Italy and to learn by heart which areas were assigned to which tribes.[366] This was a more difficult task than perhaps it sounds; for after 241 BC the old practice of creating new tribes to take in newly acquired territory was abandoned, and new lands were thenceforth assigned to one or more of the existing tribes.[367] The result was that in the first century, and particularly after the enfranchisement of the Italian communities in the eighties, the mass of Roman tribes were no longer single units, as once they had been, but collections of a large number of often widely separated units. Thus, Cicero's tribe consisted of at least five sections, one near Rome, one round Arpinum, one in Umbria, one in Samnite territory, and one in the toe of Italy. It was the mark of the able candidate, therefore, that he knew where to concentrate his effort and establish his connections. He required to control at least as many tribes as would assure him of a majority in the full assembly and to devote his attention to those particular sections of these tribes as would inevitably yield a sufficient majority of individual voters.

The importance and complexity of this exercise has commonly been obscured by the supposition that there existed some form of bond between fellow-tribesmen which disposed them frequently to vote predominantly in a single sense or for a single candidate. In fact, however, the association of citizens in a single tribe was very much an artificial one. A closer and more natural association sprang from living in close proximity, as Cicero frequently recognizes;[368] for people who lived as neighbours were subject to the same social and economic influences and were numbered among the friends and dependants of the same local notables. At best, it would seem, the tribe served as a means of contact with the uncommitted during the last stages of a campaign at Rome. There is reason to believe that each tribe had a central headquarters in the city.[369] Here full registers will have been kept, and it is not unlikely that the tribal officials there had a more detailed knowledge of those members of the tribe who were present in Rome for the vote than anyone else. Indeed, if, as we have suggested, voters were required to present credentials at the time of voting, it is not impossible that they collected some special token of identification from the tribal headquarters in advance. The information which the tribal officers could provide would, of course, have been useful to all candidates in an election, but perhaps particularly so to a candidate who came from the same tribe himself in that a noble could traditionally extend a limited amount of hospitality to his fellow *tribules* during the course of his election campaign without falling foul of the laws on corruption.

It was this particular opportunity which the candidate enjoyed to contact his own *tribules* in Rome and to confer services upon them, together of course with the natural preponderance of fellow tribesmen among his neighbours at his country seat, that accounts for the emphasis in the tradition upon candidates' special associations with their *tribules*.[370] It is undeniable that a candidate was normally expected to be able to carry his own tribe, although clearly when two candidates came from the same tribe this could not always be. But this was a very small part of the battle. It was necessary to carry at least seventeen others, and, to achieve this, a candidate had to rely substantially upon the efforts of his friends. 'Name any tribe', remarks Cicero, when speaking of the election of Plancius to the aedilate, 'and I will tell you through whom he carried it.'[371] It seems likely that Cicero is here referring to influential friends at Rome who contacted, befriended and mobilized in Plancius' cause the voters present for the vote, and who therefore effected in their own respective tribes what Plancius himself could only effect in his own.

At major elections it is likely that this last-minute activity in Rome was of considerably less importance than has commonly been suggested. The vital preparatory work was done months before the election, as we have seen, and in the case of the established noble families, of course, the foundation for a broad basis of support over a wide area had often been laid many years in advance. In her recent work *The Voting Districts of the Roman Republic*, Lily Ross Taylor lays rightful stress upon two of the

most important aspects of this long-term planning of the nobility
—the readiness of members of the governing class to change their
tribe and domicile as Rome expanded from the fourth century
onwards, and the influential role played by individual magistrates
in enfranchising new citizens and assigning them to particular
existing tribes. Unfortunately, however, her account is bedevilled
by the underlying implication that the noble was concerned
primarily to extend his influence within his own tribe.[372] In fact,
the opposite is true. When the nobles moved out onto rural
estates in new areas during the middle Republic, their change of
tribe was coincidental. Their purpose was to furnish themselves
with a wider following of clients and friends from a populous
area whence voters might reasonably be expected to travel to
Rome. The more tribes that might be represented among those
clients, the better would they be pleased. Analogous was the
later and more sophisticated practice of purchasing villas at
widely scattered points throughout Italy. Cicero himself had as
many as six. Similarly, when legislators or censors determined
the tribe to which a group of new citizens should be allocated,
they were concerned not primarily to associate the new citizens
with their own tribe, as Miss Taylor implies, but rather so to
dispose them as to ensure the greatest electoral advantage for
themselves and their descendants. Provided that they could
number the new citizens among their own potential adherents
(provided, that is, that they had themselves sponsored the grant
of citizenship), it will clearly have been in their interest to enrol
them in tribes which were *not* already firmly under their control.
Much, too, will have depended upon the geographical location
of the new area and its proximity to Rome; for if it was near at
hand a noble could gain considerably by placing it in a tribe which
had hitherto been dominated by a political opponent, whereas
if it was at some distance and could not be expected to send
many voters to Rome it could only help to allot it to a tribe in
which the control was at best evenly balanced.

THE DELIVERY OF THE VOTE IN TRIBAL ASSEMBLIES

In the centuriate assembly the result of a vote was normally determined by members of the upper property classes. In the tribal assemblies, on the other hand, wealth was theoretically of no consequence, and every citizen had an equal voice. For this reason the vote in the tribal assemblies was undoubtedly somewhat more difficult to control, and the outcome less predictable.[373] It is noteworthy, for example, that, when Cicero's friends decided that he should be recalled from exile in 57 BC, it was exceptionally a centuriate assembly rather than a tribal assembly which they summoned to pass the necessary resolution. But it is unwise to generalize too much about the tribal assemblies on the basis of evidence which relates largely to the violent and disordered days of the first century. The tight hold which the nobility kept over the lower magistracies, as well as its successful management of legislation, bears witness to its ability throughout most of the Republican period adequately to control attendances at the tribal as well as at the centuriate assemblies.

Tribal elections should be considered separately from other voting for the simple reason that they, and they alone, normally took place in the same period as the major elections. They could therefore readily be attended by most of those who had made their annual journey to Rome primarily to take part in the election of consuls and praetors. These were, of course, men of means who could hope to make their voices felt in the centuriate assembly; and, although they represented but a very small proportion of the entire citizen body, it is very probable that these voters from the first or second property classes frequently constituted a majority within their respective tribes of those who actually attended the minor elections. Certainly, there can have been few others with the time, the money, or the inclination to travel to Rome from the outlying areas, and those members of the rural tribes who were domiciled in the city cannot have been very many until the last years of the Republic.[374] It should, of course, be recognized that the primary purpose of most of these voters in coming to Rome will have been to cast their votes in the major elections, and that they will have been induced to attend by the consular or praetorian candidates rather than by the candidates for lower office. Nevertheless, there was no doubt an inclination on their part to support for minor office the political associates of those whom they had come to elect as consuls or praetors, and, if their minds were not made up, they will have been prey for organized canvassing from the moment that they arrived in the city. Indeed, there is a case for supposing that the last-minute electioneering conducted by candidates and their friends on a tribal basis, to which reference has already been made, played a very much more vital role in the run up to the minor elections than it did in the run up to the major elections.

From the middle of the second century at least it was prohibited by law to hold a legislative vote within three weeks either side of the elections (cf. p. 148). The object of this rule may not have been so much to keep political demagogy out of the electoral campaign as simply to ensure that elections retained their essential character as true tests of the candidates' standing and of the extent of their respective personal followings. Its effect was that legislative assemblies were very much more sparsely attended. There is little reason to suppose that this did not suit the purpose of the governing oligarchy, particularly as it seems to have had little difficulty in suspending the rule when the occasion demanded.[375] In the comparatively settled days of the middle Republic, when the great majority of those domiciled in the city were registered in the urban tribes, the outcome of legislative votes was determined by those members of the rural tribes, however few in number, who could be brought in from the country areas. It was therefore of no small advantage to the would-be legislator to introduce his bills at a time when the only sizable group of rural citizens present would be those whom he himself had specially arranged to bring in to Rome for the occasion. This must also have worked well for the oligarchy as a whole, so long as the magistrates remained loyal to senatorial traditions, and so long as virtually all bills were first presented to the Senate for its blessing. The assured absence of the large mass of electoral voters, whose views on the content of legislative proposals were untested, guaranteed that the tribal assemblies could be managed with the minimum of fuss.

Towards the end of the second century, of course, the situation in tribal legislative assemblies was changed radically, as senatorial authority itself came under concerted attack from the *populares*, and as individual magistrates were tempted to follow a more independent course of action. The behaviour of the Gracchus brothers and others, who used their traditional magisterial control over the tribal assembly to carry radical and anti-Senatorial legislation, may well have prompted a reversal in conservative attitudes and some substantial rethinking as to how the tribal assembly might most effectively be controlled in future. It has been remarked in an earlier chapter that the policy of confining the urban population to the four urban tribes was progressively abandoned in the post-Gracchan era; and it is not impossible that this was a development which was, if not inspired, at least abetted by those conservative elements who sought a way of reasserting their control over the tribal assembly. Now that this control was beginning to be threatened, instead of guaranteed, by the opportunity which the initiating magistrate enjoyed to regulate the attendance of voters from the country, many of the nobility may well have been quite happy to see the tribal assembly transformed gradually into a body dominated by the urban population, whose regular attendance would be predictable, and whose vote they might themselves hope to influence more directly. It is at 'east significant that several of the radical reformers of the pre-Sullan period, such as, for example, the Gracchi and Saturninus, relied heavily upon potential voters imported from outside the city, and that they were repeatedly thwarted by the mass of urban voters who lent support to the Senatorial cause.[376]

In the event, of course, the gradual transformation of the legislative body into an urban-dominated one proved to be an unmitigated disaster for the Republican regime. While the Senate may have succeeded for a time in manipulating and controlling the urban voters in the tribal assemblies, it was not long before other more sinister and disruptive elements came to recognize that the same voters could readily be bent to their own will. In the last years of the Republic several attempts were made by those ambitious for power to flood the tribal assembly with a large *clientela* of newly enfranchised freedmen,[377] and when these efforts failed, resort was had to more direct methods, first to blatant demagogy, and then to organized hooliganism and armed intimidation.

MALPRACTICE IN THE CANVASS

The accepted rules governing the conduct of the electoral canvass underwent considerable modification during the course of the Republic. The early laws directed against travel outside the city and self-advertisement soon fell into abeyance and must clearly have been recognized as unnecessary and unrealistic by the end of the fourth century, when Rome's territory and citizen population was appreciably extended. Indeed, in the later years candidates travelled widely to make contacts with the vital tribal concentrations of voters, and their advertising campaigns had become an established ritual.[378] For several months before the elections a candidate arranged for himself to be saluted each morning at his house by an imposing crowd of retainers, and during the last twenty-four days he paraded the city streets, making personal appeals in a toga conspicuously whitened with chalk (*candidata*), and often attended by a band of followers known as *sectatores*.[379] All this was accepted as unobjectionable in the days of Cicero. What concerned the legislators in this period was the manner in which the candidates used their personal wealth to buy votes.

To judge from the record of legislation on the subject, bribery on any appreciable scale first appears to have become a serious problem in the second century. This was an age of fast-growing empire and lucrative campaigning; vast wealth was consequently falling into the hands of the foremost citizens and the opportunity for profitably investing such wealth was still extremely limited. The several repressive laws of the second century were undoubtedly severe, and Polybius suggests that by comparison with those of Greek communities they were effective.[380] It is probable, however, that they were directed against the cruder and more direct forms of bribery which were easy to detect. From the spate of legislation on the subject which was found necessary in the first century[381] and from the details provided in such speeches of Cicero as the *Pro Plancio* and the *Pro Murena* it would appear that the Romans soon found more devious ways of distributing largesse. What emerges from the evidence is that many of the restrictions were extremely easy to evade, and that the distinction between criminal practice and behaviour which was hallowed by custom was so difficult to draw as to render much of the legislation virtually ineffective.

Perhaps the least offensive form of corruption consisted in finding a legal basis for the distribution of benefits at a time sufficiently close to an election as to influence the choice of the voters. Thus, the aediles frequently took advantage of their responsibility for staging public games to supplement the state funds provided for the purpose from their own pocket, and so attract support for their own imminent candicacy for higher office. Private individuals, too, were prone to choose an opportune moment to provide public banquets or shows in honour of deceased members of their families—a practice which went unchallenged until 63 BC, when a law of Cicero required that such entertainment could only be staged if provision had specifically been made for it in a will.[382]

A practice equally hallowed by ancestral custom, and yet one which was much and increasingly abused, was the adoption by an individual of the role of beneficent patron towards his fellow *tribules*. The favours he extended may have taken many forms— an invitation to a banquet perhaps, the reservation of good seats at a place of entertainment, or even the simple gift. The ancestral right of the *nobilis* to act in this way towards his *tribules* is beyond dispute and is defended by Cicero in the *Pro Murena*.[383] But of course there was a distinction between a *beneficium* conferred in the context of a personal relationship and one extended to an unidentified mass, and this was a distinction which the legislation of the late Republic clearly intended to draw when it strove to render mass entertainment at an individual's expense illegal. Unfortunately, however, to judge from the arguments employed by Cicero in defence of those of his clients who were accused of electoral bribery, such legislation had little positive effect. It proved very difficult to establish the impersonal nature of such benefits in a court of law.

As has been stressed, the success of an electoral campaign depended upon a candidate's winning the support not only of his own tribe, but of at least seventeen other tribes in addition. Bribery, therefore, to be effective, had to be widespread. Although the distribution of largesse outside one's own tribe was strictly contrary to the law, methods were undoubtedly found which proved effective. Among the most blatant was the use of those tribal officers known as *divisores*, whose legitimate business it had always been to distribute benefits and personal gifts among the members of their own tribe.[384] In fact, in the Ciceronian age at least, it was quite common for a candidate to summon and employ the *divisores* of a large number of tribes for a similar purpose.[385] In 67 BC, it is true, an attempt was made to check this abuse by making the *divisores* as well as the candidates responsible for any electoral abuse;[386] but the *divisores* themselves, who found this a very profitable service, put up a stout resistance at the time, and there were too many interested parties for the law to be rigorously enforced. Another abuse was the organization and employment of associations within the tribes known as *sodalicia*, which made it their business to keep a careful check of the tribesmen present in Rome, and which arranged for the most effective distribution of bribes in the interests of whoever was prepared to pay the highest price. These too were attacked, by a law of Crassus in 55 BC, but Cicero's successful defence of his client, Plancius, suggests that the legislation was comparatively ineffective.[387]

A less reprehensible method of influencing the votes of those who were not one's own tribesmen was to employ the services of one's political friends in other tribes. In his defence both of Murena and of Plancius Cicero is at some pains to establish that the entertainment and gifts offered to those who were not of his client's own tribe had in fact been provided by his friends. This canvass by friends was a well-established custom, which was presumably perfectly legitimate provided that the money expended came out of the pockets of the friends and not that of the candidate himself. But this it was, of course, impossible to control; and it was perhaps for this reason that the younger Cato, when he stood for the consulship, felt impelled to ask the Senate to pass a decree forbidding anyone to conduct an electoral canvass except the candidate himself. According to Plutarch, this extreme and untraditional step proved very unpopular not only with the candidates, but also with the electorate, who were cheated of their customary bribes; and it virtually ensured Cato's rejection.[388]

In most of its forms, as we have seen, bribery at elections was facilitated by respect for a traditional code of behaviour. There was, however, one practice, almost certainly encouraged by the spread of electoral corruption, which was fundamentally anathema to the Roman ethic. That was the practice known as *coitio*—the pooling of campaigning effort by two or more candidates in their common interest. It is unlikely that *coitio* was in itself illegal, as several scholars, among them Mommsen, have claimed.[389] We hear of a case as early as 184 BC, when the candidates in a censorial election banded together, albeit without success, to secure the electorate's rejection of their common rival, M. Porcius Cato;[390] and there were several other examples in Cicero's day which were common knowledge.[391] For obvious reasons, however, the practice did strike at the root of a political system in which candidates for magistracy stood solely on their own merits and not as proponents of a party policy, and in which a noble's successes and failures were viewed as measures of the strength of his *clientela*. Any suggestion of *coitio* in a bribery charge was, therefore, likely to prejudice a jury against the accused—a fact which could well partly account for the prominence of the theme in the various prosecutions of the Ciceronian period.[392] But there is also a further point. *Coitio* can hardly have served much purpose or have been particularly effective except when it found expression in some form of electoral bribery, whether it were a joint contribution to mass entertainment, or a common hiring of *divisores* and *sodalicia* to canvass with monetary gifts, or, to take a concrete example from the year 54 BC, a joint advance offer of a bribe to the prerogative century.[393] Proof of *coitio* thus offered a presumption of bribery; and it seems probable that a charge of *coitio* was one which might in certain circumstances have been considerably easier to substantiate than one of simple corruption. Evidence of a joint canvass cannot have been difficult to produce, and the voting figures themselves may frequently have been revealing. It is known from the *Pro Plancio* that the prosecution attached no small importance to the fact that in certain tribes the number of individual votes cast for two of the candidates in an aedilician election had been almost exactly equal![394]

MANIPULATION OF THE STATE RELIGION

One of the most effective ways in which members of the nobility could control or influence voting was by invoking the aid of the state religion. As the priestly colleges were in their hands, they were in a position to use their authority either to prevent voting taking place altogether, or to secure the nullification of a vote if it did not have the desired result.

A common preventative measure in the last century of the Republic was so to interfere with the calendar as to ensure that political enemies did not have the opportunity to introduce hostile legislation. Thus the college of *pontifices* might be induced to refrain from inserting the intercalary month which was due to be inserted every two years in order to correct the Roman calendar. This would often have had the effect of depriving a would-be legislator of vital extra comitial days which at a time when the number of days set aside for comitial business was considerably restricted he may well have needed.[395] But a more common manœuvre designed to achieve the same end was to arrange religious festivals and celebrations in such a way as to create the maximum interference with comitial business. In some cases established festivals were declared faulty and repeated, and special periods of thanksgiving were decreed for no other purpose than to use up comitial time. It is possible that this type of manœuvre made its appearance only in the later days of the Republic, when the threat of militant tribunes to the Establishment became serious; but there are many examples of it in that period, and it is openly and unashamedly commended by Cicero in a letter to his brother Quintus. 'Lentulus', he writes, 'is a very good consul. He has got rid of all the comitial days, for even the Latin festival is being performed again and there has been no lack of thanks-givings. In this way disastrous legislation has been prevented.'[396]

The Romans' respect for auspices also provided the politicians with a ready means of interfering with the voting in a popular assembly. Before undertaking any public act at Rome a magistrate was required by tradition to enquire the will of Jupiter through the taking of the auspices. At the time of a comitial vote he would himself repair to the voting arena before dawn and watch for favourable signs in the heavens. If the signs were not favourable, he could not technically proceed. Nor indeed could he proceed if at any time before or during the holding of the assembly an unfavourable omen was observed or reported either by himself or by any other person who was recognized by law as one who could effectively interpret such signs. Such a person could be a fellow-magistrate, a member of the augural college, or, since the passing of the *leges Aelia et Fufia* in the second century, even a tribune of the plebs.[397]

This traditional respect for the auspices naturally lent itself to abuse, and our sources provide us with many examples. A presiding magistrate might himself postpone an assembly before the start on the ground of unfavourable auspices, if he felt that the nature of the attendance was such as to militate against his interests. More commonly he would arrange to see or hear an unfavourable omen when the voting was in mid-course. Thus in 55 BC, when Pompey was presiding over the praetorian elections and the conservative Cato had already been returned by the all-important prerogative century, he claimed to hear thunder and so procured the postponement of the election until such time as bribery and intimidation could be relied upon to bring about a more acceptable outcome.[398] And again, in 44 BC, when Antonius was conducting the consular elections after Caesar's assassination, he called off the assembly on augural grounds when the centuries of the entire first class had already voted.[399] Political opponents, of course, could also effectively use such tactics. In the Ciceronian age votes were frequently held up by the announcement of some religious obstruction by a hostile magistrate or tribune. The object was either to bar some unacceptable piece of legislation or to defer the holding of elections until an electorate more favourably disposed to the cause of the obstructor could be assembled.[400] On some occasions it may even have been to prevent the holding of elections until the existing magistrates had gone out of office, and so to ensure that the responsibility for filling the vacancies would lie with an *interrex*. For those, like Pompey in 55 BC, who were in a position to ensure the nomination of a series of friendly *interreges* in such circumstances the prospect of a vote in which the populace was merely called upon to accept or reject two nominees of the *interrex* was far preferable to that of a full-scale election at which the voters exercised total freedom of selection.[401]

This form of reliance upon religious obstruction almost reached the point of absurdity in 59 BC, when during Caesar's first consulship his colleague, Bibulus, announced his intention of watching the heavens continuously for the rest of the year with a view to preventing Caesar from putting any matter to the vote.[402] Although Caesar ignored this obstruction and rode roughshod over tradition, he thereby incurred considerable public odium and provided his opponents with an unanswerable case for declaring his subsequent legislation invalid.

In earlier times the abuse of the state religion may not have been quite so blatant as it appears to have been in the age of Cicero. But, if we read less of obstructive action by individual magistrates, we hear more of corporate interference with the will of the assemblies by the entire augural college, which had the right to declare any law or election invalid on religious grounds long after all the voting procedure had been completed. During the later Republic, after the introduction of an element of popular election, the augural college was not normally as united as once it had been; but earlier, when it was a closed, self-appointing body, it often fell under the domination of one prominent political faction, which may on occasions have used it quite ruthlessly to further its policies and promote its factional interests. Cases of elections declared invalid extend from as early as 326 to as late as 163 BC,[403] and there are strong arguments for the view that for a long period before, and for some time during, the Hannibalic War the augural college was used by the controlling family of the Fabii to influence both foreign policy and military strategy.[404]

What is remarkable about these procedures is that they are accepted by Cicero and others as both necessary and salutary. The principle that it was right and proper for members of the nobility to deceive the people in matters of religion was accepted by the famous *pontifex maximus*, Q. Mucius Scaevola; and Cicero makes it very clear in his *De Legibus* that the use or misuse of the auspices and of augural authority was an essential feature in his ideal state. 'Magisterial auspices', he says, 'were meant to secure the postponement of many unprofitable assemblies by providing plausible excuses for delay. The gods have often suppressed the unjust pronouncements of the popular will by means of the auspices.'[405]

THE INFLUENCE OF THE PRESIDING MAGISTRATE

Perhaps the man who was in the best position to influence the outcome of a vote without actually violating the law was the presiding magistrate himself. This was because he alone had control of the voting procedures.

As has been argued in an earlier chapter, there is a strong case for the view that, at least in legislative assemblies, the presiding magistrate enjoyed the right personally to select the men who would be the first to cast their votes within each tribe, and so, by advertising the support given by prominent citizens for his measures, to set a pattern of voting which the majority would be prone to follow. Another useful weapon in his armoury was his right to make up the numbers of any voting unit from which less than five voters were present by transferring to it persons who were officially registered in another.[406] This right was probably only invoked at legislative assemblies, when attendances, particularly from the more distant tribal areas, were much smaller, and when the absence of a quorum of voters from any particular tribe might well on occasions have been comparatively simple to arrange. The management of the assembly responsible for Cicero's exile by the tribune P. Clodius serves as a good example of the exercise and abuse of this discretionary power. Having first ensured that the voters he did not want were barred from the voting arena by force, he then proceeded to fill up the empty voting units with chosen hirelings from among the freedmen and slaves.[407]

At an election the presiding magistrate had wider powers. He had the right to accept or to refuse any candidate's nomination, and he apparently enjoyed what might well be regarded as the logical extension of this right—the power to take no account of votes cast for a candidate whose nomination he had refused when making his voting returns. In later times, it would appear, this power was rarely invoked, and then probably only on strictly legal grounds, as for example when Marius in 100 BC refused to recognize the candidature of Glaucia for the consulship because his election would have violated the *lex annalis* which stipulated that a two-year period should elapse between praetorship and consulship.[408] But it is clear that the powers were discretionary and beyond dispute. Almost certainly they stemmed from the fact that in law the magistrate of one year was still essentially the 'creator' of his successor in office. The increasing freedom of choice exercised by the assembly in elections represented a concession which apparently had no binding force in law and which did not therefore detract from the latent authority of the presiding magistrate.

A course of action which had the same legal basis and which, though perhaps less offensive than a refusal to recognize a candidate's performance, was equally effective was that of calling a halt to voting proceedings in mid-course and demanding that they be started anew. These were the tactics employed on a number of occasions during periods of crisis in the Hannibalic War. In the elections for 214 BC, for example, the prerogative century named two persons who in the opinion of the presiding magistrate, Q. Fabius Maximus, were not suitable for taking command in the field. He therefore stopped proceedings forthwith, put his case to the assembled electorate, and called upon the prerogative century to choose again, with the result that the original selection was changed and he was himself elected both by the prerogative and all succeeding centuries to serve for another term.[409] A very similar incident occurred four years later, in which the same Q. Fabius was involved;[410] and, if we are to believe Livy, there was a precedent from the time of the Samnite Wars for interrupting the voting procedure at a much later stage—in fact after the entire first class had named its choice.[411] The lack of comment in the tradition makes it very probable that the presiding magistrates in each case were regarded as being quite within their rights. Whether there were many, or indeed any, other occasions when a presiding consul resorted to the same tactics it is, of course, impossible to say; but it appears likely that there was a tendency in the later Republic to defer to a greater extent to the principle of popular sovereignty and so to rely on more sophisticated methods, such as an appeal to faulty auspices, to reverse a comitial decision.

ILLEGALITY AND FRAUD

In an altogether different category from behaviour which had the backing of either law or ancestral custom were those activities which were manifestly illegal or fraudulent. The tactics of violence and intimidation which were so deplorable a feature of the last period of the Republic are a case in point. Sulla set the pattern in 88 BC for turning the city into an armed camp and using soldiers to frighten the voters into accepting his legislation, and his example was undoubtedly followed by Caesar when he was consul in 59 BC. More common, however, was the employment of bands of hired thugs, to intimidate, to cause a general disturbance, or simply to debar unwanted voters from entering the voting arena. These methods, as we have seen, enabled the tribune Clodius to pass the bill resulting in Cicero's exile, and exactly the same methods helped his arch-enemy, Milo, to prevent Clodius from carrying even his own tribe when he stood as candidate for the aedilate.[412] If the disruptors were not strong enough in numbers to control the attendance at an assembly, they could always resort to interfering with the actual voting procedures. As early as 133 BC the opponents of Tiberius Gracchus resorted to removing the apparatus for conducting the lot,[413] while thirty years later an attack was mounted against an assembly of the popular tribune Saturninus by the conservative Caepio which resulted not only in the removal of the voting urns but also in the dismantling of the *pontes*.[414]

The Roman voting system, like any other, was of course open to more subtle forms of abuse. At assemblies where the tribes voted successively, for example, there can have been little to stop an individual from casting his vote in more than one voting unit, if he felt so inclined. An identity check such as we have envisaged would have gone some way towards making this more difficult, particularly if the voter was required to hand in a token at the time of voting which had been specially issued for the purpose. But it would presumably always have been possible to borrow or buy proof of identity from those who had no intention of attending.

Another device which may or may not have been commonly used, but to which Cicero makes reference in the *De Domo*, was that of arranging for there to be two candidates at an election who bore the same initials.[415] As it was the custom at Rome for voters to record their votes by inscribing the initials of candidates on their ballots rather than the full names, this could lead to considerable confusion in the counting, which might be used to advantage. Technically, of course, *custodes* were nominated by each candidate to be present at the count, and it might be thought that there would be little opportunity for fraud at this stage. But, if a candidate was willing to allow himself to be used in this way, his *custodes* could presumably be appropriately instructed. Perhaps the most effective way of bringing off this manœuvre was to have a fellow candidate with the same initials as oneself who was prepared to concede all doubtful initialled votes.

More common, perhaps, was some form of interference with the actual ballots. In 61 BC, when there was a proposal before the assembly that a jury be set up to try the young P. Clodius on a charge of sacrilege, some of the *custodes*, who were Clodius' henchmen and had presumably been appointed by a friendly consul, distributed ballots which made provision only for a negative vote.[416] What sort of effect this gambit had upon the voting figures is not known; but, although it could not have prevented ardent supporters of the motion from inscribing the appropriate words—*uti rogas*—or their abbreviation on the tablet and erasing the negative *antiquo*, it was obviously expected appreciably to decrease the number of affirmative votes cast. It is very possible that the manœuvre effectively undermined the secrecy of the ballot in that those voting in favour of the of the proposal would perforce make themselves conspicuous by writing upon their voting tablets with their *stili*. In these times of mob violence there may have been many who were unwilling to expose themselves to reprisals.

On another occasion, at an election of aediles, M. Cato noticed, presumably at the time of the counting of votes, that several of the ballots had been inscribed in the same hand.[417] It is not to be supposed that any one voter could have cast multiple votes, at least within the same voting group; and therefore this pheno- menon can presumably be explained in only one of two ways. It is possible that marked ballots, inscribed with the names of candi- dates, had been distributed to some voters instead of blank ballots. In this case the result would have been much the same as at the legislative vote on Clodius' sacrilege which we have just discussed. It would have been open to voters to change the initials on the tablet, but only at the cost of drawing attention to themselves in so doing. Another possibility, and a more credible theory perhaps, is that numbers of pre-prepared ballots were somehow introduced into the ballot boxes after the completion of the voting and before the counting was far under way. This could presumably only have been engineered by one or more of the *custodes*. It is interesting that a similar malpractice—perhaps even the same malpractice—is recorded by Varro, who tells of an aedilician election in the late Republic at which someone was caught red-handed during the counting process stuffing ballots into a *loculus*.[418] There is unfortunately some dispute as to what a *loculus* may have been. One suggestion is that it was a container for discarded ballots for which the counters had no further use; if this were so, the fraud recounted by Varro consisted in the premature transference of unfavourable and as yet uncounted ballots to the discard pile. Another view, however, is that the *loculus* was either the voting urn itself or some receptacle for as yet uncounted ballots, in which case the guilty *custos* must have been introducing non-genuine ballots prior to the count.

Any opportunity for fraud on the part of the presiding magistrate at a vote must have been limited to some form of manipulation of the process of sortition. One very uncomplicated method would have been simply to give a false report of the results of the sortition, but it is unlikely that in normal circumstances this would have been possible. In Cicero's speech against the Rullan bill in 63 BC, it is true, the allegation is made that Rullus intended fraudulently to conduct a lot with a view to choosing the seventeen tribes which would constitute a special assembly under his bill and that to this end he would dispense with the services of a *custos*.[419] The charge is a wild and exaggerated one, and it forms part of his demagogic outcry against what he represented as the imminent threat of dictatorship. It provides no basis for the view that this was a known practice at the time. Later, however, when dictatorship became a reality, the sortition may well have become just such a mockery as Cicero envisaged. The poet Lucan suggests that the election of Caesar to one of his later consulships was wholly faked. 'He sings out the names of the tribes', he writes, 'and spins the urn which in fact is empty', clearly implying that the entire process of determining the order in which the results of the voting should be announced was a hollow sham and that the order was in fact predetermined.[420]

More feasible perhaps in normal times may have been prior interference with the lots designed to ensure that certain lots emerged before others. As early as the first half of the second century the playwright Plautus parodied an electoral sortition in a passage which shows him to have been aware of the advantage to be gained by using a lot of slightly smaller size or lighter wood than the others.[421] Such a lot could be relied upon to come out of the urn or pitcher first; and to this extent any person or group of persons who controlled the insertion of the lots was in a position to influence the outcome of the sortition to a limited extent. Even if it be supposed, however, that the presiding magistrate was commonly in a position so to interfere with the fairness of the lot, his opportunity by this means to determine the overall result of a comitial vote was severely limited. At a centuriate election it might have been possible to predetermine the identity of the prerogative century in this way; and, if the vote of the prerogative century had such an influence on the final outcome of the election as is suggested by Cicero and as is indicated by the heavy bribery of that century in 54 BC, this would have been a most effective manœuvre. Any tampering with the process of sortition which determined the order in which the results from the various groups was announced, however, would have been a very much more complex affair. For one thing, the technical difficulties would have been more formidable, since it would have been necessary to ensure not that one lot came out before the rest, but that at least half the lots came out before the other half. But there is the further point that in general a presiding magistrate would have found it difficult to be certain in what order the returns should be announced to produce the desired result. There may indeed have been a few occasions when the voting intentions of certain units were known before the vote; but more often than not he would have needed to have sight of the preliminary returns and to do some quite detailed calculations before being able to assess how the results could be ordered to his best advantage. There is only one suggestion in our sources that a fraud of this kind was perpetrated—a supposed allegation by Gaius Gracchus and his friends that the order of announcing the results in a tribunician election in 122 BC had been rigged to deprive him of victory.[422] The story may be quite false, but the very fact that it could be spread about is perhaps enough to indicate that the Romans looked upon such a fraudulent operation as feasible.

CONCLUSION

It would be unfortunate if any undue concentration upon the subject matter of this chapter were to convey the impression that there was something hollow and unreal about Roman voting procedures or indeed that the vote did not normally serve as a true expression of the popular will. This is very far from the truth. As far as ballot-rigging and other forms of outright fraud are concerned, it is likely that they were as rare at Rome as they are in the modern democratic state. Apart from the fact that misdemeanours of this kind invariably make news, it would in any case be wrong to assess the frequency of electoral abuse on the basis of evidence which relates exclusively to the lawless and violent days of the late second and first centuries which were so untypical of the Republican period as a whole. Similarly, it is reasonable to assume that abuse of religious taboos and undue reliance upon the overriding magisterial *imperium* were the exception rather than the rule, and that, even when magistrates did have recourse to such means in order to interfere with or revoke popular decisions, they were not regarded as doing more than imposing a legitimate sanction. The open approval which Cicero gives to these tactics is an indication that they were no more than accepted safeguards against hasty and ill-considered decisions, such as are commonly built into the most enlightened of constitutions.

To those who are accustomed to the workings of modern democracy, it is true, the elaborate preparations which preceded any comitial vote, and more particularly an election, at Rome may well appear to have made a mockery of the entire proceedings. To believe this, however, is altogether to misunderstand the nature and purpose of the Roman election. Although there were undoubtedly occasions when the outcome of major elections had some bearing upon official policy-making, the election itself was rarely, if ever, seen by the electorate as providing them with an opportunity to choose between rival political parties or opposing political programmes, as does the election of today. It was viewed as a trial of strength between two or more persons who stood entirely on their own merits. Once this is recognized, the Roman electoral campaign, the elaborate efforts which were made to regulate attendances at the *comitia*, and even the less extreme forms of bribery appear as legitimate and integral ploys in the electoral game. The important thing is that it was a game of which the voting public fully understood the rules, and one which for the greater part of the Republican era it was perfectly content to play.

CHAPTER XII

ELECTIONS IN THE IMPERIAL AGE

ELECTIONS AT ROME

DURING THE LAST YEARS of the Republican age the annual elections became the scene of increasing disturbance and the voting assembly found itself subjected repeatedly to irresistible pressures. Then in 49 BC came the Civil War and with Julius Caesar's victory the establishment of an authoritarian regime which made little pretence of preserving electoral freedom. By the *lex Antonia* of 44 BC Caesar appears to have been given the legal right to appoint half of the annual magistrates by direct nomination and in so doing to by-pass the popular assembly altogether;[423] even in cases where the assembly retained its nominal right of choice, both Caesar and the triumvirs who followed him took steps to ensure that the voters were fully aware of their own wishes and that for the most part they acted upon them. When therefore Augustus, or Octavian as he then was, emerged after the battle of Actium as the undisputed leader of the Roman world, a full quarter of a century or more had elapsed since Rome had witnessed the conduct of a free and orderly election campaign.

Anxious to learn from the mistakes of Caesar, Augustus made it his chief concern at the outset of his principate to reconcile the maintenance of his own overriding personal authority with the basic principles of the Republican constitution. To this end, therefore, he made some show of restoring the magisterial elections to their traditional form[424] and at one stage he even toyed with the notion of securing fairer representation of the more distant Italian areas by introducing some form of a postal vote.[425]

Whether he originally intended these arrangements to be permanent or temporary, however, he soon realized that they were unworkable. The restoration of free elections was an ideal which was rendered unattainable partly by the recent course of history, and partly—and perhaps more particularly—by Augustus' retention of a pre-eminence which, although in many ways less offensive than that of his predecessors, was nevertheless recognized to be very real. As has already been remarked, the active interest of the mass of the voters in the outcome of elections had begun to wane from as far back as the early second century BC, and those who had travelled to Rome to record their vote had tended to do so almost exclusively as a service to a patron. From the point of view of the nobility the elections had come to be viewed essentially as trials of strength reflecting the size and amenability of their respective *clientelae*. It follows, therefore, that once the delicate balance of influence existing between individual noble families and groups had been disturbed by the impact of the Julian family upon traditional loyalties, the popular election ceased to be a meaningful operation. The voters, who had long since stopped playing an influential role and who naturally came to look upon Augustus as their potential benefactor and patron-in-chief, were no doubt less inclined than ever to participate in an exercise which for them was of little or no consequence; while the nobles themselves were surely quite happy to rid themselves of the unrewarding and burdensome chore of a canvass which no longer served its traditional purpose and which could of course be thwarted at a stroke by Augustus' giving the merest hint of his own personal preferences.[426]

In AD 5 Augustus took the realistic step of transferring the effective voice in the major elections from the *comitia centuriata* to a select assembly consisting of senators and those members of the equestrian order who sat on the public courts. The function of this body is defined in the Tabula Hebana as *destinatio* (literally, a 'marking out' for office), and the object of the proceedings was to produce a single list of candidates containing only as many names as there were offices to be filled. This is made absolutely clear by the detailed provisions of the inscription. The senators

and *equites* were grouped together for voting purposes into artificial 'centuries' numbering at first ten and later fifteen and twenty;
and the procedure prescribed for announcing the results of the
voting followed very closely the pattern established in the full
assemblies of the Republican period. The lot was used to determine the order in which the various centuries should have their
results announced, and the declaration ceased as soon as a sufficient
number of candidates to fill the offices had been secured by a bare
absolute majority of units. How exactly *destinatio* was related to
creatio (formal election), which remained the prerogative of the
comitia, is a controversial problem, the solution to which depends
to some extent upon the interpretation to be given to a partially
corrupt section of the epigraphical text. There are those who argue
that at first the centuries of this select assembly were viewed as
performing a function analogous to that of the prerogative century
of the Republic, and that the full *comitia* could technically take into
account the claims of those candidates whom the select assembly
had rejected. There are others who urge that the *comitia* must
have been restricted to accepting or rejecting the names of the
destinati.[427] But the issue is largely an academic one; for, even if
the *comitia* had been left with some freedom of choice in law, it is
difficult to believe that they would have been disposed to exercise
it. Even in Cicero's day the vote of the prerogative century had
been regarded as an omen. The prerogative vote of a select
body which was known to have been set up with Augustus'
approval and whose voting units were significantly named after
members of the Julian family can have been little short of decisive.

The inclusion of important elements from the equestrian order
in this select body has been variously explained. Perhaps the most
attractive suggestion is simply that Augustus wished his new
assembly to appear as a microcosm of the first property class of
the Republican *comitia centuriata*, and that he assigned a part to the
equites in tactful recognition of the controversial role which the
more influential among them had played in the electoral contests
of the late Republic.[428] But at all events their participation in the
major elections was fairly short-lived; for there is evidence enough
that at least from the time of Caligula the outcome of these and

of all other elections was determined by the Senate alone.[429] There are those, indeed, who maintain that the select assembly of senators and *equites* was virtually superseded by the Senate at the very start of Tiberius' principate, basing their conclusion upon Tacitus' statement that in AD 14 'the elections were for the first time transferred from the Campus to the Senate'.[430] But the words of Tacitus are at best ambiguous,[431] and the fact that the continued existence of the select assembly is proved for AD 19 by the Tabula Hebana is damaging to this thesis. A more attractive view is that the *equites* progressively came to recognize their own role in the new election process as an anachronism and an irrelevance and so began voluntarily to absent themselves from the select assembly in ever-increasing numbers. Presumably, when attendances had been drastically reduced, possibly before the death of Tiberius, the new assembly could readily have been disbanded and the move to the Senate effected without occasioning adverse comment.

Augustus could no doubt argue that these modifications in electoral procedure involved no fundamental breach of Republican precedent. Technically, the popular assembly remained the body which was formally responsible for the *creatio* of magistrates; and there is evidence that this remained the case in the time of Trajan and possibly even into the third century.[432] Nevertheless, the proceedings at comitial level are likely to have been reduced at a very early stage to a pure formality. As in the *comitia curiata* of the later Republic, the centuries and tribes are likely to have been represented by lictors who attended merely to witness the *renuntiatio* of the presiding magistrate; and it is noteworthy that already in the principate of Tiberius the magnificent marble *saepta* which had been constructed under Caesar and Augustus to house the voters on the Campus Martius were being used for such purposes as the display of wild animals.

Yet another factor which served to reduce elections to a mere shadow of what they had once been was the very considerable influence exercised by the Princeps over their outcome. This is to be explained partly in terms of his overriding *auctoritas*—that quality of pre-eminence which resulted in the expression of his every wish being treated as a virtual command—and partly in terms of a legal authority of which he exceptionally enjoyed continuous tenure.

The effect of *auctoritas* was seen most clearly in the use which the Princeps made of *commendatio*. As has been observed, it had been common practice in Republican days for prominent members of the governing class and of society at large both to canvass for their friends in person and to send candidates written recommendations in which they pledged their support and invited that of others. This had been an inoffensive enough practice so long as the influence exerted by the various leading noble families was reasonably balanced; but as soon as one man and one family acquired an authority and a personal following which far exceeded that of any of his contemporaries it naturally became a most potent threat to electoral freedom. Caesar, it has been said, secured the legal right to appoint half of the annual magistrates direct; but he also ensured himself effective control over the selection of the other half by arranging for his own recommendations to be circulated to all the tribes.[433] Augustus, of course, almost certainly behaved with more circumspection, but he did not abandon the Roman noble's traditional right to make his wishes publicly known. He indulged in canvassing,[434] and, when he grew too old for this activity, he formed the custom of publishing an official list of those whose candidature he favoured.[435] His *commendatio* was not of course binding in law, but that it was treated as binding in practice first by the *comitia*, and then in later years by the select assembly of senators and *equites* and by the Senate itself, there can be little question.[436] The candidates so indicated were officially described as *candidati Caesaris*;[437] and at the beginning of the Flavian period the *lex de imperio Vespasiani* went so far as to give them official recognition by providing that they should be returned as a group before the other candidates at the formal *renuntiatio*.

Needless to say, the Princeps had to show some restraint in his use of *commendatio* if the elections, even in their emasculated form, were to retain any semblance of reality. In AD 14, for example, Tiberius contented himself with recommending only four candidates for the praetorship, when the complement of the college was twelve; and this proportion of one third may have been accepted as the norm.[438] The position regarding the consulship is more doubtful. There were of course only two places to fill, and it is possible that Augustus himself rarely commended anyone. According to Tacitus, however, Tiberius occasionally hinted at his own preferences, even if he did not cite the candidates concerned by name,[439] and we know from an inscription of at least one consul who publicly claimed to have secured office on Tiberius' recommendation.[440] Later, intervention is likely to have become more common; and the younger Pliny indicates that by Trajan's time the control of the consulship by the Princeps was openly recognized.[441]

More problematical is the extent of the influence exerted over the elections by the Princeps through the exercise of his legal *imperium*. Augustus, of course, held the consulship continuously until 23 BC, and it is very likely that as from 19 BC he and his successors enjoyed full consular authority divorced from the office.[442] That this gave the Princeps the right to accept the *professio* of candidates, which was of course a magisterial prerogative, is generally accepted. What is in dispute is the manner and extent to which he chose to make use of this right. One common view is that he regularly published his own list of 'nominated' candidates alongside those of the two consuls, and that there was therefore each year, in addition to the recommended *candidati Caesaris*, a further and larger group of candidates who could claim the distinction of being upon the Princeps' own list. In this case, however, it is difficult to understand why candidates should ever have chosen to minimize their chances by making *professio* to one of the consuls rather than to the Princeps; and it is a more attractive suggestion that the Princeps gradually assumed sole responsibility for accepting the names of would-be candidates and in consultation with the consuls of the year producing a single, approved list.[443] In itself such a practice need have had little effect upon the conduct and outcome of an election—and indeed there are several cases of elections for the major magistracies in the early Principate which appear to have been keenly and genuinely contested;[444] but in practice it is likely that the Princeps came to exercise a very much more stringent control over nominations than did the Republican consuls. Both in AD 7, for example, and again in AD 14, when Augustus was on his deathbed and anxious to ensure a trouble-free succession for Tiberius, the number of candidates nominated for particular offices appears to have been restricted to the number of places to be filled.[445] At other times there is little doubt that the Princeps was responsible for at least some measure of pruning, as is clear from the fact that the publication of the official list of candidates was keenly awaited.[446]

All things considered, therefore, the electoral contests of the imperial age bore little practical resemblance to those of the free Republic. Within a very short space of time the effective right of suffrage came to be confined to members of the Senate, and even *their* freedom of choice was appreciably restricted both by the Princeps' use of *commendatio* and by the control which he chose to exercise over the composition of the lists of candidates. Not surprisingly the practice of the early Empire soon developed into theory. Whereas Dio, commenting on Augustus' restoration of popular elections, is content to remark simply that 'nothing was done of which the Princeps disapproved',[447] the later jurist expresses himself more bluntly. 'The appointment of magistrates', he writes, 'is the concern of the Princeps.'[448]

MUNICIPAL ELECTIONS

If the coming of the Principate quickly brought about the demise of the popular election at Rome, there is reason to believe that, for a time at least, it actually stimulated interest in the local elections in the municipalities. Some contribution to the vitality of local government had already been made by the municipal law of Julius Caesar, which in many places had been responsible for introducing forms and procedures directly analogous to those observed at Rome; and when the more influential members of Italian society found themselves no longer directly involved as pawns in the political game at Rome they quite naturally began to devote more time and interest to their local township.

The evidence which bears on municipal elections in the early

Empire is limited but none the less illuminating. Detailed information about procedures is provided by the extant text of the *lex Malacitana*, the charter given to the Spanish colony of Malaga in AD 84.[449] This reveals that the assembly used at elections was in almost every respect a model of the *comitia tributa* of the Roman Republic. Its component units were known as *curiae* rather than tribes, but, like the Roman tribes, these *curiae* were local divisions to which the citizens were assigned without distinction of wealth or birth. In the voting the secret ballot was employed, and the groups voted simultaneously as in the Campus Martius at Rome. Furthermore, the principle of election by absolute majority was observed in the declaration of results, and the other rules of procedure were in most other respects identical with those which were applied in the Republican assemblies.

But perhaps of even greater interest than the *lex Malacitana* are the many hundreds of political notices which have been found inscribed upon the walls and buildings of the once thriving township of Pompeii.[450] These throw welcome light upon the nature of local electoral campaigns, and they illustrate beyond dispute both that the contests for municipal office in this period were less contrived than contests for state magistracy had ever been, and that elections were events of immediate concern not only to members of a governing class or to a selection of their influential clients, but also to the great mass of private citizens in almost every walk of life.

The posters appear to deal with two stages in the electoral campaign. Some of them contain notices of nomination for office made either by named individuals or unnamed groups. Thus one inscription reads: 'M. Cerrinus Vatia is proposed for the aedilate by Nymphodotus and Caprasia', and another, less specifically, 'T. Claudius Veres is named for the post of duovir by his neighbours'. Others—by far the larger group—are concerned with the canvass for votes. These take many and various forms. There are of course the usual recommendations from citizen notables, which, as in the Republican state elections, may have been tantamount to directives addressed to clients and dependants. But the great majority were clearly less binding and were designed to do no more than influence public opinion. Some supposedly advertise the official line being adopted by groups in society or by particular trade guilds such as the goldsmiths, the fruit-dealers, the bakers, the muleteers, the fishmongers and others. Others leave the author unidentified and are aimed at drawing the attention of the populace to the particular merits and demerits of the candidates named. Thus one notice reads: 'If upright living is considered to be any recommendation, Lucretius Fronto is worthy of office', another 'I ask you to elect Julius Polybius to the aedilate. He procures good bread', and a third in more hostile and scurrilous a vein, 'Vatia is supported for the aedilate by all the petty thieves'.

It would appear, therefore, that the electoral campaign at Pompeii, and presumably in other municipalities in the early Empire, bore strong resemblances to the sort of campaign conducted in a small township of a modern democratic state. *Clientela* of course played its part, as it does in any community, but its role was not decisive. Those who posted these notices were clearly convinced that the votes of many of the townsmen could be affected by consideration of the political programme, efficiency, and integrity of the candidates. They must also have had faith in the cumulative effect upon the uncommitted of the advertisement of the voting intentions of others.

The inscriptions found at Pompeii date from the time of Augustus to the year AD 79, when the town was destroyed in the Vesuvian eruption. There is, however, good reason to believe that the lively interest in local institutions which they display was comparatively short-lived in the Roman Empire at large. Already in the *lex Malacitana* there are indications that it was declining, for the charter contains a section on the nomination of candidates which suggests that there might commonly be a deficiency in the number of persons who voluntarily allowed their names to go forward for local office. The fact was that, owing to increasing interference in local affairs by the central government, which robbed municipal officers of much of their responsibility and dignity, and owing too to the very heavy financial burden which came in time to be laid upon them, the citizens of the municipalities became progressively more loath to stand for election. By the middle of the second century their disinclination had become so great that the participation of the populace in the process of magisterial appointment was almost as meaningless as it had been at Rome during the early years of Augustus' principate. There were consequently modifications of procedure, and the responsibility for appointing local magistrates was transferred from the assembly to their predecessors in office. Even the local Senate did no more than formally ratify their choice.

APPENDIX I

NON-COMITIAL VOTING
AT ROME

IN THE MAIN BODY of the text we have concerned ourselves solely with voting in
the Roman assemblies. Voting also took place, however, both in the Senate and in
the special criminal courts—*quaestiones*—which were at first set up *ad hoc*, and
then, from the middle of the second century onwards, on a permanent basis and
in ever increasing numbers.

Voting in the Senate was normally the culmination of a protracted debate,
during the course of which the presiding magistrate sought the views of the leading members in an established order of precedence. Cicero's account of the famous
debate which took place in 57 BC regarding the restoration of Ptolemy Auletes of
Egypt throws considerable light on the preliminaries of the vote and upon the
prerogatives of the presiding magistrate in particular.[451] The proposals and formal
motions which were put forward during a debate could clearly be many and
various; and it was the magistrate's responsibility first to sort these out into those
whose terms were mutually exclusive and those which were in some way recon-
cilable, and then, in the case of the latter, to determine which should be put to the
vote. He further decided the order in which all the motions should be put; and it
need hardly be said that he would normally arrange to present first a motion of
which he approved rather than one of which he disapproved.

Although the presiding magistrate was therefore in a strong position to influence a senatorial decision, he did not himself have a vote. Nor, it would appear,
did any of his magisterial colleagues. This is virtually confirmed by the fact that
there is no record in our sources either of a magisterial vote or even of a magisterial
expression of opinion, and also by the knowledge that the order in which members of the Senate were traditionally asked for their views was headed by the ex-
magistrates and not the magistrates themselves. The explanation of this probably
lies not simply in the fact that a magistrate could not properly give an answer to
his own question—for this would not account for the exclusion of magistrates
other than the presiding magistrate from the vote—but rather in the clear distinction which always existed between the executive authority of the magistrate,
which was derived from the people, and the purely advisory authority of the
Senate.

The vote in the Senate was taken by division[452] and, at least in Republican
times, was entirely open, as in the democratic parliaments of modern times.[453]
The question called for an answer in the form of a simple 'yes' or 'no'; and the

'ayes' and the 'noes' separated themselves not by exiting through different doors, but by changing their positions in the body of the chamber. There was not even one side of the chamber reserved for 'ayes' and another for 'noes', for it was apparently customary for those who supported a motion to assemble around the person with whom it was associated and for those who opposed it to separate themselves off in another part of the house. According to Pliny, it was normal for the presiding magistrate to indicate the positions which he wished the senators to take up with his hands as he uttered a set form of words—'Those who approve this motion, cross over here; those who hold a different view, go there.'[454]

It might be thought that this frequent process of changing sides in a body of some three to four hundred persons would have resulted in something of a *mêlée*. In fact, however, there is evidence to indicate that many senators often took up their positions long before the call to divide, and that they deliberately used the system of division and grouping to advertise their feelings and proclaim their adherence to a particular viewpoint during the course of the debate. Indeed, in some debates, notably in that which took place in 63 BC on the fate of the Catilinarian conspirators, there was a constant change of stand on the part of certain senators, who by their movement across the chamber showed themselves to be convinced first by one speaker and then by another.[455] After all, Roman senators were not bound by any claims of party allegiance. They were open to persuasion; and it was quite possible for the proposer of a motion to end up by voting in another sense.

The formula of words used for announcing the result of the vote was simply 'This side appears to be the larger'.[456] This suggests that there did not normally take place a count of heads, and that a presiding magistrate may sometimes have been in a position to interpret a close verdict according to his own whim. On the other hand, it should be supposed that a precise count could be demanded by any one of those present. This is nowhere clearly stated; but we do know that the demand for a count was in order when any senator had reason to believe that the necessary quorum of members was not present.[457]

The methods of voting used in the criminal courts at Rome were very similar to those employed in the assemblies. When the first permanent court was set up in 149 BC to try cases of extortion it is probable that oral voting was the order of the day, as it still was in the *comitia*. It is also likely that the introduction of the written ballot came in 137 BC with the law of L. Cassius Longinus. The fact that this measure concerned itself with the only existing criminal court of that time as well as with the assemblies acting in their judicial capacity is strongly suggested by the portrayal of a tablet on a commemorative coin of the Cassii which bears the letters A and C for *absolvo* and *condemno*, terms normally reserved for the public courts (Fig. IX).[458] Even after 137 BC, however, the written vote did not become the universal rule. There is evidence in Cicero's speech in defence of Cluentius that at the trial of Oppianicus the choice as to whether a secret written ballot or an open oral vote should be used lay with the defendant. In fact, Oppianicus on this occasion opted for the oral vote, and as a consequence the order in which the various jurymen cast their vote was determined by a process of sortition.[459] It may well be that this provision for alternative methods of voting applied to all the criminal courts at this particular time and that it had been introduced by the Sullan

Fig. IX *Coin probably commemorating the*
lex Cassia *of 137 BC, and showing both a voting*
urn and a ballot such as was used in the criminal courts.

legislation of 81 BC. If so, it had a comparatively short life. Certainly, in the courts manned by equestrian jurors which were set up by Gaius Gracchus in 123 BC and in the courts of mixed senatorial and equestrian jurors established by the *lex Aurelia* of 70 BC the use of the written ballot appears to have been mandatory; the jurors were actually bound by oath not to divulge the sense either of their own vote or of the vote of their neighbour.[460]

The manner of conducting the secret ballot was as follows. On the tribunal was set either one voting urn or, when as normally the jury was drawn from members of distinct social groups, as many voting urns as there were groups represented.[461] (As to the purpose of this practice of using different voting urns for different groups, we can only suppose that it was designed to minimize the chance of either excessive bias or corruption on the part of any one group. The verdict of each group, senators, *equites*, and, after 70 BC, *tribuni aerarii*, was made public along with the overall verdict of the court; and any undue divergence of view would have been certain to induce suspicion.) Waxed tablets were then distributed to all the jurors, similar to those used in comitial voting, and inscribed on one side with the letter A and on the other with the letter C. The jurors were then instructed to erase one of the letters and to place the tablet in the appropriate voting urn, taking particular care to cover the letter remaining as they did so. The count was conducted by the president of the court, but not before one juror appointed by lot for the purpose had run through all the ballots that had been cast, discarding those that were invalid and sorting out the remainder into two groups—those for condemnation and those for acquittal.[462]

APPENDIX II

THE USE OF THE LOT
AT ROME

AT ROME SORTITION WAS not used, as it was at Athens, as a substitute for popular election. It did, however, play a not insignificant role, and it is right that some of its more important uses should be listed.

Reference has been made in the main body of the text to the principal functions of the lot at the voting assemblies. Before any voting began, it was employed to select the particular voting unit in which certain inferior groups who had no fixed tribe of registration should record their vote. The tribe in which those who held the Latin rights and happened to be present in Rome should cast their vote was regularly determined in this way, and for a short period during the second century so was the tribe—necessarily an urban tribe—to which the freedmen voters present should be assigned.[463] A more vital function of the lot, as we have fully explained, was to determine the order in which the individual voting units should be called to the vote, or, at assemblies where they all voted simultaneously, the order in which the results of the voting in the various units should be announced. In the first case, what was involved was simply the selection of one tribe, known as the *principium*, which then voted first and was followed by the remaining tribes in an established order. In the second case, of course, the process of sortition actually followed the voting, and in the case of elections which were closely contested it may often have been a determining factor in deciding the outcome. Finally, there was a use for the lot at elections which occurred more rarely—to decide the issue between two tying candidates, between two candidates, that is, who had obtained the absolute majority of votes necessary for success with the announcement of the returns from one and the same unit.[464]

[Although the lot was never used as a substitute for election by the people, there were occasions when it was used to select individuals for specific duties from out of a larger group. Thus, the jurors to be assigned to a particular criminal case were chosen by lot from among those who had previously been enrolled on the judicial panel.[465] There is reason to believe also that the Senate resorted frequently to the lot when faced with the job of choosing a board of commissioners or ambassadors from among its own number. In this last case it is unlikely that the outcome of the lot process was viewed as binding; for Cicero tells us that the Senate rejected both himself and Pompey when choosing an embassy to the Helvetii in 60 BC, on the grounds that both men were indispensable at Rome.[466] But the use of sortition for this purpose was well established; it may well have originated as early as the third or even fourth century, when the Senate tended to fall under the dominant influence of one particular group of families for comparatively long periods. It was advisable that boards of ambassadors or commissioners charged with conducting negotiations of long-term effect should be as representative as possible of all interests and shades of opinion in the Senate; and the use of the lot will have gone some way to ensure an unbiased selection.]

The only other common function of sortition in the political sphere was to determine how the particular responsibilities of a collegiate magistracy should be shared between the individual members of the college. The Romans very soon learnt that some apportionment of duties was essential if the existence of two or more colleagues enjoying exactly equal authority and the right of veto one over the other was not to result in anarchy. The system of the turn, by which each of the two consuls took precedence over the other in Rome itself in alternate months, was an early device designed to meet this problem on the domestic front; but, as the size of colleges of magistrates grew and their duties became more manifold and more particularized, other methods had to be found of ensuring a proper demarcation of responsibility; the lot emerged as the most convenient solution to the problem. The first examples of the use of sortition in this way are credited to the fifth century. When the Senate advised the consuls that a dictator should be nominated, it was the lot, we are told, which decided which of the consuls should nominate him;[467] and frequently, in cases where there had been no prior agreement, it was the lot which determined which consul should hold the elections, returning, if necessary, from the field of battle to do so.[468] The two censors also commonly drew lots to decide which of them should perform the all-important task of completing the *lustrum*,[469] as did the consuls to determine to which of two fighting fronts they should go and which of two armies they should command. Later, with the growth of overseas provinces and the proliferation of the criminal courts, each the responsibility of a praetor, the problem of allocating responsibility became more complex, and the lot became an accepted procedure for assigning provinces to both magistrates and pro-magistrates and particular judicial duties to members of the praetorian college.[470] Of course, although sortition became the accepted method of making these decisions, it is probably correct to say that in none of these cases was its use more than an optional convenience. A private, amicable agreement between colleagues could have served as well and probably did in many cases where the number of persons involved was only two or three.

We know very little of the equipment which was used for *sortitio* at Rome. But it is most unlikely to have been anything like as complicated as that used at Athens; and it may well have varied according to the complexity of the selection to be made. The receptacle commonly used is variously described as a *sitella* and an *urna*, both words, like the Greek *hydria* which is used in Plutarch,[471] being names for a form of vessel which held water. As Professor Lily Ross Taylor has recently argued,[472] it is probable that when there was a simple choice to be made and when therefore the number of lots to be employed did not exceed three or four, as for example when magistrates drew lots to determine their provinces, the *sitella* would have been in the form of a simple water-pitcher with a small spout, and the process of lot-taking would have consisted simply of swinging the pitcher and gently pouring until a lot appeared at the spout. This is what is suggested in a parody of certain political practices in the *Casina* of Plautus, and it is in keeping with the use of the word *effundere* (to pour out) to describe the drawing of lots.[473] It is notable too that the augurs, who appear to have had some special responsibility for the supervision of lot-taking, should have used a pitcher as one of their symbols of office. When the process of sortition was more complex, however, as for example when lots had to be drawn between all thirty-five of the tribes, the simple operation of pouring would have been less effective, as a number of lots would have tended to get jammed in the spout at the same pouring. On such occasions, therefore, the Romans appear to have used what they called an *urna versatilis*—a revolving urn. This also was presumably filled with water and may have been a large vessel affixed to some form of revolving base. The lots presumably flew out of their own accord (*effugere*) as the vessel was spun round.

The lots themselves were almost certainly made of wood and were shaped in the form of balls (*pilae*). An inscription from the early Imperial age prescribes for their preparation. They are to be made 'as equal in size and in weight as possible'.[474] Exact equalization, of course, will have been impossible to achieve; and, as we have noted in the text, there may have been some opportunity here for the less scrupulous operator to rig the lot, if he was so disposed. Any lots which were to any degree lighter than the rest, whether by reason of their being slightly smaller or because they were made of a less weighty wood, would be certain to float higher in the water; and, whether the container was tilted or whirled round, they could be guaranteed to emerge before the rest.

APPENDIX III

THE *LEX MALACITANA*

THE *lex Malacitana* dates from *circa* AD 84, when Domitian conferred a Latin charter upon the Spanish township of Malaga in accordance with his father's earlier decision. The extant part of this charter, which covers sections 51 to 69 was discovered near the ancient site of the town in 1851 and is inscribed on bronze tablets. It is of particular interest to the constitutional historian in that it contains virtually in their entirety the regulations laid down for the conduct of the local elections.

For the convenience of readers those clauses of the charter which are most relevant to the study of voting and electoral procedure are reproduced below in an English version. It should be emphasized that this is at best a free translation, or paraphrase, of the Latin text, which may conveniently be consulted in Bruns, *Fontes Iuris Romani*[7] (1909). In the interests of clarity and conciseness I have dispensed with a certain amount of legal periphrasis and have on occasions altered the sentence construction of the original text.

Section 51—*The Nomination of Candidates*

If no person announces his candidature before the appointed day or if fewer do so than there are offices to be filled, or again if there should prove to be fewer qualified persons among those who have announced their candidature than there are offices to be filled, then the presiding magistrate shall himself post up the names of as many qualified persons as are required to make up the necessary number. . . . If they so desire, those whose names are so posted may then themselves go before the presiding magistrate and each nominate one other person who possesses the same qualifications as himself, and again, if they so desire, this second group of nominees may go before the presiding magistrate and each nominate a further individual. The magistrate before whom these nominations are made shall post up all their names . . . and shall conduct the election on the entire list as if they had all professed their candidature by the appointed day and as if they had all stood for office on their own accord from the outset.

Section 52—*The Conduct of the Elections*

The elections and bye-elections for the appointment of duumvirs, aediles and quaestors shall be conducted by the elder of the two duumvirs who are in office in this town at the time, or, in the event of his not being available, by his colleague. Voting shall take place in accordance with the division of the population by *curiae* which has been outlined above, and it shall be conducted by ballot. The persons who are so elected shall hold the office into which they are voted for one year, or, if they be suffects, for that part of the year which remains.

Section 53—The Curia for the Vote of Foreign Residents
The presiding magistrate at the election of duumvirs, aediles and quaestors in this township shall draw a lot to determine the one *curia* in which resident aliens who are Roman citizens or Latins shall cast their vote.

Section 54—Qualifications for Candidature
The presiding magistrate shall ensure that the duumvirs in charge of jurisdiction, the aediles and the quaestors are chosen from among those who are of free birth, as defined by this law. A candidate for the office of duumvir must be at least twenty-five years old and must not have held the office within the preceding five years. A candidate for the aedilate or the quaestorship must be at least twenty-five years old and free from any of the impediments which would debar him from becoming a decurion or senator if he were a Roman citizen.

Section 55—The Casting of the Vote
The presiding magistrate shall call the townsmen to vote by *curiae*. All the *curiae* shall be summoned together and they shall severally register their votes by ballot in separate compartments. The presiding magistrate shall further arrange for three townsmen to be assigned to each ballot-box to act both as guards and as tellers. These persons shall themselves be members of a different *curia* and, before acting, they shall be required to swear on oath that they will conduct the count and report the results in good faith. Likewise the candidates shall be permitted to assign one guard to each ballot-box. Each of these guards, whether he be appointed by the presiding magistrate or one of the candidates, shall cast his own vote in the particular *curia* to whose ballot-box he is assigned, and his vote shall be treated as legally valid just as though he had cast it in his own *curia*.

Section 56—Rules Governing Ties in the Voting
When announcing the results of the voting in any one *curia*, the presiding magistrate shall first return the candidate who has obtained the largest vote and shall then return others in an order determined by the size of their votes until he has returned as many as there are offices to be filled. In the event of two or more candidates obtaining an equal number of votes in a *curia*, he shall give precedence in making the returns to a married man, or a man who enjoys the rights of a married man, over a bachelor who has no children and does not enjoy the rights of a married man, to a man who has children over one who has none, and to a man who has a greater number of children over one who has a smaller; and for this purpose two children lost after they have been named or one boy or girl lost after reaching puberty or marriageable age shall be treated as the equivalent of one living child. If two or more candidates obtain an equal number of votes whose circumstances in these respects are the same, he shall put their names into the lot and return them in the order in which they are drawn.

Section 57—Rules Governing the Selection of Curiae by Lot and Ties in the Number of Curiae Won

When the voting returns from all the *curiae* have been brought in, the presiding magistrate shall put the names of the *curiae* in the lot and shall draw the lots one by one to determine the order in which their several results shall be announced. As soon as any one candidate secures a majority of the *curiae*, he shall take the oath and give security for public money and shall then be declared duly elected. This procedure shall continue until as many magistrates are declared elected as are required. In the event of two or more candidates securing a majority with the announcement of the same set of results, the procedure to be followed by the presiding magistrate in breaking the tie shall be the same as that prescribed above for breaking ties in the number of votes cast, and on the same principle the candidate in whose favour the tie is broken shall be given precedence in the declaration.

NOTES

ABBREVIATIONS

AJP   *American Journal of Philology*

AP   The *Athenaion Politeia* (Constitution of Athens) of Aristotle

ASI   *Ancient Society and Institutions.* Studies presented to Victor Ehrenberg (Oxford, 1966)

BS   Busolt-Swoboda, *Griechische Staatskunde* (Munich, 1920–6)

CIL   *Corpus Inscriptionum Latinarum*

CQ   *Classical Quarterly*

HAC   C. Hignett, *A History of the Athenian Constitution to the end of the Fifth Century B.C.* (Oxford, 1952)

IG   *Inscriptiones Graecae*

ILS   H. Dessau, *Inscriptiones Latinae Selectae* (Berlin 1892–1916)

JHS   *Journal of Hellenic Studies*

JRS   *Journal of Roman Studies*

PP   L. R. Taylor, *Party Politics in the Age of Caesar* (Berkeley, 1949)

RA   G. W. Botsford, *The Roman Assemblies* (New York, 1909)

RE   Pauly-Wissowa, *Real-Encyclopädie der Classischen Altertumswissenschaft*

RVA   L. R. Taylor, *Roman Voting Assemblies* (Ann Arbor, 1966)

St.   Th. Mommsen, *Römisches Staatsrecht* (Leipzig, 1887–8)

VDRR   L. R. Taylor, *The Voting Districts of the Roman Republic* (Rome, 1960)

CHAPTER I

1 For a useful discussion of the origins of voting in the ancient world see J. A. O. Larsen, 'The Origin and Significance of the Counting of Votes', *Classical Philology*, 1949, 164ff.

2 As M. I. Finley writes in *The World of Odysseus* (1956), 51, 'The world of Odysseus was not that of the seventh century B.C., neither was it the Mycenaean age five or six hundred years earlier. If it is to be placed in time . . . the most likely centuries seem to be the tenth and

ninth.' This excellent book by Finley is indispensable as a guide to the value of Homer as a historical source. See also M. P. Nilsson, *Homer and Mycenae* (1953) and D. Page, *The Homeric Odyssey* (1955).

3 *Odyssey* II, 26ff, 42ff.

4 *Odyssey* II, 386.

5 *Odyssey* II, 12.

6 The evidence bearing on the role of the Homeric assemblies is discussed in detail by Finley, *The World of Odysseus*, 84ff, 119ff.

7 *Iliad* I, 22ff, 376ff.

8 *Iliad* II, 74ff.

9 *Iliad* II, 190.

10 *Iliad* II, 255ff.

11 A useful general survey of early Spartan history, which avoids the most highly controversial issues, is to be found in H. Michell, *Sparta* (1952). See also the brief summary in V. Ehrenberg's *From Solon to Socrates* (1968), 27ff. Some of the other more specialized studies are detailed below (note 15).

12 Pausanias 3, 3, 2–3.

13 Aristotle, *Politics*, 1313 A, 26–33; Plutarch, *Lycurgus*, 7, 2.

14 Plutarch, *Lycurgus*, 6, 2.

15 The dates suggested for the Rhetra by scholars vary from the ninth century to the late seventh. In recent times the subject has been treated in detail in K. M. T. Chrimes, *Ancient Sparta* (1949), W. den Boer, *Laconian Studies* (1954), G. L. Huxley, *Early Sparta* (1962) and F. Kiechle, *Lakonien und Sparta* (1963), and in articles by A. Andrewes (*CQ*, 1938, 89ff), H. T. Wade-Gery (*CQ*, 1943, 62ff and 1944, 1ff), N. G. L. Hammond (*JHS*, 1950, 42ff), W. G Forrest (*Phoenix*, 1963, 157ff) and A. H. M. Jones (*ASI*, 165ff). It should be mentioned that many of these scholars propound theories on the institutions and early development of Sparta which are totally at variance with the views I have expressed in the text.

16 This, for example, is the gist of the case argued by Jones, *ASI*, 165ff.

17 Plutarch, *Agis*, 11, 4–5. This and other examples of the rights of the ephors as against the kings—the right to fine (Plutarch, *Agesilaus*, 2, 6), the right to summon (Plutarch, *Cleomenes*, 10, 5), the right to arrest (Thucydides, 1, 31), the exchange of oaths (Xenophon, *Respublica Lacedaemoniorum*, 15, 7)—do not imply that the ephors had ever been 'the representatives and the champions of the people against the kings' (Jones, *ASI*, 170). They are entirely consistent with the view expressed in the text that they represented the claims of the aristocracy to a larger share in executive government. See below, pp. 32f.

18 Plutarch (*Cleomenes*, 10, 3, 4) preserves the tradition that the ephors were originally appointed by the king. Aristotle (*Politics*, 1313 A, 27) and Plato (*Laws*, 692 A) stress that the ephorate from early times acted as a check on the regal authority.

19 The controversial issue of the powers of the Spartan Assembly is one which is discussed by all the authors cited in note 15. It is very doubtful whether the Assembly ever enjoyed a right of amendment, as Plutarch himself surmised; for Aristotle (*Politics*, 1273 A, 12; *cf.* also 1272 A, 11) clearly implies that it had no authority other than to ratify the proposals of the *gerousia*. I believe that the rider reserved for the *gerousia* the right to overrule the Assembly when it rejected what were deemed to be essential measures.

20 Herodotus 1, 65, 1; Thucydides 1, 18, 1.

21 Plutarch, *Theseus*, 32, 1; Thucydides 2, 15, 1. For the view that both these passages refer to the origin of the aristocratic Council of the Areopagus, which was at one time composed exclusively of Eupatrids, see H. T. Wade-Gery, *CQ*, 1931, 6ff.

22 The stages of the transition from monarchy to magistracy in eighth- and seventh-century Athens are obscure. The rival traditions and modern theories are carefully examined by Hignett, *HAC*, 38ff.

23 So BS II, 141; Hignett, *HAC*, 83. The rule that the Areopagus should be recruited from ex-archons may have been of post-Solonian origin.

24 *AP*, 8, 2. *Cf.* Isocrates, *Areopagiticus*, 7, 22.

25 1273 B, 40.

26 *Cf.* 1274 A, 15–17: 'Solon himself probably gave the people no more power than was absolutely necessary: without the right of electing magistrates and calling them to account, they would have been virtually slaves and hostile to the government'; 1281 B, 33: 'it was on these grounds that Solon and other legislators gave them (*scil.* the general body of citizens) the power of electing magistrates and calling them to account'.

27 A. Ledl, *Studien zur älteren athenischen Verfassungsgeschichte*, 1914, 388f, cited apparently with approval by Hignett, *HAC*, 79.

28 Thucydides 1, 126; Herodotus 5, 71, 1; Plutarch, *Solon*, 12, 1.

29 *AP*, 7, 1; Plutarch, *Solon*, 17, 1.

30 See Hignett, *HAC*, 97ff. For the name '*heliaea*' as applied to the Assembly acting in a judicial capacity *cf.* Lysias 10, 16; Demosthenes 24, 105.

31 The arguments against the Solonian origin of a second Council are set out by Hignett, *HAC*, 95ff.

32 *AP*, 7, 3. *Cf.* Plutarch, *Solon*, 18, 2.

33 *IG*, I², 114.

34 *Cf.* Herodotus 6, 136; Plutarch, *Themistocles*, 23, 4ff.

35 *AP*, 21, 2.

CHAPTER II

36 1300 A, 10ff.

37 *Politics*, 1318 B, 23ff.

38 Plutarch, *Lycurgus*, 5, 12f; 26, 1; Herodotus 6, 57, 5; Plato, *Laws*, 692 A; Pausanias 3, 5, 2.

39 *Politics*, 1271 A, 10. Aristotle considered that it was 'improper for the person to be elected to canvass for the office'.

40 Aristotle repeatedly implies that the councillors were drawn in practice, if not in law, from a limited group of families. He stresses that the *gerousia* represented the oligarchical element in the constitution (1265 B, 38; 1270 B, 24), and suggests that the selection of its members was based on the principle of δυναστεία, or hereditary succession (1306 A, 18). This view, however, is rejected by Jones, *ASI*, 173, n. 36.

41 *Politics*, 1270 B, 15.

42 Compare the five *agathoergoi* (Herodotus 1, 67, 5) and various other five-man commissions (Thucydides 5, 19, 2; Xenophon, *Hellenica*, 2, 4, 39; *AP*, 38, 4). Little definite is known of the structure of Spartan society, and scholars are divided on whether it was the local tribes or the obes which numbered five. For detailed discussion see *BS* II, 645, and the works on early Sparta cited in note 15 above.

43 1294 B, 30. *Cf.* 1265 B, 39, 1270 B, 8, and 1272 B, 36, for emphasis on the point that all Spartan citizens were eligible to stand for the ephorate.

44 *Politics*, 1270 B, 34.

45 'The Government of Classical Sparta', *ASI*, 9.

46 *AP*, 3, 1. As Hignett writes (*HAC*, 78), 'this may have been a condition not legally prescribed but observed in practice, as impoverished aristocrats would be unable to maintain their position among richer members of their class.'

47 *AP*, 8, 1; 47, 1.

48 *AP*, 26, 2.

49 This assumption is made without comment by Hignett, *HAC*, 101f, 142f, 156. As evidence for the view that the archonship was not thrown open to the second class until some date between the time of Solon and 457 BC may be cited Plutarch, *Aristides*, 1, 2 (a suggestion that the office was still confined to the first class in the early fifth century) and *AP*, 4, 2 (a coupling of archons with the Treasurers of Athena as officers drawn from the first class in the spurious constitution of Draco).

50 *AP*, 8, 1.

51 The two passages are those already cited in notes 25 and 26 above (1273 B, 40; 1274 A, 15–17). In the first the author is concerned to stress continuity, and he uses the term 'elected magistracy' to signify an essentially aristocratic element in the constitution which Solon both inherited and preserved. For the same reason that the term 'elected' should not be supposed to imply the participation of a popular assembly it should not be regarded as excluding an element of sortition. In the second passage Aristotle is concerned with the minimum concession which Solon felt himself obliged to make to the people. 'Election', therefore, need

bear no more precise a meaning than 'participation in the process of selection'.

52 The Licinio-Sextian plebiscite of 367 BC provided that one of the two consuls each year *must* be a plebeian (Livy 6, 35, 5). It thus technically imposed a restriction upon the freedom of the voters to elect the men of their choice.

53 *AP*, 13, 1–2.

54 *Revue de Philologie*, 1924, 144ff. This view is favoured also by Wade-Gery, *CQ*, 1931, 79f.

55 Thucydides 6, 54, 6.

56 See T. J. Cadoux, *JHS*, 1948, 109ff. The list contains the names of Miltiades and Cleisthenes as well as of members of the tyrant's family.

57 *AP*, 22, 5.

58 *AP*, 55, 1.

59 Hignett (*HAC*, 174) would emend the text of Aristotle to read that the number of *procritoi* was one hundred, not five hundred. On his own admission, however, this would involve rejecting Aristotle's reference to the role of the demes as an error. Although the archons were chosen from the whole tribe in the fourth century, there is no reason to suppose that the Athenians did not experiment for a period with selection at deme level.

60 *AP*, 8, 1; 55, 1.

61 Yet this appears to be the contention of R. J. Buck, *Classical Philology*, 1965, 96ff. He rules out any earlier use of the lot, but suggests that the double sortition of later times was developed from a two-stage election process of Solonian origin.

62 This is the generally accepted view. *Cf. BS* II, 881; Hignett, *HAC*, 169ff; W. Schwahn, *RE*, Supplement VI, 1071f.

63 *AP* 22, 2. They were certainly elected by the full Assembly in the early fifth century (Herodotus 6, 104, 2).

64 Thus Hignett writes (*HAC*, 773): 'Perhaps the assumption by the ekklesia in 501/500 of the right to elect the generals was simply a fresh affirmation of the sovereignty of the demos, and the consequent increase in the prestige of the generals was an unexpected by-product of the change.'

65 Herodotus 6, 109–10. Although the archons were at this time still appointed by direct election, the allocation of particular offices on the board may traditionally have been left to the lot. This is the implication of Herodotus' statement that the polemarch owed his office 'to the bean'.

66 My treatment of this difficult subject here is to a large extent a summary of the arguments and conclusions expounded in my recent article, 'Voting Procedures at the Election of *Strategoi*', *ASI*, 275ff. Among other discussions should be noted Wade-Gery, *CQ*, 1931, 89f, 309ff; Ehrenberg, *AJP*, 1945, 113ff; Hignett, *HAC*, 348ff; M. H. Jameson, *Transactions of the American Philological Association*, 1955, 63ff; D. M. Lewis, *JHS*, 1961, 118ff. See also the works cited in *ASI*, 286, n. 1.

67 For the evidence see *ASI*, 286, n. 2.

68 So *BS* II, 890ff; U. Kahrstedt, *Untersuchungen zur Magistratur in Athen* (1936), 29.

69 The point is particularly well made by Jameson, op. cit., 67f.

70 *AP*, 61, 1.

71 This is possibly true even of a much later period. Among the five known generals of 97/96 BC there were no two from the same tribe (*IG* II, 2336).

72 The tendency has been to explain

Aristotle's supposed silence by underestimating the significance of the fifth-century reform (*cf.* Jameson, op. cit., 68, who describes the new procedure as 'not very different' from the old). But in actual fact the known lists from the fifth century show that it had a more radical effect upon the composition of the board than any change which may be supposed to have come later.

73 *AP*, 50–61.

74 For a brief survey of the various Athenian magistracies see G. Gilbert, *Constitutional Antiquities of Sparta and Athens* (1895), 230ff; J. W. Headlam-Morley, *Election by Lot at Athens* (1933), 105ff.

75 The tribes, of course, continued to choose their own local officials. They were also occasionally assigned the responsibility for electing certain extraordinary state officials such as the *teichopoioi* (builders of walls), when the work involved could be apportioned among the tribes (*cf.* Aeschines 3, 30).

76 *AP*, 62, 1: 'For some of the magistracies chosen by lot (including those of the nine archons) candidates were at one time drawn from the tribe as a whole, whereas those to which appointment is now made in the Theseion were distributed over the demes.'

77 So, recently, M. Lang, 'Allotment by Tokens', *Historia*, 1959, 83ff.

78 *AP*, 62, 3; Demosthenes 24, 150; *cf.* Aristotle, *Politics*, 1298 A.

79 See below, p. 111.

80 *Cf.* Lysias 6, 4; 31, 33; Isocrates 15, 150 for examples of personal application for offices which were filled by lot. Harpocration, *s.v.* ἐπιλάχων, also refers to 'those who seek to hold office or to serve as councillors'. Voluntary candidature, as opposed to conscription, is further attested by several references to the appointment of magistrates 'without the lot' in the fourth century. These are most naturally interpreted in terms of unopposed selection (see below, pp. 110f).

81 *AP*, 22, 2.

82 *AP*, 62, 3; Xenophon, *Memorabilia*, 1, 2, 35.

83 Harpocration, s.v. ἐπιλάχων; Aeschines 3, 62. On the reserves see Headlam-Morley, op. cit., 53ff.

84 For these estimated figures see in particular A. W. Gomme, *The Population of Athens in the Fifth and Fourth Centuries B.C.* (1933), 29 (Table II). Gomme further calculates that less than a quarter of those attaining the age of thirty lived to be sixty.

85 Members of the Council were in receipt of state pay in 411 BC (Thucydides 8, 69, 4). This amounted to five obols a day in Aristotle's time (*AP*, 62, 2).

86 Significantly the evidence of the extant lists shows at least twenty-five to thirty per cent of the councillors of any one year to have been drawn from well-to-do families. It is likely that the actual proportion was very much higher.

87 Hignett, *HAC*, 230. General discussions of the principle of sortition are to be found in Headlam-Morley, op. cit., 1ff, and in *RE*, s.v. *Lösung*, XIII, 1461ff.

88 It is, of course, not apt to point to Rome as an example of a state where the principle of rotation was successfully coupled with direct election (*cf.* Hignett, *HAC*, 230). Rome was ruled in practice, if not in law, by a narrow oligarchy; and rotation here served the useful purpose of ensuring that offices were equitably shared among the comparatively few highly qualified persons who laid claim to them.

89 *Politics*, 1303 A, 15. *Cf.* Plato, *Laws*, 757 E.

90 See Ehrenberg, *RE*, XIII, 1461ff, on the confusion of the secular and religious aspects of sortition. Even in the Homeric world people had resort to the lot not only out of respect for the divine will but in order the more easily to settle their differences. Later writers, of course, all regard sortition as an essential constituent of democracy (*cf.* Aristotle, *Politics*, 1294 B, 8; 1300 A, 32; 1317 B, 20; Herodotus 3, 80, 6; Xenophon, *Memorabilia*, 1, 2, 9).

91 Wade-Gery (*CQ*, 1931, 88) has suggested another motive for the introduction of sortition at this time. He considers that it was viewed as a concession to religious sentiment at a time when the archonship was being thrown open to families which did not have the close connections with the gods claimed by the Eupatrids. It seems perverse, however, to argue that Eupatrid claims to divine preferment were in some way responsible for the institution of a process of selection which can only have been less favourable to aristocratic interests than direct election.

92 It is probable that the reintroduction of sortition and the opening of the office of archon to members of the second class went hand in hand (see above, p. 38). Once it was accepted in principle that the archonship should rotate among a wider cross-section of the citizens than hitherto and that it should therefore be held by those who were not to be chosen essentially for their ability, the institution of election by lot rather than by vote was the logical step to take.

93 For a slightly different emphasis see Hignett, *HAC*, 185f. He accepts that Themistocles was involved in

the changes but stresses his concern to
provide Athens with a body of
trained and efficient executive magistrates who would be eligible for
repeated re-election.

94   Cf. AP, 45, 2; Demosthenes 20,
90; Lysias 26, 12.

95   Cf. AP, 55, 2; Demosthenes 40,
34; Lysias 15, 2; Aeschines 3, 14;

Pollux 8, 44.

96   Lysias 16, 9.

97   Lysias 13, 10; Aeschines 1, 19.

98   Hignett, *HAC*, 232.

99   For a brief discussion of the
various views on the origin of the
scrutiny see Hignett, *HAC*, 206ff.

100   Cf Headlam-Morley, op. cit.,
97ff.

CHAPTER III

101   Thucydides 8, 69, 4; cf. Demosthenes 39, 10; Xenophon, *Memorabilia*, 1, 2, 9.

102   *Ecclesiazusae*, 681.

103   *AP*, 64.

104   These machines were described
and discussed in detail by Sterling
Dow in *Hesperia*, Supplement I (1937),
198ff.

105   J. D. Bishop, 'The Clero-
terium', *JHS*, 1970, 1ff, who also
suggests that the counters when
released might have been arranged in
some form of display gallery for the
benefit of those who were there to
witness the allotment.

106   For what follows I am much
indebted to Sterling Dow's article,
'Aristotle, the Kleroteria, and the
Courts', which appeared in *Harvard
Studies in Classical Philology*, 1939, 1ff.
It is generally agreed that Dow's
examination of Aristotle's account in
the light of the archaeological evidence has cleared up once and for all
many of the misconceptions which
previously existed about the procedure.

107   Cf. Demosthenes 14, 18; Plato,
Laws, 745 C. A process of simultaneous sortition is described by Aristotle

in *AP*, 66.

108   W. S. Ferguson, in *Athenian
Tribal Cycles* (1933), 51ff, argues that
the three senior archons at least were
taken each year from different tribes
and that there were definite periods
during which individual offices could
not be held again by a member of a
tribe which had already been represented in them. His evidence, however, relates only to the third century
and after, when the number of tribes
had in any case been increased from
ten to twelve.

109   In other words, the first counter
to appear would have related to the
first *valid* ticket in the vertical row of
slots, reading from the top, the
second counter to the second valid
ticket, and so on.

110   Cf. *Hesperia*, 1951, 51f. The
evidence is discussed in detail by
Lang, *Historia*, 1959, 80ff.

111   This is the view of Lang (op.
cit., 84), although she speaks, I think
mistakenly, in terms of fifty candidates who presented themselves at the
allotment. See above, p. 50, for the
view that no candidates were in fact
involved at this stage of the proceedings.

CHAPTER IV

112   Thucydides 1, 87. Cf. Xenophon, *Hellenica*, 2, 2, 19; 5, 2, 11;

Plutarch, *Agis*, 5.

113 *Hellenica*, 2, 4, 38; 3, 2, 23; 4, 6, 3.

114 Plutarch, *Agis*, 8, 1.

115 *Politics*, 1271 A, 10.

116 *Lycurgus*, 25.

117 See above, note 19.

118 For intervention in debate *cf.* Thucydides 1, 79ff; Diodorus 11, 50, 6; Xenophon, *Hellenica*, 6, 4, 2; Plutarch, *Agis*, 8. In all cases where the speakers in question are not known to have been ephors or members of the *gerousia* they can be identified as members of the upper hierarchy. Only a somewhat dubious anecdote in Aeschines (1, 180) indicates a different view. For the introduction of envoys at the invitation of the ephors *cf.* Thucydides 6, 88; Xenophon, *Hellenica* 5, 2, 11; 6, 2, 33; 6, 3, 3.

119 See most recently Andrewes, *ASI*, 1ff, who regards the *gerousia* as playing a relatively unimportant role. Jones, *ASI*, 169f, is also prepared to concede that the *gerousia* could be bypassed.

120 *Agis*, 11, 1.

121 *Cf.* Herodotus 5, 39–40 (ephors and *gerousia* consult on the advice to be given to the king on marriage); Xenophon, *Hellenica* 3, 3, 8 (consultation at the time of the conspiracy of Cinadon). It is possible that the 'little assembly' referred to in this last passage was in fact no more than a gathering of kings, Council and ephors for emergency debate. On the election of ephors see above, p. 31.

122 Thucydides 1, 87.

123 *Cf.* Aristotle, *Politics*, 1275 B 10; 1294 B, 33; Xenophon, *Hellenica*, 5, 4, 24f; Plutarch, *Lycurgus*, 26, 2; *Agis*, 24–25.

124 Pausanias 3, 5, 2.

125 Thucydides 1, 20, 3.

126 Herodotus 6, 27, 5.

127 *Politics*, 1270 B, 28.

128 *Laws*, 692 A.

129 Thucydides 8, 72, 1. This statement, however, may to some extent reflect the propaganda of the moderate oligarchs who aimed in 411 BC to restrict the franchise to a body of five thousand citizens.

130 *Politics*, 1318 B–1319 B; Aristophanes, *Peace*, 296; 540ff; *Birds*, 489ff. *Cf.* Plato, *Politicus*, 565 A; Xenophon, *Memorabilia*, 3, 7, 6.

131 Aristotle specifically connects the introduction of state payment—probably in the first decade of the fourth century—with the difficulties encountered in securing a reasonable attendance at the Assembly (*AP*, 41, 3).

132 On procedure see *BS* II, 992ff; Gilbert, op. cit., 285ff. The chief source is *AP*, 43, 3ff. For other details see Demosthenes 18, 169; Pollux 8, 95; Plutarch, *Alcibiades*, 34, 1.

133 *Cf.* Philochorus, fr. 79 B; Plutarch, *Aristides*, 7.

134 *Cf.* Demosthenes 19, 60; Lysias 13, 32 (Peiraeus); Demosthenes 21, 9; Aeschines 2, 61 (theatre). There is also the plentiful evidence of inscriptions. Thucydides 8, 94 provides an early example of the use of the theatre.

135 *Cf.* Thucydides 8, 97; Plutarch, *Nicias*, 7; Aeschines 3, 34; Demosthenes 18, 169; and frequent references in the plays of Aristophanes. For the Pnyx as the established venue for the elections even in later time see Pollux 8, 133.

136 *Cf.* Pollux 8, 104; *IG* II², 1257.

137 Pollux 8, 104: 'they dyed a rope and used the *toxotai* to drive the people from the market-place into the place of assembly'.

138 *Ecclesiazusae*, 289ff.

139 Xenophon, *Hellenica*, 1, 7, 9.

140 Plutarch, *Pericles*, 11, 2; Thucydides 6, 13, 1; 24, 4. *Cf.* Demosthenes 18, 143; Aristophanes, *Ecclesiazusae*, 2, 89.

141 See *Hesperia*, 1932, 104f.

142 Xenophon, *Memorabilia*, 1, 1, 18; 4, 4, 2; Aristophanes, *Acharnians*, 40ff.

143 *AP*, 44, 2.

144 *AP*, 43, 1; Thucydides 3, 49, 1; Xenophon, *Hellenica*, 1, 7, 7; Aristophanes, *Ecclesiazusae*, 264; Lysias 12, 44; Aeschines 2, 13.

145 *AP*, 43; Lysias 30, 5; Demosthenes 26, 5; 58, 27.

146 Harpocration, s.v. προχειροτονία. *Cf. AP*, 43, 6; Demosthenes 24, 11; Aeschines 1, 23.

147 *BS* I, 455.

148 Yet this is the explanation favoured by Larsen, *Classical Philology*, 1949, 174.

149 Almost the same scene is depicted in two distinct paintings by Douris and the Brygos Painter (see J. D. Beazley, *Attic Red-Figure Vase-Painting*, 2nd ed. (1963), II, 369, no. 2; 429, no. 26). The relevance of these paintings to the use of *psephoi* in the open vote was stressed by A. T. Boegehold in his article, 'Towards a Study of Athenian Voting Procedure', *Hesperia*, 1963, 366ff.

150 Lysias 13, 37. Compare the similar use of an open voting token at Megara in 424 BC (Thucydides 4, 74, 3).

151 *Cf.* Herodotus 6, 63, 2; Aristophanes, *Wasps*, 656, for the use of fingers in counting. See also the remarks of Lang, *Hesperia*, 1957, 271 and Boegehold, *Hesperia*, 1963, 370.

152 *Cf.* Aeschines 1, 18; Demosthenes 18, 149; 19, 122.

153 *Laws*, 755 D.

154 See above, p. 45.

155 *Cf.* Demosthenes 59, 89; 24, 45; 24, 59; Andocides 1, 87; and the sources cited in note 156 below.

156 Philochorus, fr. 79 B; Plutarch, *Aristides*, 7. The evidence and the procedure on which it throws light are discussed in full by J. Carcopino, *L'Ostracisme Athenien* (1935), 72ff.

157 This is implied by the anecdote of the country voter who approached Aristides in the market-place with the request that he fill in his own name on an *ostrakon* (Plutarch, *Aristides*, 7, 7).

158 *Cf.* Pollux 8, 20; schol. on Aristophanes, *Knights*, 855.

159 For a full exposition of this argument and for a useful bibliography on the controversy see Carcopino, op. cit., 90ff.

160 Plutarch, *Nicias*, 11, 5; *Alcibiades*, 13, 6.

161 Xenophon, *Hellenica*, 1, 7, 9. *Cf.* Demosthenes 59, 90.

162 Aeschines 1, 35.

163 Harpocration, s.v. ἐκφυλλοφορῆσαι; Aeschines 1, 111.

164 Philochorus, fr. 119.

165 See Sterling Dow, *Hesperia*, Supplement I, 1937, 211f.

166 *AP*, 24, 3; 27, 4. *Cf.* Aristophanes, *Wasps*, 661ff.

167 *AP*, 63ff.

168 Aristophanes, *Wasps*, 332, 349, 887; Pollux 8, 16; Harpocration, s.v. καδίσκος.

169 Lysias 13, 37. *Cf.* Demosthenes 12, 91; 19, 239. It is clear too from a passage in Aeschylus, *Eumenides*, 744, that the results of a vote could not normally be determined by observation and that it was necessary to wait for the official count.

170 *Agamemnon*, 813. See on this text J. T. Allen, *Classical Review*, 1904, 456ff.

171 So Boegehold, *Hesperia*, 1963, 368.

172 Pollux 8, 16.

173 Demosthenes 43, 10.

174 *AP*, 53, 3; Demosthenes 24, 9.

CHAPTER V

175 *Politics*, 1271 A.

176 *Phocion*, 8.

177 The question of candidature and the electoral campaign at Athens was treated by C. Baron in 'Political Candidature at Athens', *Revue des Etudes Grecques*, 1901, 372ff. Despite its age this still remains the only serious examination of the subject.

178 This is probably true at least of Aristides, Cimon, and Thucydides, son of Melesias, the chief political opponent of Pericles.

179 *Cf.* Thucydides 4, 29, 1; 66, 3; 6, 30, 1; 64, 1; 7, 14, 2; Xenophon, *Hellenica*, 1, 4, 10; 1, 5, 16.

180 *Characters*, 24, 5. That Theophrastus is referring to the regular magistracies is denied, however, by Kahrstedt, op. cit., 40.

181 *Cf.* Pollux 8, 55; Demosthenes 19, 122, 124; Aeschines 2, 94f; Harpocration, s.v. ἐξωμοσία.

182 *Respublica Atheniensium*, 1, 3.

183 *Cf.* Euripides, *Iphigenia in Aulis*, 337.

184 Even Aristophanes (*Acharnians*, 598) admits that elections lent themselves to manipulation by wealthy cliques.

185 Demosthenes 3, 30.

186 Aeschines 2, 41.

187 The most comprehensive treatment of the composition and activities of the Athenian political clubs is still G. M. Calhoun, *Athenian Clubs in Politics and Litigation* (1913).

188 Thucydides 8, 54, 4.

189 *Cf.* Aristophanes, *Lysistrata*, 576; Demosthenes 21, 139; 58, 39; Plato, *Theaetetus*, 173 D; *Republic* 365 D.

190 Sophocles, *Ajax*, 1135.

191 Demosthenes 13, 19.

192 Isocrates 15, 116.

193 Xenophon, *Memorabilia*, 3, 4, 1.

194 Isocrates 8, 50.

195 Aeschines 1, 86.

196 Lysias 19, 57. *Cf.* Aeschines 1, 107.

197 Demosthenes 19, 7.

198 Aeschines 1, 106.

199 Aeschines 3, 3.

200 *AP*, 27, 5.

201 *AP*, loc. cit.; Plutarch, *Coriolanus*, 14.

202 *AP*, 64–6.

203 The evidence is discussed by O. Broneer, *Hesperia*, 1938, 228ff.

204 Demosthenes 57, 8f.

205 Pollux 8, 18.

206 Compare the provisions for appointing ticket-setters at the original selection process. Significantly, too, the magistrates did not themselves draw to determine the courts over which they were to preside. On the other hand, perhaps because there was no other practicable method, the selected jurors did themselves draw for their courtrooms. This was possibly the weakest link in the whole procedure.

207 Aeschines 3, 62, 73.

208 Demosthenes 39, 12.

CHAPTER VI

209 Livy 1, 13, 6; Dionysius 2, 7,; Cicero, *De Republica*, 2, 14. Compare Mommsen, *St.* III, 99ff; G. W. Botsford, *RA*, 8ff. The *curiae* were associations of *gentes* which played a prominent part in the religious life of early Rome. Whether they originated before or after the creation of the state is still disputed. On this point see particularly *RE* IV, 1819 (Kübler), and P. de Francisci, 'La comunita sociale e politica romana primitiva', *Studia et Documenta Historiae et Iuris*, 1956, 1ff.

210 Livy 1, 49, 7; Dionysius 2, 14, 3; 2, 60; 5, 6; Pomponius in *Digest* 1, 2, 2, 2.

211 For the role of the *curiae* at the appointment of the king see Livy 1, 17, 10; 1, 32, 1; 1, 35, 1; 1, 36, 1; Cicero, *De Republica*, 2, 25; 31; 33; 35. The traditional view of the early role of the *comitia curiata* is presented by Botsford, *RA*, 168ff. Against this it has been forcibly and convincingly argued by U. Coli that the assembly did no more than witness the proceedings ('Regnum', *Studia et Documenta Historiae et Iuris*, 1951, 60ff).

212 Cicero, *De Lege Agraria*, 2, 26–31.

213 Asconius, *In Cornelianam*, 76 (Clark); Dionysius 6, 89; 9, 46.

214 The constitutional significance of the *lex curiata* has been the subject of much controversy. For a defence of the view here expressed and for bibliographical detail see my treatment in *Historia*, 1956, 84ff.

215 Cicero, *De Lege Agraria*, 2, 26.

216 Livy 1, 43; Dionysius 4, 16ff.

217 For a defence of the view that at least some parts of the centuriate organization were in fact of Servian origin see in particular H. Last, 'The Servian Reforms', *JRS*, 1945, 30ff. Last here accepted the arguments earlier expounded by P. Fraccaro in *Atti del 20° Congresso Nazionale di Studi Romani* (1931), 91ff and in *Athenaeum*, 1934, 57ff. A summary of some of the more important theories concerning the development of the centuriate political system is given in *Historia*, 1956, 75ff. For the basic evidence on the subject see Botsford, *RA*, 66ff, 201ff.

218 Cicero, *De Republica*, 2, 40. The

centuria of the *proletarii* contained all those whose property did not qualify them for enrolment in the classes, and in the fully developed political system it ranked as the counterpart of one of the five non-combatant centuries of the original Servian organization.

219 *De Republica*, 2, 39. This vital text reads as follows: 'Now you see that the system is this. The centuries of *equites* and the *sex suffragia*, together with the centuries of the first class and one additional century of carpenters which serves the city's essential needs, number 89. If only 8 centuries are added to these from among the remaining 104, an absolute majority is achieved.' Recently an attempt was made to revive old doubts concerning the authenticity of Cicero's text by G. V. Sumner, *AJP*, 1960, 136ff. This was shown to be unfounded by L. R. Taylor, *AJP*, 1961, 337ff, *AJP*, 1963, 66ff (questions of text), and by E. S. Staveley, *Historia*, 1962, 299ff, and J. J. Nicholls *Classical Philology*, 1964, 102ff (questions of interpretation).

220 Livy 1, 43, 12: 'nec mirari oportet hunc ordinem qui nunc est post expletas quinque et triginta tribus, duplicato eorum numero centuriis iuniorum seniorumque, ad institutam ab Servio Tullio summam non convenire.'

221 Livy 29, 37, 13; Livy, *Periochae*, 49; Cicero, *De Lege Agraria*, 2, 4; *Philippics*, 11, 18; Polybius 6, 14, 7; Lucan 5, 391ff.

222 Mommsen, *St.* III, 274, n. 3. *Cf.* A. D. Momigliano, *Studia et Documenta Historiae et Iuris*, 1938, 509ff.

223 The evidence is contained in the document known as the Tabula Hebana (lines 22–32), which was discovered in 1947. The text can be found in *AJP*, 1954, 225ff, and that part of it which concerns elections has been conveniently reproduced by L. R. Taylor, *RVA*, 159ff. For a translation see Johnson, Coleman-Norton and Bourne, *Ancient Roman Statutes* (1961), 131ff. The case for regarding the procedure detailed in this document as relevant to the Republican centuriate assemblies was first argued by G. Tibiletti, 'Il funzionamento dei comizi centuriati alla luce della Tavola Hebana', *Athenaeum*, 1949, 210ff.

224 I have stated my own reasons for treating the evidence of the Tabula Hebana in this connection with caution in *AJP*, 1953, 10ff, and *Historia*, 1956, 112ff. For the view that only the first or the first two classes were coordinated with the tribes see particularly A. Rosenberg, *Untersuchungen zur römischen Zenturienverfassung* (1911), 73ff; P. Fraccaro, *Studi in honore di P. Bonfante* I (1929), 117ff; Staveley, *AJP*, 1953, 17ff.

225 *De Republica*, 2, 39–40.

226 Compare Mommsen, *St.* I³, 470. The right of choice is unlikely to have been original if the centuriate assembly was at its outset a purely military gathering, but it is difficult to believe that its introduction was delayed long after selection had begun to be exercised in the purely plebeian assembly (possibly in 471 BC). For a different view and a much later date see H. Siber, *Römisches Verfassungsrecht* (1952), 47. For the particular circumstances which obtained during an *interregnum* see Staveley, 'The Conduct of Elections during an Interregnum', *Historia*, 1954, 193ff.

227 Cicero, *De Legibus*, 3, 11. *Cf. De Domo*, 43; *Pro Sestio*, 65, 73; *De Republica*, 2, 61; *De Legibus*, 3, 44. On the early judicial activity of the centuriate assembly see Staveley, 'Provo-

cation during the Fifth and Fourth Centuries B.C.', *Historia*, 1955, 412ff. More recently the view of Mommsen that the assembly functioned essentially as a court of appeal has been challenged by W. Kunkel, *Untersuchungen zur Entwicklung des römischen Kriminalverfahrens in vorsullanischer Zeit* (1962) (reviewed and discussed by P. A. Brunt, *Revue d'Histoire du Droit*, 1964, 440ff, and A. N. Sherwin-White, *JRS*, 1964, 208ff).

228 Cicero, *De Legibus*, 3, 44–5. Cicero significantly refers to the voters of the centuriate assembly as 'the whole of Italy', and he comments that 'when the people are divided by wealth, rank, and age, their decisions are wiser than when they meet in the assembly of tribes'.

229 Pseudo-Sallust 2, 8 (123 BC); Cicero, *Pro Murena*, 47 (66 BC).

230 See below, pp. 218ff. It is likely that this change is reflected in Dionysius 4, 21, 3, where reference is made to a 'more democratic form' of voting in his own times (*cf.* Fraccaro, *Studi Bonfante* I, 108ff). Some scholars still insist, however, that Dionysius is referring here to the third-century reform (*cf.* Nicholls, *AJP*, 1956, 252; Brunt, *JRS*, 1961, 82f; Taylor, *RVA*, 87).

231 Tabula Hebana, lines 8ff. See below, p. 219.

232 Livy 2, 56, 2; 58, 1; Dionysius 9, 41; 10, 4. On the origins of the tribal assembly see Botsford, *RA*, 119ff.

233 I have discussed the evidence relating to the use of the tribal assembly in the official sector in 'Tribal Legislation before the *Lex Hortensia*', *Athenaeum*, 1955, 3ff. Suggestions for the use of tribal assemblies of the whole people are to be found in Livy 3, 71, 2; 6, 21, 5; 7, 16,

7; Tacitus, *Annals*, 1, 22. For the possible part played by the tribal assembly in the election of consular tribunes between 445 and 367 BC see Staveley, *JRS*, 1953, 30ff.

234 Frontinus 129.

235 On this point see my discussion in *Athenaeum*, 1955, 4ff, where the case against the later exclusion of patricians is argued in detail (*cf.*

Botsford, *RA*, 302). An attempt has recently been made by Taylor, *RVA*, 60f, to revive the older view of Mommsen that patricians were excluded throughout the Republic; but the vital evidence of the extant legislation has been ignored (*cf.* Bruns, *Fontes Iuris Romani*[7] (1909), III, 16, lines 29, 39; 17, lines 13, 20–21).

CHAPTER VII

236 See, in particular, Larsen, *Representative Government in the Greek and Roman World* (1955), *passim*, for details of voting arrangements in the Hellenistic federations.

237 This is also the view favoured by U. Hall in her important article, 'Voting Procedure in Roman Assemblies', *Historia*, 1964, 269ff.

238 For a comprehensive treatment of the distribution of the tribal areas in Italy see Taylor, *VDRR*, *passim*, and in particular 79ff, 151ff.

239 This question, and the possible motives of the censors in failing to take the necessary action, is discussed above, p. 201.

240 Suetonius, *Divus Augustus*, 46. The unrepresentative nature of the assemblies at Rome in the later Republic is considered in detail by G. Tibiletti, 'The *Comitia* during the Decline of the Roman Republic', *Studia et Documenta Historiae et Iuris*, 1959, 94ff.

241 Livy 9, 46, 11; Diodorus 20, 36, 4.

242 See Staveley, 'The Political Aims of Appius Claudius Caecus', *Historia*, 1959, 410ff. A very similar view has also been propounded by F. Cassola, *I Gruppi politici Romani nel III secolo A.C.*, 1962, 128ff. For different interpretations of the censorship of Appius Claudius see, among

others, P. Lejay, *Revue de Philologie*, 1920, 105ff; A. Garzetti, *Athenaeum*, 1947, 175ff.

243 Livy 9, 46, 14; Valerius Maximus 2, 2, 9. The emphasis on the new concept of the urban tribes as an underprivileged group is inherent in these texts.

244 On the importance of *clientela* in Roman voting see below, pp. 192ff.

245 Appian, *Bella Civilia*, 49, 4; Sisenna, fr. 17; Velleius 2, 20, 2. See Taylor, *VDRR*, 102ff for a detailed discussion of the problems which are raised by the evidence on this issue.

246 Livy, *Periochae*, 84. Taylor expresses the orthodox view when she writes that 'the problem was tremendous, and there was a danger that the old citizens would be outvoted by the large numbers of new citizens' (*VDRR*, 102). It is improbable, however, that the new voters represented a political threat in this sense, as they were not sufficiently a single entity to take a united stand on legislation or to promote their own candidates at an election. The fear of the nobility was no doubt simply that, if they were registered immediately in the existing tribes, they would upset by dint of their numbers the very well laid plans of individual families and groups to marshal the vote (see below, pp. 191ff). Time was needed by the nobles to extend their *clientelae* and adjust their calculations for the delivery of the vote, so that they might continue to fight elections among themselves in accordance with the established and accepted code of rules.

247 Livy, *Periochae*, 20. The date is uncertain, as this book of Livy covers four censorships between 234 and 220 BC.

248 Livy 45, 15, 7; Cicero, *De Oratore*, 1, 38.

249 Livy 41, 50, 8; *cf.* 45, 15, 1–2. I

accept here the interpretation of Botsford, *RA*, 85, and Taylor, *VDRR*, 139. An alternative view, favoured by A. H. McDonald, *Cambridge Historical Journal*, 1938, 134, and H. H. Scullard, *Roman Politics 220–150 B.C.* (1951), 182f, is that Livy's words refer to some further reform of the centuriate assembly.

250 Livy, *Periochae*, 77 (*lex Sulpicia*); Dio 36, 42, 2; Asconius, *In Cornelianam*, 64 (Clark) (*lex Manilia*).

251 See below, p. 201.

CHAPTER VIII

252 Cicero, *Pro Sestio*, 72; Dio, 42, 23 (whitened tablet); Cicero, *Pro Milone*, 87; Suetonius, *Divus Julius*, 28, 3 (bronze).

253 Cicero, *Pro Sestio*, 135. *Cf. De Legibus*, 3, 11; Festus 224.

254 The ban on meeting for comitial business on market-days (*nundinae*) dated from the *lex Hortensia* of 287 BC (Macrobius 1, 16, 30; Pliny, *Naturalia Historia*, 18, 3, 13). The ban on the use of *dies fasti* was confirmed, and possibly introduced, by a *lex Fufia* in the middle of the second century BC (*cf.* Cicero, *Pro Sestio*, 56), although it was removed, at least for a period, by a law of the tribune Clodius in 58 BC (Cicero, *Pro Sestio*, 33; *De Provinciis Consularibus* 46–7). See below, note 397.

255 Cicero, *De Domo*, 41; *Pro Sestio*, 135; *Ad Atticum*, 2, 9, 1; *Philippics*, 5, 8.

256 Mommsen, *St.* III, 375ff. *Cf.* Livy 3, 35, 1; Dionysius, 7, 58, 3; 10, 3, 5.

257 Livy 4, 58, 8; 7, 33, 9; 25, 2, 4, 27, 6, 2; 41, 14, 3; 42, 28, 1; 43, 11, 3; 44, 17, 2.

258 Cicero, *Philippics*, 1, 25; Appian, *Bella Civilia*, 4, 7.

259 *Pro Sestio*, 129. *Cf.* Quintilian 2, 4, 35 for the concept of the *dies idoneus* (the proper day).

260 Livy 26, 18, 7 (P. Scipio Africanus announces his candidature when the people are already assembled in the Campus Martius); Plutarch, *Aemilius Paulus*, 10, 2 (L. Aemilius Paulus is prevailed upon to accept the consulship). The candidature of Q. Pompeius is also represented as a last-minute bid, calculated to surprise his opponents on the eve of the election (Plutarch, *Apophth. Scip. Min.*, 8). Examples of the election of individuals who had not professed their candidature are cited in Livy 10, 9, 10; 10, 22, 2; 26, 22, 2–6; Cicero, *De Amicitia*, 11; Dio 54, 6, 10.

261 Cicero, *De Oratore*, 2, 260: 'ex eodem hoc vetus illud est, quod aiunt Maluginensem illum M. Scipionem, cum ex centuria sua renuntiaret Acidinum consulem praecoque dixisset "dic de Manlio": "virum bonum" inquit "egregiumque civem arbitror." ' It is clear from this anecdote that the standard form of enquiry which was made of the returning officers of the individual

units by the herald was 'dic de X'
('Tell me about X'), where X in each
case was the name of a specific
candidate on the published list. See
above, pp. 177f.

262 In at least two cases persons
who had been nominated and elected
in consular elections declared themselves unwilling to take up office.
This was true of Augustus in 21 BC
(Dio 54, 6, 10), and of T. Manlius
Capitolinus in 211 BC, who pleaded
his physical unsuitability for military
command and prevailed upon the
presiding magistrate to restart the
voting, when the prerogative century
had already declared itself in his
favour (Livy 26, 22). On each
occasion the presiding consul is
likely to have been responsible for
nominating the person concerned (*cf.*
Scullard, *Roman Politics*, 64f, on 211
BC). The only suggestion of a 'write-
in' vote comes from Suetonius' story
that at the elections for 43 BC certain
votes were found to have been given
to two persons who had recently
been deposed by Caesar from the
tribunate (*Divus Julius*, 80, 3). But it
is very clear from Suetonius' language
that this was a protest vote, and that
no official note was taken of it at the
election itself.

It is possible that these rules governing candidature and official nomination were not so strictly observed by
the tribunes in the plebeian assemblies. According to A. H. M. Jones,
*Proceedings of the Cambridge Philo-
logical Society*, 1960, 36ff, the account
in the sources of the elections of
Gaius Gracchus in 123 BC and of
Saturninus in 101 BC can reasonably
be taken to indicate that formal note
was taken at tribunician elections of
votes cast for persons who were
strictly ineligible on account of their
having held the office in a previous

year. If then by any chance less than
the full quota of other candidates
managed to secure a majority of
votes, Jones argues, these 'ineligible'
persons could legally be elected, if
they won a majority of the votes, to
make up the college of tribunes to its
full complement. Whether he
believes that the presiding tribunes
accepted, and so advertised, the
names of such persons in the first
instance, or merely that he formally
acknowledged the votes cast in their
favour at the *renuntiatio*, is not clear.

263 Cicero (*De Lege Agraria*, 2, 24)
states that the Rullan bill of 63 BC
required personal *professio*, 'which
had not been demanded by any earlier
law'. Plutarch's suggestion that such
a rule applied in 104 BC (*Marius*, 12, 1)
is surely mistaken. On Caesar's *professio* see Suetonius, *Divus Julius*, 18,
2; Plutarch, *Caesar*, 13; Dio 37, 54, 2.
Under Roman law, as soon as a pro-
magistrate entered the city his
imperium lapsed, and with it his right
to claim a triumph.

264 Suetonius, *Divus Julius*, 28, 3;
Dio 40, 56, 1.

265 Sallust, *Catiline*, 18, 2. Compare also Appian, *Bella Civilia*, 2, 8;
Dio 39, 27, 3; Cicero, *Ad Familiares*,
16, 12, 3.

266 On the refusal of a presiding
magistrate to put the names of
would-be candidates before the
electorate see Livy 3, 64, 5; 7, 22, 8;
8, 15, 9; 10, 15, 11; 27, 6, 5; 39, 39, 4;
Cicero, *Brutus*, 224; *Ad Brutum*, 1, 5,
3. For the later emphasis on the consul's refusal to announce the votes
cast in favour of particular candidates
see Valerius Maximus 3, 8, 3;
Velleius 2, 92; and—probably a
reflection of the practice of his own
time—Livy 3, 21, 8. That a consul
could still refuse to accept the candidature of a disqualified person in the

first century is proved by Asconius, *In Toga Candida*, 89 (Clark). For a recent discussion of the problems connected with *professio* see D. C. Earl, *Historia*, 1965, 325ff, who has justly stressed (*contra* A. E. Astin, *Historia*, 1962, 252ff) that *professio* as a formal requirement of candidature was closely associated with the concept of the time limit.

267 On this rule, which was probably embodied in the *lex Fufia, cf.* Schol. Bob., 148 (Stangl). Dispensation from the rule was occasionally granted by the Senate, as for example to facilitate the passing of laws on electoral bribery (*cf.* Dio 36, 39, 1; Cicero, *Ad Atticum*, 1, 16, 13; 4, 16, 5). For the *lex Fufia* see the works cited in note 397.

268 *Cf.* Livy 3, 63, 8; 10, 7, 1; 10, 8, 12; 34, 1, 4; 34, 4, 20; 45, 21, 6; Dio 39, 35, 1; Cicero, *Pro Lege Manilia*, 69; *De Legibus*, 3, 11; Asconius, *In Cornelianam*, 71 (Clark). On the subject of *contiones* in general see Mommsen, *St.* III, 394ff; Botsford, *RA*, 139ff.

269 Cicero, *Ad Atticum*, 1, 19, 4.

270 Gellius 3, 2, 10; Censorinus 23, 4. See Mommsen, *St.* I³, 103ff.

271 Varro, *De Lingua Latina*, 6, 92; Plutarch, *Gaius Gracchus*, 3, 4; Dionysius 7, 59, 1 (summoning at dawn); Livy 39, 16, 4 (end at sunset).

272 Varro, *De Lingua Latina*, 5, 155.

273 Gellius 15, 27, 5; Livy 6, 20, 10; Cicero, *Pro Rabirio*, 11.

274 Dio 37, 27; Varro, *De Lingua Latina*, 6, 92; Macrobius 1, 16, 5.

275 Livy 7, 16, 7.

276 *Cf.* Plutarch, *Gaius Gracchus*, 3, 2; Cicero, *Pro Plancio*, 16; *Ad Atticum*, 1, 1, 1; 4, 3, 4; Varro, *De Re Rustica*, 3, 2; Suetonius, *Divus Julius*, 80, 4.

277 Cicero, *Ad Atticum*, 4, 16, 8; Dio 53, 23, 2.

278 'La procedura del voto nei comizi tributi romani', *Atti della R. Accademia delle Scienze di Torino*, 1913–14, 600ff. On the introduction of simultaneous voting in the tribal electoral assemblies see above, pp. 172f.

279 Livy 3, 54, 15; *cf.* 3, 63, 7. For an assembly in the late third century see Livy 27, 21, 1; Plutarch, *Marcellus*, 27, 3.

280 *Cf.* Varro, *De Lingua Latina*, 5, 155; *De Re Rustica*, 1, 2, 9. The Comitium was an enclosed space in the north-east corner of the Forum. It was partly separated from the Forum proper by the *rostra*, which was commonly used as a speakers' platform at informal gatherings and as a voting tribunal at *comitia*. The case for the one time regular use of the Comitium by the tribes is convincingly argued by Taylor, *RVA*, 40f. On topography see Taylor, *RVA*, 21ff.

281 Livy 25, 3, 15; 33, 25, 7; 34, 1, 4; 43, 16, 9; 45, 36, 6; Appian, *Bella Civilia*, 1, 16, 2; 1, 25, 8; Plutarch, *Tiberius Gracchus*, 16f; *Gaius Gracchus*, 13. This evidence relates to the period before 120 BC.

282 Appian, *Bella Civilia*, 1, 12, 5; Dio 38, 6, 2; Cicero, *Post Reditum*, 18; *Ad Atticum*, 1, 14, 5; Valerius Maximus 8, 1; Plutarch, *Cato Minor*, 27; Frontinus 129. This evidence relates to the period from 133 BC onwards. Where Livy and Dionysius refer to the use of the Forum in the early Republic (Livy 3, 17, 4; Dionysius 6, 17, 7), they are probably speaking of the Comitium (see above, note 280).

283 Livy 9, 46, 11. It is unlikely that Livy used these words to distinguish between the tribal and the centuriate assemblies, as has sometimes been thought. They appear in his reference to the reforms of Appius Claudius, the censor, who changed the system of registration in the tribes. At this time, in 312 BC, the composition of the centuries had nothing to do with the tribes.

284 *De Re Rustica*, 1, 2, 9. *Cf.* Cicero, *Laelius*, 96. Plutarch (*Gaius Gracchus*, 5, 3) ascribes this move to Gaius Gracchus. But he is almost certainly mistaken in dating it so late and in attributing a political motive to its author. See on this Taylor, *RVA*, 25f.

285 Livy 25, 3, 14; 34, 1, 14; 45, 36, 6.

286 Cicero, *Pro Sestio*, 79, where reference is made to the use of *fragmenta saeptorum* (pieces of the barrier fences) as weapons in a riot. The tribal contingents were divided off one from another (*cf.* Cicero, *Philippics*, 1, 25; 5, 9). For the use of ropes compare Appian, *Bella Civilia*, 1, 30; Dionysius 7, 59 (probably an anachronism).

287 *Cf.* Mommsen, *St.* III, 390f.

288 Asconius, *In Cornelianam*, 58 (Clark); Appian, *Bella Civilia*, 1, 11; Dio 37, 43, 2; Plutarch, *Cato Minor*, 28, 1.

289 Cicero in Asconius, *In Cornelianam*, 71 (Clark).

290 *Cf.* Asconius, *In Cornelianam*, 71 (Clark): 'adstat populus confusus ut semper alias, ita in contione'. For examples of *contiones* held prior to the vote *cf.*, for example, Livy 2, 56, 10; 3, 11, 4; 25, 3, 15; Cicero, *Pro Flacco*, 15. The Romans used the term *summovere populum* to denote the breaking up of the *contio* and the transformation of the gathering into a voting assembly, from which those not qualified to vote were excluded.

291 The permanent enclosures on the Campus Martius appear to date from at least the late third century (*cf.* Livy 26, 22, 11). According to one source (Schol. on Vergil, *Eclogues*, 1, 33), these were wooden structures

during the Republic. Caesar, however, planned the construction of marble enclosures with a roof, which were completed only after his death (Cicero, *Ad Atticum*, 4, 16, 8).

292 Asconius, *In Cornelianam*, 71 (Clark). *Cf.* Livy 2, 56, 12; 3, 11, 4; Cicero, *De Lege Agraria*, 3, 4, 11.

293 Livy 25, 3, 14.

294 Livy 25, 3, 16. Compare the provisions of the municipal charter of the colony of Malaga in Spain for the votes of Roman citizens and Latins (*lex Malacitana*, 53). A translation of the most relevant clauses of the *lex Malacitana* appears in Appendix III.

295 Livy 24, 7, 12 (*Aniensis iuniorum*); 26, 22, 7 (*Voturia iuniorum*); 27, 6, 3 (*Galeria iuniorum*). For the view that the prerogative century was chosen from all the centuries of juniors except those drawn from two of the urban tribes see Taylor, *RVA*, 92f.

296 *De Divinatione*, 1, 103; *cf.* 2, 83; *Pro Murena*, 38. Cicero writes (*Pro Plancio*, 49) that no one who was returned first by the *centuria praerogativa* ever failed to secure election as consul for the year in question. The importance attached to the vote of the *praerogativa* is further illustrated by Pompey's dismissal of the assembly on a religious pretext when the prerogative century had voted against his interests (Plutarch, *Cato Minor*, 42, 3), and by the attempt to bribe the as yet undetermined *praerogativa* at the elections for 54 BC (Cicero, *Ad Quintum fratrem*, 2, 14, 4).

297 Cicero, *Pro Plancio*, 35.

298 For the established *ordo tribuum* see Cicero, *De Lege Agraria*, 2, 79. Hall, op. cit. (note 237, above), 278, believes lots were drawn throughout to determine the order in which results were to be announced, as was the case in the electoral *comitia*. But this would have been a purposeless and time-wasting procedure; and, as the tribes had to be moved in succession into a restricted voting enclosure, it would have been administratively more convenient if the order in which they were to be called were known from the outset of the proceedings.

CHAPTER IX

299 See M. Rothstein, *Festschrift Hirschfeld* (1903) 30ff.; Botsford, *RA*, 156f; Taylor, *RVA*, 2.

300 Botsford (*RA*, 157) suggests that individual voting began with the centuries; but it is not easy to accept that the assertion of individuality was fostered in the military sphere.

301 Cicero, *De Legibus*, 3, 33f. See Mommsen, *St.* III, 403ff.

302 Cicero, *Laelius*, 41; *De Legibus*, 3, 35, 36; *Pro Sestio*, 103; *Brutus*, 37; 106. A fourth law, a *lex Coelia*, probably of 107 BC, extended the ballot to the somewhat rare judicial proceedings on a charge of *perduellio* (high treason) which took place before the *comitia centuriata*.

303 Auctor ad Herennium, 1, 21 (*cistae*); Plutarch, *Tiberius Gracchus*, 11, 1 (ὑδρίαι); Dionysius 10, 41 (ἀγγεῖα); 11, 52 (καδίσκος). Voting receptacles portrayed on coins of the late Republic appear variously as vases and as wicker baskets (*cf.* E. A. Sydenham, *Roman Republican Coinage* (1952) nos. 502, 917, 935, 963; Figs. VI and IX in the text). The Tabula Hebana, line 18, refers to them as *cistae vimineae grandes* (large willow baskets).

304 Auctor ad Herennium, 1, 21; Cicero, *Ad Atticum*, 1, 14, 5; Suetonius, *Divus Julius*, 80, 4; Festus 452.

305 Cicero, *De Legibus*, 3, 38.

306 Mommsen, *St.* III, 401. On the basis of the Marble Plan of Rome, discovered in 1937, it has been estimated that the overall size of the new *saepta* designed at the end of the Republic was approximately 100 by 300 yards. This would suggest that there were thirty-five parallel compartments, each from 7 to 8 feet in width. The evidence has been discussed by Taylor, *RVA*, 47ff.

307 For a detailed consideration of the structures in the Roman Forum which may have been used for voting purposes see Taylor, *RVA*, 41ff.

308 See Cicero, *Divinatio In Caecilium*, 24; Tabula Hebana, line 19 (*tabella e eratae*); *lex Bembina* of 122 BC (*CIL*, 1, 2², 583, lines 50ff) (*sorticulae*).

309 Cicero, *De Domo*, 112. *Cf.* Plutarch, *Cato Minor*, 46, 2; Suetonius, *Divus Julius*, 80, 4.

310 Sometimes, however, in a court of law provision was made for the letters to be on opposite sides of the voting tablet (*cf.* the *lex Bembina*, 50ff, which governed procedure in the extortion courts), and it is clear that practice was not uniform. A coin of Cassius Longinus (Sydenham, no. 935 —Fig. VI in text) clearly shows a legislative ballot with only the letter U (for *uti rogas*) on the one side.

311 Cicero, *Ad Atticum*, 1, 14, 5.

312 That the Romans were normally expected to mark their tablets is clearly indicated by Plutarch's story of the riot at an assembly of Gaius Gracchus, at which the voters used their *stili* as weapons (*Gaius Gracchus*, 13, 5).

313 Tabula Hebana, lines 18–19. It should be noted that this was a vote at which the attendance was small compared with that at the full electoral assemblies of the Republic (see below, pp. 218f).

314 Sydenham, no. 548. For the orthodox interpretation of this, the only voting scene to be depicted in any detail on Roman coinage, see Mommsen, *St.* III, 400, n. 4; Taylor, *RVA*, 39.

315 See T. E. Carney, *Numismatic Chronicle*, 1959, 87. The identity of the moneyer, P. Licinius Nerva, is, however, uncertain.

316 Tabula Hebana, line 20.

317 The argument summarized in this section has been developed more fully in my recent article, 'The Role of the First Voter in Roman Legislative Assemblies', *Historia*, 1969, 513ff.

318 *Cf.* the *lex Quinctia* of 9 BC: 'tribus Sergia principium fuit, pro tribu Sex. L.f. Virro primus scivit' (Frontinus 129); the *lex agraria* of 111 BC: 'pro tribu Q. Fabius Q.f. primus scivit' (CIL, 1.2², 585).

319 Cicero, *Pro Plancio*, 35; 'nam quod primus scivit legem de publicanis tum cum vir amplissimus consul id illi ordini per populum dedit quod per senatum, si licuisset, dedisset, si in eo crimen est quia suffragium tulit, quis non tulit publicanus? si quia primus scivit, utrum id sortis esse vis, an eius qui illam legem ferebat? si sortis, nullum crimen est in casu; si consulis, *splendor etiam Planci* hunc a summo viro principem esse ordinis iudicatum.'

320 Compare Mommsen, *St.* III, 411, n. 2: 'Cicero's words indicate that it was at least possible for the *rogator* to make the choice himself, but this must have been exceptional', and Hall, *Historia*, 1964, n. 37: 'In this passage Cicero says that it was either *sors* (the lot) or the consul (Caesar) which determined that Plancius senior was the first man to vote on a particular law. Presumably all that Caesar could have done to ensure

this was, knowing Plancius' importance in his own tribe and expecting him to vote first in it, to see that his tribe was the first to vote.'

321 Livy (9, 38, 15), for example, indicates that the choice of the *principium* in the *comitia curiata* was left to the lot. The *lex Malacitana* shows that at Malaga it was the lot which determined the order in which results were announced, when the units voted simultaneously (see below, p. 235).

322 *De Domo*, 79–80. We gather that Clodius had had the name of C. Fidulius inscribed in the prescript of his* measure as being the individual who had been the first to cast his vote, and that Fidulius had subsequently denied having been present. Whether he was or was not present is irrelevant to Cicero's argument, for his object was simply to draw attention to the fact that Clodius had been forced to rely upon the services of such a lowly person. The implication is clearly that Fidulius was a man of Clodius' own choosing.

323 This is implied clearly by the complaints which were made against Plancius on the ground that he voted first, as also by Cicero's designation of the first voter as *auctor* in *De Domo*, 79.

324 See Livy 1, 43; Dionysius 4, 20, for the Servian organization of the centuries. It is suggested by Livy (10, 22, 1) and Festus (290) that the centuries of *equites* acted as *praerogativae*. So Mommsen, *St.* III, 290f. See, however, Ch. Meier, *RE*, Supplement VIII, 567ff.

325 Cicero, *Philippics*, 2, 82–3: 'sortitio praerogativae ... renuntiatur ... prima classis vocatur: renuntiatur; deinde, ita ut adsolet, suffragia; tum secunda classis.' This is the clearest statement we have of the order of procedure in the *comitia centuriata*. For the attempts to upset the strict calling of the centuries by classes see Pseudo-Sallust, 2, 8, 1 and Cicero, *Pro Murena*, 67.

326 *Lex Malacitana*, 55.

327 Livy 10, 13, 11.

328 Livy 26, 22, 11.

329 'La procedura del voto', 605ff. See also Hall, op. cit., 276ff, and Taylor, *RVA*, 128.

330 Valerius Maximus 8, 1, 7; Asconius, *In Cornelianam*, 72 (Clark). Other references to successive voting are contained in Livy 4, 5, 2; 40, 42, 10; 45, 36, 7. A passage in Dionysius (7, 59, 9) which had been thought to indicate simultaneous voting at an early Republican tribal assembly is almost certainly irrelevant (see Hall, op. cit., 277f; Taylor, *RVA*, 130).

331 See above, pp. 155f.

332 Cicero, *Pro Plancio*, 49; Varro, *De Re Rustica*, 3, 2, 1.

333 This was convincingly argued by Taylor, 'Was Tiberius Gracchus' Last Assembly Legislative or Elective?', *Athenaeum*, 1963, 51ff, and again, in answer to objections raised by Earl (*Athenaeum*, 1965, 95ff), in 'Appian and Plutarch on Tiberius Gracchus' Last Assembly', *Athenaeum*, 1966, 238ff. Taylor notes that an assembly supposedly called for the election of colonial commissioners in 194 BC is said to have been held on the Capitol (Livy 34, 53, 1–2), and she explains this by suggesting that Livy has mistaken the election for the carrying of the subsequent *lex curiata* (on which see above, p. 123). There is, however, no reason to suppose that Livy was in error. The appointment of commissioners was a routine matter, which was not dealt with in the official election period. The attendance is likely, therefore, to have been small, and the voters could probably well have been accommodated on the Capitol.

334 'La procedura del voto', 251f. Fraccaro is followed in this view by Hall, op. cit., 291ff.

335 *Cf.* Taylor, *RVA*, 46, who also accepts the case for a much earlier change to simultaneous voting at tribal elections.

CHAPTER X

336 On the master *tabula*—Cicero, *In Pisonem*, 11; Varro, *De Re Rustica*, 3, 18; Q. Cicero, *Commentariolum Petitionis*, 8: on *puncta*—Cicero, *Pro Murena*, 72; *Pro Plancio*, 53; *Tusculanae Disputationes*, 2, 62; Horace, *Satires*, 2, 2, 50: on *loculi*—Varro, *De Re Rustica*, 3, 18; Ausonius, *Gratiarum actio ad Gratian*, 3.

337 For *custodes* as counters of the votes—Cicero, *Post Reditum*, 28; *In Pisonem*, 36; *lex Malacitana*, 55.

338 Pliny, *Naturalia Historia*, 33, 31; *lex Malacitana*, 55.

339 *Lex Malacitana*, 55. Cicero (*In Pisonem*, 11) claims that he was given the first or principal *tabula* for the prerogative century by Piso. It would appear, therefore, that candidates had several *custodes* of their own to supervise the count in the all-important *praerogativa*.

340 See in particular G. De Sanctis, *Storia dei Romani* III, 1, 365f, summarized by Hall, *Historia*, 1964, 305f. The suggestion that the reference to *renuntiatio* in para. 56 of the *lex Malacitana* implies an official announcement of results prior to that which is prescribed in para. 57 is unwarranted.

341 *Lex Malacitana*, 57. On Cicero, *De Oratore*, 2, 260 see above, note 261.

342 *Lex Malacitana*, 57; Cicero, *Pro Plancio*, 53.

343 Livy 6, 38, 5; 40, 42, 10; 45, 36, 7; Appian, *Bella Civilia*, 1, 14, 4.

344 This point is established beyond all question by the *lex Malacitana*, 57, and the Tabula Hebana, lines 40ff, as also by a number of passages in the literary sources which stress the importance attached to being declared elected before the other candidates (Livy 7, 5, 9; Cicero, *Pro Murena*, 18; *In Pisonem*, 2; *De Legibus*, 2, 16; Plutarch, *Tiberius Gracchus*, 15, 5; *Gaius Gracchus*, 3, 2).

345 This was, of course, because the entire assembly disposed of a total of 350 votes (35 × 10), whereas only 344 votes were theoretically needed to give an absolute majority (18 votes) to each of 19 candidates.

346 *Lex Malacitana*, 57.

347 'La procedura del voto', 616ff. See also Hall, op. cit., 285, who accepts this extraordinary piece of time-wasting.

348 *Tiberius Gracchus*, 15, 4. For references to 'all the tribes' see Livy 3, 63, 11; 29, 13, 7; 8, 37, 10; 30, 43, 3; 43, 8, 9.

349 Hall (op. cit., 295) draws attention to the alleged complaint of Gaius Gracchus that he was robbed of election by an unjust *renuntiatio* after he had secured the majority of the votes. The basis and substance of this complaint is at best a matter of dispute (see above, p. 215, with note 422). But in any case this was an election at which all the tribes had in fact voted simultaneously, and Gracchus might well have claimed to have ascertained the sense of all the votes through unofficial channels. The

important point is that this is the sort of complaint about which we should expect to hear far more if the results from all the tribes had been officially announced.

350 It is indeed difficult to see why the use of the lot should not have satisfied the demands for full democratic expression of which Fraccaro speaks ('La procedura del voto', 619). Furthermore, it is surely unrealistic to suppose that the voters at a legislative assembly would have been so concerned to assert their democratic rights that they would have been prepared to spend their time voting on an issue which had already been decided.

351 Cicero in Asconius, *In Cornelianam*, 85 (Clark): 'nescis me praetorem primum esse factum, te concessione competitorum et collatione centuriarum et meo maxime beneficio ex postremo in tertium locum esse subiectum?'. These words, of course, could also be meaningfully interpreted if the Roman voter disposed of only a single vote at elections, irrespective of the number of places to be filled. This view was given some consideration by Hall, op. cit., 297ff, but she showed that it runs counter to much of the evidence and is wholly untenable.

352 The calculation is a simple one. Time for 50 men to pass over the *pontes* (100 in two parallel columns) —4 minutes; number of centuries in the first class and *centuriae equitum*— 88; therefore total voting time—352 minutes. The suggested total of nine hours for vote and *renuntiatio* could, of course, have been reduced to approximately six hours, if at a successive vote the announcement of results had been made during the course of the voting.

353 It has been estimated that each

compartment in the later marble *saepta* could have contained approximately two thousand voters in reasonable comfort (*cf.* Taylor, *RVA*, 54). Although the attendance in some tribes was poor, it is not unlikely that others were very well represented. Cicero (*Pro Plancio*, 21–23) tells us that there was a very large attendance on one occasion from the Teretina tribe, and Plutarch records that the crowds were so great at the election of Gaius Gracchus that many voters were actually excluded from the voting arena (*Gaius Gracchus*, 3, 1).

354 *De Re Rustica*, 3, 2–17.

355 The 'maximum' is the time which would have been required on occasions when it proved necessary to call the centuries of all the classes to the vote. The 'minimum' is the time which would have been required on occasions when the issue of an election was decided by the centuries of the *equites* and the first and second classes alone.

356 It should be remembered that the length of time taken up by the count was not affected by the number of centuries in each group. Thus the count of the votes in the prerogative century alone will have taken as long as the count for the remaining centuries of the first class.

CHAPTER XI

357 The classic work on the Roman nobility is still M. Gelzer, *Die Nobilität der römischen Republik*, 1912, which as recently as 1969 was published in an English translation by R. Seager. See also Scullard, *Roman Politics*, Chapter I; E. Badian, *Foreign Clientelae*, 1958, 1ff; and—for a most valuable survey of the operation of *clientela* and the political activity of the nobles in the first century BC— Taylor, *PP*.

358 See the important recent contributions to the study of third-century domestic history by Cassola (*I Gruppi Politici*) and A. Lippold (*Consules: Untersuchungen zur Geschichte des römischen konsulates von 264 bis 201 v. Chr.*, 1963), summarized and reviewed by myself in *JRS*, 1963, 182ff, and *JRS*, 1964, 197f. A similar and more cautious approach was earlier applied by Scullard in his *Roman Politics* to the study of late third- and early second-century history.

359 *Commentariolum Petitionis*, 53.

Occasionally in the late Republic, when a candidate fought from a position of strength, he could afford to raise a political standard. Thus, Pompey in 71 BC announced his intention of restoring the powers of the tribunes which had been curtailed by Sulla (Cicero, *In Verrem*, 1, 45; Appian, *Bella Civilia*, 1, 121, 2). The circumstances on this occasion, however, were exceptional. In normal times the association of a candidate with strongly held views on matters of policy was less significant for its effect upon the attitude of the voting public than for its effect upon the enthusiasm of his fellow nobles in promoting and assisting his campaign.

360 *Cf.* Livy 2, 41; Dionysius 8, 70ff; Diodorus 1, 37, 7 (Spurius Cassius): Livy 6, 11, 4–6 (M. Manlius).

361 Livy 4, 25, 13; 7, 15, 13.

362 In the second century all nobles were required to do a ten-year period of military service before entering upon their political careers (Polybius

6, 19, 2). This rule appears to have been relaxed later, but the young *nobilis* commonly served a period as a military tribune, or, failing that, as a companion of a commander in the field.

363 Cicero, *Paradoxa Stoicorum*, 40; Plutarch, *Lucullus*, 5–6.

364 Cicero, *Ad Quintum fratrem*, 3, 1, 10; 3, 8, 3; Suetonius, *Divus Julius*, 23, 2.

365 The evidence comes largely from inscriptions. *Cf. ILS*, 8205–7, and, for the many slogans written upon walls and buildings in Pompeii calling for votes at the municipal elections, *ILS*, 6398ff. See below, pp. 224ff.

366 *Commentariolum Petitionis*, 30: 'Learn by heart the tribal divisions of the whole of Italy, so that you may have adequate strength in every single municipality, colony, prefecture, or other place in Italy.'

367 These assignments are discussed in detail by Taylor, *VDRR*, 79ff, 150ff.

368 Cicero, *Pro Murena*, 69; *In Vatinium*, 39; *Pro Plancio*, 43; *De Haruspicum Responsis*, 56; *cf.* Q. Cicero, *Commentariolum Petitionis*, 17.

369 This can be inferred from the fact that there were tribal officers, as well as from the evidence which suggests the existence of a tribal secretariat and of central tribal accommodation (*cf.* Cicero, *Pro Murena*, 72; Suetonius, *Divus Julius*, 41, 3). For their probable siting see Taylor, *RVA*, 69.

370 Cicero, *Pro Plancio*, 45: 'We must not stop our children from attending upon, and showing affection to, their fellow-tribesmen or from being able to deliver the votes of their tribes for their friends.' *Cf.* Q. Cicero, *Commentariolum Petitionis*, 18.

371 *Pro Plancio*, 48.

372 See my remarks in the *Classical Review*, 1962, 73ff.

373 *Cf.* in particular *Pro Plancio*, 7, where Cicero contrasts the major and minor elections and emphasizes the part played by *diligentia* and *gratia* in the latter.

374 The size of the contingent in the city who remained registered in the rural tribes has for long been a matter of dispute. Compare the different views of F. B. Marsh, *History of the Roman World, 146 to 30 BC* (1935), 370ff, and Last's review of it, *AJP*, 1937, 467ff. Both scholars took up somewhat extreme positions, and it is likely that they both overstated their case. Certainly the much quoted statement of Cicero that there were certain tribes which at some assemblies did not manage to muster the required quorum of voters (*Pro Sestio*, 109) does not prove that the retention of rural registration by urban dwellers was a fiction, for a poor attendance might often have been ascribable to apathy and should not be taken to indicate that there were no eligible voters near at hand. On the other hand, it is probably a mistake to assume that the country folk could not influence the way in which the voting went, if they wished to do so. Perhaps it should be said that the numbers of city-dwellers registered in the rural tribes were large enough to determine the outcome at most, if not all, legislative votes, which the country people did not normally travel to attend, but not large enough to have any real impact at the tribal elections.

375 The evidence is cited in note 267 above.

376 Appian asserts that for his last assembly Tiberius Gracchus attempted to summon his supporters from the country areas, but that in the event he was forced to rely upon the urban folk on account of the former's preoccupation with the harvest (1, 14, 2–3). He also represents the conflict in the assembly during Saturninus' tribunate in 100 BC as one between the rural dwellers, who supported the tribune's proposals, and the urban element which opposed them (1, 30, 2).

377 Livy, *Periochae*, 77; Dio 36, 42, 2; Cicero, *Pro Milone*, 87; 89; Asconius, *In Milonianam*, 52 (Clark).

378 Among the most profitable areas to canvass appear to have been the regions both north and south of the Po, probably because the inhabitants were distributed over a large selection of tribes (*cf.* Taylor, *VDRR*, 126ff). They were visited by Cicero before his election in 64 BC (*Ad Atticum*, 1, 1, 2; *Philippics*, 2, 76), and Caesar travelled widely in the area in preparation for his second consular candidature (Hirtius, *Bellum Gallicum*, 8, 50).

379 See in particular Q. Cicero, *Commentariolum Petitionis*, 34–38; Varro, *De Lingua Latina*, 5, 28; Livy 39, 39, 2; Cicero, *Pro Murena*, 70ff. Further evidence is quoted by Mommsen, *St.* I³, 478ff.

380 Polybius 6, 56, 1. Laws were carried in 181 BC (Livy 40, 19, 11) and in 159 BC (Livy, *Periochae*, 47) which appear to have carried the death penalty.

381 Laws are recorded as follows: 81 BC (?)—Schol. Bob., 78 (Stangl); 67 BC—Dio 36, 38, 4; Cicero, *Pro Murena*, 46; 67; Asconius, *In Cornelianam*, 69 (Clark); 63 BC—Dio 37, 29; Cicero, *Pro Murena*, 3; 5; 67; *Pro Sestio*, 133; *Pro Plancio*, 83; *In Vatinium* 37; 55 BC—Dio 39, 37, 1; Schol. Bob. 162 (Stangl); and 52 BC —Cicero, *Ad Atticum*, 10, 4, 8;

Caesar, *Bellum Civile*, 3, 1; Velleius 2, 47; Plutarch, *Cato Minor*, 48; Appian, *Bella Civilia*, 2, 23, 5. The penalties prescribed ranged from a ten-year ban on office to possibly a long period of exile. See Mommsen, *Römisches Strafrecht* (1899), 874.

382 Cicero, *In Vatinium*, 37; *Pro Sestio*, 133.

383 See in particular 72–3. This speech is packed with valuable information concerning the legitimacy of various practices in the canvass.

384 *Cf.* Cicero, *Ad Atticum*, 1, 18, 4.

385 *Cf.* Cicero, *In Verrem*, 1, 22, where it is suggested that Verres arranged for the summoning of the *divisores* of all the tribes by night. Similar abuses are mentioned in Cicero, *Pro Plancio*, 35; *Ad Atticum*, 1, 16, 12; *In Verrem*, 3, 161; Suetonius, *Divus Augustus*, 3, 1.

386 Cicero in Asconius, *In Cornelianam*, 74 (Clark). It was recognized, said Cicero, that there was no means of checking bribery except by imposing penalties on the *divisores*.

387 On the common use of *sodalicia* as a means of suborning the members of the rural tribes see Taylor, *PP*, 210, n. 101.

388 Plutarch, *Cato Minor*, 49, 3.

389 Mommsen, *Römisches Strafrecht* (1899), 872ff; Taylor, *PP*, 84. The case for regarding *coitio* as a legitimate, if somewhat unethical, practice has been convincingly argued by Hall, *Historia*, 1964, 301ff.

390 Livy 39, 41.

391 Apart from the two cases cited in the text there should be mentioned the likely association of Pompey and Crassus in the bid for the consulship of 70 BC (Plutarch, *Pompey*, 22, 1), and the attested *coitio* formed against Cicero by his two rivals, Antonius and Catiline, in 64 BC—see Asconius, *In Toga Candida*, 83 (Clark). For examples from an earlier period see Livy 7, 32, 12; 9, 26, 8.

392 Cicero (*Paradoxa Stoicorum*, 46) specifically refers to what he calls *intercessiones pecuniarum in coitionibus candidatorum*.

393 Cicero, *Ad Quintum Fratrem*, 2, 14, 4.

394 *Pro Plancio*, 53. The charge, however, was not *coitio*, but the employment of *sodalicia* in contravention of the *lex Licinia*.

395 Censorinus 20, 7; Dio 40, 62, 1.

396 *Ad Quintum fratrem*, 2, 4, 4ff. *Cf.* Cicero, *Ad Familiares*, 8, 11, 1; Caesar, *Bellum Gallicum*, 2, 35; Plutarch, *Sulla*, 8, 3; Appian, *Bella Civilia*, 1, 55, 5; 59, 6.

397 On the auspices in general see Mommsen, *St.* I³, 101ff; Botsford, *RA*, 110ff. The date and content of the *leges Aelia et Fufia*—which not only dealt with auspical *obnuntiatio* but also regulated the days on which comitial business could be transacted (see above, note 254)—have been the subject of much controversy. So too has the measure of success achieved by Clodius in securing their repeal in 58 BC. Among the many contributions to the study of these problems should be mentioned W. McDonald, 'Clodius and the lex Aelia Fufia', *JRS*, 1929, 164ff; G. V. Sumner, 'Lex Aelia, Lex Fufia', *AJP*, 1963, 337ff; and A. E. Astin, 'Leges Aelia et Fufia', *Latomus*, 1964, 421ff.

398 Plutarch, *Pompey*, 52; *Cato Minor*, 42, 2.

399 Cicero, *Philippics*, 2, 82f.

400 *Cf.* Cicero, *Ad Atticum*, 4, 3, 4; 4, 9, 1; *Ad Quintum fratrem*, 3, 3, 2; *Pro Sestio*, 78; *In Vatinium*, 16; *Philippics*, 2, 99; Plutarch, *Crassus*, 15, 3ff; Appian, *Bella Civilia*, 2, 18, 3.

401 I have attempted to interpret the circumstances of the elections for 55 and 52 BC in *Historia*, 1954, 202ff.

402 Dio 38, 4ff; Suetonius, *Divus Julius*, 20, 1.

403 *Cf.* Livy 8, 15, 6; 8, 17, 3; 8, 23, 14; 9, 7, 13; 21, 63, 2; 23, 33, 11; 23, 31, 13; Cicero, *De Divinatione*, 1, 33–36.

404 See, in particular, Scullard, *Roman Politics*, chs. III and IV *passim*, together with his remarks in the *Bulletin of the Institute of Classical Studies*, 1955, 19.

405 Cicero, *De Legibus*, 3, 27.

406 Cicero, *Pro Sestio*, 109.

407 Cicero, *Pro Sestio*, 53; *De Domo*, 79ff; *De Legibus*, 3, 45.

408 Cicero, *Brutus*, 224. *Cf.* the action of the consul of 66 BC in refusing to recognize the candidature of Catiline on the ground that he was to be prosecuted for extortion— Asconius, *In Cornelianam*, 89 (Clark). On this question see also above, pp. 147f.

409 Livy 24, 7–9.

410 Livy 26, 22.

411 Livy 10, 22, 1.

412 Cicero, *De Domo*, 49; *Pro Sestio*, 111.

413 Plutarch, *Tiberius Gracchus*, 11, 1.

414 Auctor ad Herennium, 1, 21. At a later date the tribune Clodius resorted to much the same tactics (Cicero, *Ad Atticum*, 1, 14, 5).

415 Cicero, *De Domo*, 112.

416 Cicero, *Ad Atticum*, 1, 14, 5. See above, p. 160, for an interpretation of this manœuvre.

417 Plutarch, *Cato Minor*, 46, 2.

418 *De Re Rustica*, 3, 7.

419 *De Lege Agraria*, 2, 21.

420 Lucan, 5, 392ff.

421 Plautus, *Casina*, 295ff, and especially 380ff for suspicions concerning the possibility of a fraudulent operation of the lot.

422 Plutarch, *Gaius Gracchus*, 12, 4. If indeed there was a fraud, this must

be where it lay. There can have been
no question of the presiding tribune's
falsifying the returns which will have
been reported to him by the tribal
custodes (see above, p. 177). Jones
(*Proceedings of the Cambridge Philological Society*, 1960, 37) suggests that

Gracchus' allegation was prompted
by a different interpretation of the
rules governing re-election to the
tribunate, and he therefore presumably believes that the question of
fraud did not arise.

CHAPTER XII

423 Suetonius, *Divus Julius*, 41, 2:
'comitia cum populo partitus est, ut
exceptis consulatus competitoribus de
cetero numero candidatorum pro
parte dimidia quos populus vellet
pronuntiarentur, pro parte altera
quos ipse dedisset'; *cf.* Dio 43, 51, 3;
Cicero, *Philippics*, 7, 16. Mommsen
(*St.* II³, 730), along with others,
interpreted this power of Caesar as a
form of compulsory *commendatio*, but
this concept is a legal anomaly (see
below, note 460). For a full and recent
discussion of the *lex Antonia* see R.
Frei-Stolba, *Untersuchungen zu den
Wahlen in der römischen Kaiserzeit*
(1967), 60ff.

424 Suetonius, *Divus Augustus*, 40,
2: 'comitiorum quoque pristinum ius
reduxit'; Dio 53, 21, 1; Velleius 2, 89,
3.

425 Suetonius, *Divus Augustus*, 46,
2.

426 This point is well illustrated by
the attitude which the Senate adopted
to Caligula's schemes for restoring
the popular elections. In a successful
attempt to thwart the exercise the
senators held a preliminary unofficial
election among themselves with the
object of producing only as many
candidates as there were offices. *Cf.*
Dio 59, 20.

427 The literature on the nature and
significance of the *destinatio* procedure
as outlined in the Tabula Hebana is
very extensive. Among the more

important contributions may be
mentioned G. Tibiletti, *Principe e
Magistrati Repubblicani* (1953), 49ff
(with a complete bibliography of
material published up to that date);
Jones, 'The Elections under Augustus', *JRS*, 1955, 9ff; R. Syme, *Tacitus*
II (1958), app. 67, 756ff; Frei-Stolba,
op. cit. (note 423, above), 120ff.

428 The most accessible discussions
of the role of the *equites* in the select
assembly are those of Jones, *JRS*,
1955, 14ff, and of P. A. Brunt, 'The
Lex Valeria Cornelia', *JRS*, 1961,
71ff. Whereas Jones interpreted their
inclusion as a deliberate move to
promote the electoral chances of new
men from outside the old nobility,
Brunt saw it as an attempt to confer
upon them a mark of distinction
which befitted their social status.
Neither gives sufficient weight to the
political tradition, the relevance of
which is recognized by Tibiletti (op.
cit., 60ff).

429 The first formal reference to
the Senate as a body which had a part
to play in the electoral process is contained in the *lex de imperio Vespasiani*
of AD 70. The literary authorities,
however, make no mention of the
interest of the *equites* either in their
references to Caligula's proposed
liberal reform or in any other connection. Furthermore, it is significant
that a consul of the late Tiberian age
described himself as *destinato ab senatu*

(*cf. ILS*, 944). *Destinatio* was a technical term, and its use in this context must imply that the Senate was then already playing the official role previously played by the select assembly.

430 Tacitus, *Annals*, 1, 15, 1; 'tum primum e campo comitia ad patres translata sunt: nam ad eam diem, etsi potissima arbitrio principis, quaedam tamen studiis tribuum fiebant.' For this interpretation *cf.* Jones, *JRS*, 1955, 19f; Syme, op. cit., 756ff; Frei-Stolba, op. cit., 136ff.

431 Tibiletti, for example, explains Tacitus by suggesting that it was not until AD 14 that the popular assembly was completely deprived of its freedom of choice by being compelled to accept or reject the candidates selected by the process of *destinatio* (op. cit., 164ff). Frei-Stolba, on the other hand, denies that the words relate to *destinatio* at all and suggests that they refer to the Senate's responsibility for producing a final list of candidates (although it is difficult to grasp the subtlety of the distinction). In my view scholars have tended to create difficulties for themselves by their readiness to put too much faith in Tacitus' factual and chronological accuracy. The sentence in question is sandwiched between two references to the arrangements made for the appointment of praetors in AD 14 and it might naturally be thought, therefore, either specifically to relate to, or at least to cover, the praetorian elections. But clearly either this is not the case or, if it is, Tacitus is guilty of a manifest inaccuracy; for in the case of the major elections, as we know from the Tabula Hebana, the abandonment of the active participation of the tribes to which he alludes was something which came about at least as early as AD 5. Tacitus, therefore,

was either confused about his facts or deliberately careless in his manner of presenting them. As likely as not the minor elections were all transferred from the Campus to the Senate in AD 14; and it could well be that, when relating the fact that the praetorian candidates for the year did not exceed the number of offices, Tacitus found himself tempted to represent the change as one which newly affected the major elections as well. This is not to allege that he did not know of the arrangements of AD 5 or of the part which at one time had been played by equestrian elements: it is simply to say that he did not consider them to be of sufficient significance for the principate of Tiberius or of sufficient long standing to warrant a special mention.

432 Pliny, *Panegyricus*, 63, 2 refers to *longum illud carmen comitiorum* in the time of Trajan. *Cf.* also Dio 58, 20 for the early third century.

433 Suetonius, *Divus Julius*, 41, 2: 'et edebat per libellos circum tribus missos scriptura brevi: "Caesar dictator illi tribui. commendo vobis illum et illum, ut vestro suffragio suam dignitatem teneant."' Levick (see note 436) is surely mistaken in affirming that the candidates whom Caesar chose directly are those whom he recommended in this way to the tribes. See Frei-Stolba, op. cit., 63.

434 Suetonius, *Divus Augustus*, 56, 1.

435 Dio 55, 34, 2.

436 An excellent account of the use and significance of *commendatio* in the early Empire is to be found in B. M. Levick's article, 'Imperial control of the Elections in the early Principate', *Historia*, 1967, 209ff, where the case against treating *commendatio* as in any sense legally binding is convincingly argued. See also, among recent treatments of the same theme, W. K. Lacey, 'Nominatio and the Elections under Tiberius', *Historia*, 1963, 167ff, and Frei-Stolba, op. cit., 11ff; 109ff.

437 Velleius 2, 124.

438 Tacitus, *Annals*, 1, 15, 2.

439 Tacitus, *Annals*, 1, 81.

440 *ILS*, 944.

441 *Cf.* Pliny, *Panegyricus*, 92, 3: 'tuo iudicio consules facti, tua voce renuntiati sumus, ut idem honoribus nostris suffragator in curia, in campo declarator existeres.'

442 For this interpretation of Dio 54, 10, 5, see in particular Jones, 'The Imperium of Augustus', *JRS*, 1951, 117ff.

443 On this whole matter and on the vexed question of the Princeps' alleged right of 'nominatio' see recently Lacey, *Historia*, 1963, 169ff; Levick, *Historia*, 1967, 214ff. It is the view of Miss Levick which for the most part I have followed here.

444 *Cf.* Tacitus, *Annals*, 14, 28; Suetonius, *Vespasian*, 2, 3; Pliny, *Epistulae*, 2, 9; 3, 20; 4, 25; 6, 6; 6, 16.

445 Dio 55, 34, 2; Tacitus, *Annals*, 1, 14, 3; *cf.* Suetonius, *Nero*, 43. The decision of Augustus to appoint the magistrates himself in AD 7 has sometimes been explained in terms of an assumption of quasi-dictatorial authority or of an extended use of *commendatio* (compare Mommsen, *St.* II³, 916; Tibiletti, op. cit., 115; Frei-Stolba, op. cit., 116); but Augustus is likely to have given less offence if he achieved his ends by restricting the number of candidates and leaving the forms of the electoral procedure unimpaired.

446 *Cf.* Pliny, *Panegyricus*, 69, 1. Even Tiberius, when absent in Capri, made himself responsible for sending official lists of candidates to Rome each year for consideration by the Senate (Dio 59, 20, 4).

447 Dio 53, 21, 6.

448 *Digest*, 48, 14, 1.

449 An English version of the relevant sections of this document appears in Appendix III, pp. 233ff.

450 *ILS*, 6398ff.

APPENDIX I

451 Cicero, *Ad Familiares*, 1, 1; *Ad Quintum fratrem*, 2, 2.

452 Livy 7, 35, 2; Gellius 14, 7, 12; *cf.* Pliny, *Epistulae*, 2, 11, 22.

453 The introduction of secret voting was recommended by the author of Pseudo-Sallust, 2, 11, but the change does not appear to have been implemented except in cases when during the Empire the Senate acted as a judicial court (*cf.* Tacitus, *Annals*, 1, 74).

454 Pliny, *Epistulae*, 8, 14, 19–20.

455 Suetonius, *Divus Julius*, 14; Cicero, *Ad Quintum fratrem*, 2, 1, 3.

456 Seneca, *De Vita Beata*, 2. *Cf.* Livy 26, 33, 14 for the use of what

was probably a technical term— *maxima pars*.

457 Festus 170; Cicero, *Ad Familiares*, 8, 11, 2; *Ad Atticum*, 5, 4, 2.

458 Sydenham, no. 917.

459 Cicero, *Pro Cluentio*, 75. The vote at the trial of Verres in the same period was to be taken by ballot (Cicero, *In Verrem*, 4, 104; *De Divinatione*, 7, 24).

460 *Cf.* the *lex Bembina* (*CIL*, 1, 2², 585), 44; Cicero, *Pro Flacco*, 99; *Pro Rabirio*, 11; Asconius, *In Milonianam*, 54 (Clark).

461 Asconius, *In Toga Candida*, 89 (Clark), suggests that each section voted in a separate urn in 65 BC. Dio

38, 8 suggests that this was standard practice after 59 BC; *cf.* Asconius, *In* *Milonianam*, 53, 55 (Clark).

462 *Lex Bembina*, 52–4.

APPENDIX II

463 Livy 45, 15, 1.

464 *Lex Malacitana*, 57.

465 Asconius, *In Milonianam*, 39 (Clark). The lots, it appears, were inscribed with the names of the jurors.

466 *Ad Atticum*, 1, 19, 3.

467 Livy 4, 26, 11. *Cf.* Livy 2, 8, 6 for a similar use of the lot to determine who should dedicate a temple.

468 Livy 24, 10, 2; 35, 20; 41, 6, 1.

469 Livy 38, 36, 10; Varro, *De Lingua Latina*, 6, 87.

470 Livy 22, 35, 5; 28, 45, 9; 30, 1, 2; 32, 8, 5; 37, 1, 7; 42, 31, 9.

471 *Tiberius Gracchus*, 11, 1.

472 *RVA*, 70ff.

473 *Historia Augusta*, Probus 8, 6.

474 Tabula Hebana, line 23.

INDEX

INDEX

acclamation, voting by, 16, 74, 76, 78, 121f, 130, 135, 157, 170
aediles, election of, 172, 177, 188, 197, 206, 211, 213; and games, 203
Aeschines, 106, 110, 117
Agamemnon, 16, 108
Agis, 75
Alcibiades, 81, 104f
allotment machines, 62ff, 72, 95, 112, 116f
Antonius, C. (cos. 63 BC), 184, n. 391
Antonius, M., triumvir, 207
apella, in early Sparta, 19ff; legislative functions of, 21f, 74f; electoral functions of, 30, 74; presidency of, 73; voting procedures in, 74ff
archons, archonship, origins of, 23f; method of selection for, 24, 33ff, 38f, 48, 56f, 68; qualifications for, 33, 38, n. 49; scrutiny of, 59; preside at sortition, 64, 66; preside at *ecclesia*, 89, 93; *see also* presiding magistrate
Areopagus, Council of the: origins of, 23f; selection of, 24; elects magistrates, 25, 33f, 37; and the scrutiny, 59
aristocracy, in early society, 15, 18f, 22ff, 123, 126; in Spartan government, 30, 32, 101f; in democratic Athens, 78, 106f; in Rome, *see* nobility
army, at Rome, 124f, 128, 134f, 150
assemblies, in early Greek society, 16ff; of demes, 49, 114f; of Athenian tribes, 35, 37, 41, 48, 59, 86; under Augustus, 127ff; *see also apella, comitia centuriata, comitia tributa, concilium plebis, ecclesia*
attendance, at Athenian assemblies, 78f, 89ff, 107, n. 131; at Roman assemblies, 134, 137, 139, 142, 154, 173, 187ff, 199, 209, nn. 313, 333, 353, 374
augurs, 208ff, 232
Augustus, 127, 129, 137, 217ff, n. 262
auspices, 77, 87, 123, 134, 149ff, 207f, 211, n. 397

ballot laws, at Rome, 158, 161, 228f, n. 302
ballot receptacles, 92ff, 96ff, 114, 158, 160ff, 168, 176, 212ff, 229, n. 303
ballots, used in Athenian assemblies, 84ff, 93f (*psephoi*), 89, 91ff, 114 (*ostraka*); used in Athenian courts, 96ff; used at Rome, 160f, 168, 176, 212ff, 229; distribution of, 94, 97, 99, 115, 161f
balloting, as a form of vote, 93f, 96ff, 99, 158f, 168, 172f, 175f, 187ff, 228, 234
beans, use of in sortition, 61f, 67
Bibulus, M. Calpurnius (cos. 59 BC), 208
bribery, at Sparta, 32, 101; at Athenian elections, 39f, 48, 50, 103, 108ff; in Athenian courts, 111ff; at Roman elections, 202ff, 207, 216; legislation regarding, 197, 202f, nn. 267, 296, 380, 381

Caesar, C. Julius, 137, 147, 165f, 208, 211, 217, nn. 262, 291, 378
calendar, at Rome, 143, 206
Campus Martius, use of for voting, 150ff, 156, 159, 179ff, 220, n. 260
candidate lists, at Athenian elections, 87f, 102, 104; at Roman Republican elections, 143, 145f, 153, 162; in early Principate, 222f; at Malaga, 233
candidature, voluntary or compulsory at Athens, 40, 51ff, n. 80; profession of at Athens, 104; profession of at Rome, 146f, 222f, n. 260; profession of at Malaga, 233
canvass, electoral, at Athens, 102ff; at Sparta, 101f; at Rome, 135f, 146, 159, 192ff, 204f, 221; at Pompeii, 224ff
Capitol, use of for voting, 151f, 154, n. 333
Cassius, Sp. (cos. 502 BC), 193
Cato, M. Porcius (cos. 195 BC), 205
Cato, M. Porcius (praet. 54 BC), 147, 204f, 207, 213